Opportunities and Challenges of Tourism Financing

A Study on Demand and Supply;
Status, Structure, Composition and Effectiveness of
Tourism Financing in Nepal

Bishnu Prasad Gautam

DISSERTATION.COM

Boca Raton

Opportunities and Challenges of Tourism Financing:
A Study on Demand and Supply; Status, Structure, Composition and
Effectiveness of Tourism Financing in Nepal

Copyright © 2007 Bishnu Prasad Gautam
All rights reserved. No part of this book may be reproduced or transmitted in any form or by any means, electronic or mechanical, including photocopying, recording, or by any information storage and retrieval system, without written permission from the publisher.

Dissertation.com
Boca Raton, Florida
USA • 2008

ISBN-10: 1-59942-661-7
ISBN-13: 978-1-59942-661-7

OPPORTUNITIES AND CHALLENGES OF
TOURISM FINANCING

*A Study on Demand and Supply;
Status, Structure, Composition and Effectiveness of
Tourism Financing in Nepal*

BISHNU PRASAD GAUTAM
MBA, Ph. D.

PREFACE

Tourism as widely understood, being the temporary or short-term movement of people outside their normal place of residence has become an indispensable subject matter in various disciplines and emerged as an important sector in the economy of every country. It has become a subject of considerable interest for many scholars as well as for business entrepreneurs. It has been generator of income and employment. The economic impact of tourism is such that it not only attracts the attention of the people but also of the country.

The establishment, nursing and growth of the business require the finance. It is also required for the expansion, growth and sustaining of the business. Various aspects of tourism including the contribution, impacts, problems and prospects have been analyzed through academic research. On tourism financing scarcity of the academic literature was observed. This made it worthwhile to explore the status of tourism finance especially with reference to Nepal.

Despite the abundant potentialities for the development of tourism in Nepal, the country is not yet fully able to achieve the benefits from tourism industry. Realizing the high prospects of tourism development, the study is made in triangular form. The first is the impact of tourism and tourism financing on the development of tourism and economic growth. The second is views of the TBE (demand side) about the effectiveness of financing and the third is the views of the banks and financial institutions (supply side). The study also incorporated the magnitude of tourism financing, structure, pattern and the indicators of financing as well as the effectiveness of tourism financing.

The study is based on primary data collected from the tourism business enterprises as well as from banks and financial institutions using a structured questionnaire and also on secondary data collected from various publications.

It has employed various mathematical and statistical tools such as annual rate of change in percentage, ratio analysis, correlation coefficient, Phi-coefficient (r_ϕ), correlation coefficient, Chi-square (χ^2) test, t-Test for two sample means and regression analysis (OLS).

The present study is divided into seven chapters. Chapter 1 is an introductory chapter covering the background, concept of tourism and tourism financing, significance objectives and methodology of the study. Chapter 2 presents a theoretical underpinning for the tourism and tourism financing.

Chapter 3 presents the profile of the Nepalese tourism industry. Chapter 4 examines the sources of tourism financing and explores about the impact of tourism and tourism financing in the economy.

Based on the responses Chapter 5 analyses the structure of finance of various tourism business enterprises and examines the variation in the structure based on types and ownership of business. Chapter 6 analyses the responses of banks and financial institutions. It attempts to examine the methods of proposal analysis and techniques of credit appraisal.

Finally, chapter 7 summarizes the findings and conclusions of the research including the policy implications and suggestions.

ACKNOWLEDGEMENT

I would like to take this opportunity to appreciate and acknowledge the valuable contribution and cooperation of various persons and organizations in completion of this research work. Primarily, I would like to express my sincere and deep sense of gratitude to **Prof. (Dr.) Amita S. Kantawala** for her valuable guidance, continuous flow of inspiration and scholarly suggestions. I am heavily indebted for her skilful, genuine and timely guidance, thus, I owe her a lifetime debt. I would like to thank Prof. G. C. Maheshwori, Dean, Faculty of Management Studies and cooperative staffs in the faculty. In particular, I would like to thank Prof. Bhavana S. Kantawala, Professor of Economics for useful direction and suggestions.

I am greatly indebted to **Nepal Rastra Bank, the central bank of Nepal** for the study leave for this research work. I am especially grateful to my intimate friends Dr. Khem Raj Bhetuwal and Mr. Jyoti Adhikari and equally grateful to Prof. Parashar Koirala, Prof. Devraj Adhikari, Dr. Gopal Krishna Shrestha, Prof. Samartha Bahadur Singh, Dr. Rajendra Shrestha, Dr. Hari Prasad Shrestha and Mr. Lok Bahadur Khatri for their respective support.

I am really proud of my wife Mrs. Bindu Devi Gautam (Khanal) and would like to express my deep sense of gratitude for the continuous encouragement and cooperation. It would have been impossible to complete this work without her instant support during the entire study. I would like to record the moral support and forbearance of my children Sefalika Gautam and Sarthak Gautam during the research.

I have been greatly benefited from the study grant of ICSSR Mumbai as well as from the consultation of various libraries. I take pleasure in thanking several friends and staffs of Nepal Rastra Bank, different commercial banks, financial institutions and various tourism business enterprises viz., Mr. T. P. Koirala, Mr. Govinda Shrestha, Bhuvan Dahal, Sugam KC, Dhruba Gautam, Takaraj Gurung, Hem Neupane, Bharat Lamsal, Suresh Gnawali, Rishi Pandey, Chiranjivee Jyawali, Suman Poudyal, B. K. Lamsal, Purushottam Giri, and Mani Subedi, Mr. Deepak Rasaily.

The divine blessing of my parents Mrs. Tika Devi Gautam and Mr. (Pan.) Taranga Raj Gautam "Shastri" has always enabled and encouraged me for the further study. I bow down at their feet. I would like to mention a special respect and regard to Pan. Nandikeshar Khanal and Tarkaraj Gautam, Hon'ble Justice Rajendra K. Bhandari, Mr. Hari Prapanna Gautam, Dr. Baburam Gautam, Mr. Govinda Khanal, Mr. Padampani Gnawali, Mr. Phanindra Nath Gnawali, Dr. Pitambar Gautam, Mr. Lilamani Poudyal, Er. Gir Bahadur KC. However, all the deficiencies remained in this thesis are entirely mine.

– Bishnu Prasad Gautam

TABLE OF CONTENTS

		Page
	Preface	ii
	Acknowledgement	iii
	Contents	iv
	List of Tables, Figures and Exhibits	v
	Acronyms	x
Chapter I	Introduction	1-16
Chapter II	Review of Literature on Tourism and Tourism Financing	17-60
Chapter III	Tourism Industry in Nepal: A Profile	61-90
Chapter IV	Tourism Financing: An Impact Analysis	91-122
Chapter V	Tourism Investment: An Analysis of Respondents of Tourism Business Enterprises	123-194
Chapter VI	Tourism Financing: An Analysis of Respondents from Banks and Financial Institutions	195-216
Chapter VII	Summary of Findings and Suggestions	217-227

LIST OF TABLES, FIGURES AND EXHIBITS

Number	Name of the Table, Figure and Exhibit	Page No.
Table: 1.1	Population and Sample of Tourism Business Enterprises	10
Table: 1.2	Population and Sample of Banks and Financial Institutions	10
Table: 3.1	Growth in Tourism	65
Table: 3.2	Regional Distribution of the Tourist Arrivals	66
Table: 3.3	Tourist Arrivals by Purpose of Visit	67
Exhibit: 3.1	Introduction and Essential Information for Tourists	69
Exhibit: 3.2	A Glimpse of Tourism Products and Infrastructure	70
Table: 3.4	Manpower Trained by Nepal Academy of Tourism and Hotel Management	82
Table: 3.5	Distribution of Tourism Business (Licensed)	84
Figure: 3.1	Distribution of the Tourism Business Enterprises	84
Table: 3.6	Tourism Acts and Regulation	85
Table: 4.1	Direct Government Investment	98
Table: 4.2	Foreign Aid and Loan Disbursement	99
Figure: 4.1	Foreign Aid and Loan Disbursement	99
Figure: 4.2	Nepalese Financial System	100
Table: 4.3	Purpose-wise Loan Disbursement of Commercial Banks	101
Figure: 4.3	Loan Disbursement of Commercial Banks by Purpose	101
Table: 4.4	Loan Disbursement and Outstanding of Commercial Banks in Tourism	102
Figure: 4.4	The Ratio of Tourism in Total Credit Disbursement and Credit Outstanding	103
Table: 4.5	Outstanding Financial Assistance of NIDC (Classified by Industry)	104
Table: 4.6	Loan Disbursement and Outstanding in Tourism (NIDC)	105
Figure: 4.5	The Share of Tourism in Total Credit Disbursement and Outstanding	106
Table: 4.7	Loan Disbursement in Tourism by Financial Institutions	107
Table: 4.8	Foreign Direct Investment and Share of Tourism Industry	109
Table: 4.9	Regression Results on Development Indices (Simple Linear)	111
Table: 4.10	Regression Results on Development Indices (Log Linear)	112
Table: 4.11	A comparison of R2 and comparable R2	112
Table: 4.12	Regression Analysis on Various Development Indices (Simple Linear C - O Two Step)	113
Table: 4.13	Regression Results on Development Indices (log linear C - O Two Step)	113
Table: 4.14	Regression Results of Ln. GDPN as Dependent Variable	114
Table: 4.15	Regression Results on Tourism Financing	116
Table: 4.16	Further Regression Results on Tourism Financing	117
Table: 4.17	Regression Result of GDPT (Simple Liner)	118

Number	Name of the Table, Figure and Exhibit	Page No.
Table: 5.1	A comparison of the Population with Survey Response (Representativeness of Sample)	126
Table: 5.2	A Proportional Distribution of the Tourism Business Enterprises (Population and Sample)	127
Table: 5.3	Distribution of Sample and Response of Tourism Business	128
Figure: 5.1	Sample of Tourism Business	128
Figure: 5.2	Respondents of Tourism Business	128
Table: 5.4	Types of Business vs. Ownership Pattern	129
Table: 5.5	Nationality of Business Executives	129
Figure: 5.3	Duration of Business Operation	130
Table: 5.6	Duration of Business Operation	131
Table: 5.7	Share Capital Financing of Tourism Business Enterprises	133
Table: 5.8	Debt Financing of Tourism Business Enterprises	135
Table: 5.9	Current Assets Financing of Tourism Business Enterprises	136
Table: 5.10	Composition of the Total Financing	137
Figure: 5.4	Total Financing of Tourism Business Enterprises	138
Table: 5.11	Aggregate Balance Sheet of Tourism Business Enterprises	139
Table: 5.12	Fixed Assets of Tourism Business Enterprises	140
Table: 5.13	Total Assets of Tourism Business Enterprises	141
Table: 5.14	Working Capital of Tourism Business Enterprises	142
Table: 5.15	Sources and Uses of Funds of Accommodation Agencies	146
Table: 5.16	Sources and Uses of Funds of Travel Agencies	147
Table: 5.17	Sources and Uses of Funds of Adventure Agencies	148
Table: 5.18	Sources and Uses of Funds of Other Agencies	149
Table: 5.19	Sources and Uses of Funds of TBE (Based on Types of Business)	150
Table: 5.20	Analysis of the Variance According to the Type of Business	150
Table: 5.21	Results of t-Test for Two Sample Means (Average Percentage) Based on Type of the Business	151
Table: 5.22	Sources and Uses of Funds of Proprietorship Firms	152
Table: 5.23	Sources and Uses of Funds of Partnership Firms	153
Table: 5.24	Sources and Uses of Funds of Private Limited Companies	154
Table: 5.25	Sources and Uses of Funds of Public Limited Companies	155
Table: 5.26	Sources and Uses of Funds Based on Ownership of Business	156
Table: 5.27	Analysis of the Variance According to the Ownership of Business	157
Table: 5.28	Results of t-Test Based on Ownership of the Business	157
Table: 5.29	Sources and Uses of Funds of Respondents Based on Type of Business (Average Amount for the period)	158

Number	Name of the Table, Figure and Exhibit	Page No.
Table: 5.30	Sources and Uses of Funds of Respondents Based on Ownership of Business (Average Amount for the period)	159
Table: 5.31	ANOVA Summary (Type of Tourism Business)	159
Table: 5.32	ANOVA Summary (Ownership of Tourism Business)	160
Table: 5.33	Results of t-Test for Two Sample Means (Average Amount) Based on Type of the Business	160
Table: 5.34	Results of t-Test for Two Sample Means (Average Amount) Based on Ownership of the Business	161
Table: 5.35	Financial Planning of the Company	162
Table: 5.36	Average Interest Rate on Borrowing (in percentage per annum)	163
Table: 5.37	Distribution of the Financing Sources	165
Table: 5.38	Sales Revenue of Tourism Business Enterprises	166
Table: 5.39	Net Profit to Sales Ratio of Tourism Business Enterprises	167
Table: 5.40	Interest Coverage Ratio of Tourism Business Enterprises	168
Table: 5.41	Debt Equity Ratio of Tourism Business Enterprises	169
Table: 5.42	Debt to Total Assets Ratio of Tourism Business Enterprises	170
Table: 5.43	Proprietorship Ratio of Tourism Business Enterprises	171
Table: 5.44	Current Ratio of Tourism Business Enterprises	171
Table: 5.45	Current Asset Turnover Ratio of Tourism Business Enterprises	172
Table: 5.46	Fixed Asset Turnover Ratio of Tourism Business Enterprises	173
Table: 5.47	Working Capital Turnover Ratio of Tourism Business Enterprises	173
Table: 5.48	Response on Raising Equity Capital	174
Table: 5.49	Easy to Raise Equity Capital	174
Table: 5.50	Raising Debt Capital (Borrowing)	175
Table: 5.51	Easy to Get Borrowing	175
Table: 5.52	Received the Loan as Proposed	176
Table: 5.53	Utilization of the Loan (Borrowing)	176
Table: 5.54	Impact of Loan (Borrowing)	176
Table: 5.55	Project Drop out	177
Table: 5.56	Number of Project Drop out During the Period	177
Figure: 5.5	Reasons for Project Drop out	178
Table: 5.57	Time and Cost Over-runs	179
Table: 5.58	Year of Time and Cost Over-run	179
Table: 5.59	Reasons for Time and Cost Over-run	180
Table: 5.60	Enterprises having Other Business Related to Tourism	181
Table: 5.61	Types of Other Business Related to Tourism	181
Table: 5.62	Business Agreements (TSA or Franchise)	182

Number	Name of the Table, Figure and Exhibit	Page No.
Table: 5.63	Details of Business Agreements (TSA or Franchise)	182
Table: 5.64	Purpose of Proposed Investment	183
Table: 5.65	Amount of Proposed Investment (Rs. '000)	184
Table: 5.66	Financial Planning for Proposed Project	185
Table: 5.67	Number of Employees in the Tourism Business	186
Table: 5.68	Average number of Employees and Ratio	186
Table: 5.69	Existence of Trade Union Labour Relation	187
Table: 5.70	Lacks or Problems	188
Table: 5.71	Comments on Hindering Factors	188
Table: 5.72	Hindering Factors for the Development of the Business	189
Table: 5.73	Results of the Test Statistics for the Hindering Factors	190
Table: 5.74	Rating of the Factors for the Development of the Business	191
Table: 6.1	Distribution of Respondents (Banks and Financial Institutions)	198
Figure: 6.1	Sample of the BFI	198
Figure: 6.2	Response of the BFI	198
Figure: 6.3	Duration of Tourism Financing by Banks and Financial Institutions	199
Table: 6.2	Establishment vs. Duration of Tourism Financing	200
Table: 6.3	Specific Formats for Loan Application	201
Table: 6.4	Response on Feasibility Report or Project Proposal	202
Table: 6.5	Average Time for Loan Processing (in week)	203
Table: 6.6	Negotiations with the Clients	203
Table: 6.7	Intimation to Customers about Loan Processing	204
Table: 6.8	General Practice of Credit Disbursement	204
Figure: 6.4	General Practice of Credit Disbursement	205
Table: 6.9	Difference in Loan Processing between Tourism and Other Loans	205
Figure: 6.5	Difference in Loan Processing between Tourism and Other Loans	205
Table: 6.10	Proposal Analysis	206
Table: 6.11	Relationship Between the Factors Related to Proposal Analysis	207
Table: 6.12	Relation Between the Factors Related to Proposal Analysis	208
Table: 6.13	Credit Appraisal	209
Table: 6.14	Relationship Between the Aspects Related to Credit Appraisal	210
Table: 6.15	Relationship Between the Aspects Related to Credit Appraisal	210
Table: 6.16	Relationship Between Proposal Analysis and Financial Aspects	211
Table: 6.17	Repayment Habit of the Borrower	212
Table: 6.18	Quality of Credit Documentation	212
Table: 6.19	Existence of Restructuring of Loan	213

Number	Name of the Table, Figure and Exhibit	Page No.
Table: 6.20	Difference in Loan Quality	213
Table: 6.21	Loan Classification Related to Tourism	214
Figure: 6.6	Total Loan, Non-Performing Assets and NPA Ratio (Tourism Sector)	214
Table: 6.22	Impact of Lending	215

ACRONYMS

ADB	=	Asian Development Bank
ADB/N	=	Agricultural Development Bank, Nepal
Banks	=	Commercial Banks
BFIS	=	Banking and Financial Institutions Statistics
BFIs	=	Banks and Financial Institutions
C/D Ratio	=	Credit Deposit Ratio
CBS	=	Central Bureau of Statistics
Disb.	=	Disbursement
DW (d)	=	Durbin Watson 'd' statistics
ESCAP	=	Economic and Social Council for Asia and the Pacific
FADOT	=	Foreign aid disbursement in other sector including tourism
FDI	=	Foreign Direct Investment
FI (FIs)	=	Financial Institutions
FINCOOPS	=	Financial Cooperatives Societies
FINGO	=	Financial Non Government Organization
Forex	=	Foreign Exchange
FXET	=	Foreign Exchange Earning from Tourism
FY (F. Y.)	=	Fiscal Year (year ending mid-July)
GDP	=	Gross Domestic Product
GDPN	=	Nominal Gross Domestic Product
GDPT	=	Contribution of Hotel, Trade and Restaurant on GDP
GICA	=	Government investment in civil aviation
GIR	=	Government's internal revenue
GON	=	Government of Nepal
HAN	=	Hotel Association of Nepal
HMG/N	=	His Majesty's of Government of Nepal now Government of Nepal
ICC	=	International Chamber of Commerce
ICIMOD	=	International Centre for Integrated Mountaineering Development
IGIDR	=	Indira Gandhi Institute of Development Research
IMF	=	International Monetary Fund
INVT	=	Investment
IUCN	=	International Union for Conservation of Nature and Natural Resources
JV	=	Joint Venture
LDSCB	=	Service sector loan disbursement of Commercial banks
LDTNIDC	=	Tourism sector loan disbursement of NIDC
Ln. (ln.)	=	Log Value (base of 10)
M1	=	Money Supply (Narrowly defined)

M2	=	Money Supply (Broadly defined)
MOCTCA	=	Ministry of Culture, Tourism and Civil Aviation
MOF	=	Ministry of Finance
MOL	=	Ministry of Law
MOTCA	=	Ministry of Tourism and Civil Aviation
NARA	=	Nepal Association of Rafting Agents
NATA	=	Nepal Association of Travel Agents
NBFI	=	Non Bank Financial Institutions
No.	=	Number
NRB	=	Nepal Rastra Bank
NTB	=	Nepal Tourism Board
OLS	=	Ordinary Least Square
QEB	=	Quarterly Economic Bulletin
RGDPT	=	Ratio of GDPT to Gross Domestic Product (GDPN)
Rs.	=	Rupees (Nepalese Currency)
TAAN	=	Trekking Agents Association of Nepal
TAX	=	tax revenue
TB	=	Tourism Business
TBE	=	Tourism Business Enterprises
TEXP	=	Development expenditure of government in tourism sector
TFSD	=	Tourism Financing (Supply)
TNHB	=	Total number of Hotel Beds
TNHR	=	Total number of Trained Human Resources
TNTB	=	Total number of Tourism Business
TRAV	=	Trade Volume (Total trade)
TTAR	–	Total number of Tourists Arrival
UN	=	United Nations
UNCTAD	=	United Nations Commission for Trade and Development
WB	=	World Bank
WDR	=	World Development Report

CHAPTER I

INTRODUCTION

1.1 BACKGROUND OF THE STUDY
1.2 CONCEPT AND SCOPE OF TOURISM
1.3 CONCEPT AND SCOPE OF TOURISM FINANCING
1.4 OVERVIEW OF NEPALESE ECONOMY
1.5 RATIONALE OF THE STUDY
1.6 OBJECTIVES OF THE STUDY
1.7 RESEARCH METHODOLOGY AND DATA SOURCES
- Research Design and Sources of Data
- Preliminary Survey, Interviews and Questionnaires
- Population and Sample
- Data Collection Procedure

1.8 METHOD OF ANALYSIS AND MODEL
1.9 POSSIBLE SOURCES OF BIAS
1.10 CHAPTER SCHEME OF THE STUDY

CHAPTER I
INTRODUCTION

1.1 BACKGROUND OF THE STUDY

Tourism has been considered as fundamental instrument for the economic development of the country. It should be the main reason that many governments, developing or developed are involved in the design, development and operation of the tourism industry. It has been a focal issue in most of their Periodical Plans. The investment, involvement and participation of the public sector have been a real fact over the years. Similarly, private sector has also equally been involved in this industry.

As tourism is growing rapidly, it has attracted the attention from several sectors, formal informal, public private and national international. Consequently, various aspects of tourism including contribution, impacts, problems and prospects have been analyzed by various scholars, such as Pearce Douglas (1981, 1989), Ritchie (1980) Ghali (1976), Diamond (1977) and Jamieson and Jamal (1997) etc. Several analysis have also been performed to find out the linkages of tourism by Emanual de Kadt (1978), Goeldner, Ritchie and McIntosh (2000), Smith (1989), Douglas Frechtling (1987), Seaton and et al. (1994), John Tribe (1999), and Norbert Vanhobe (2005). Initiatives in tourism industry is aimed at creating awareness and cooperation among people, earning foreign currency, providing the employment opportunities, and thereby benefiting the people, society, country and region. Every investment is aimed at creation and accumulation of facilities, for ensuring the required services and proper infrastructures for the efficient operation and optimum utilization of the industry. For this purpose, financing is must. Proper modes of finance ensure proper growth, efficiency and effectiveness.

Tourism industry, unlike some other industries, is critical enough to be affected and often damaged by a change in weather/season, occurrence of incident and even by rumor or propaganda. Despite of joint efforts from public and private sectors to overcome problems and continuous investment, the outcome has been usually embarrassing.

1.2 CONCEPT AND SCOPE OF TOURISM

Tourism nowadays has been an essential activity all over the world. The form of tourism can be of various types. It is an activity, discipline, industry or profession depending upon the application method and criteria. Most of the people are quite familiar with the meaning of tourism though they are not well aware about its prospects and consequences.

The word tourism is related to "TOUR" which is derived from a Latin word "TORNUS". It means a tool for describing a circle of turners' wheel (Bhatia, 2002: 85). The notion of a round tour or a package tour has come from this word. In fact, it is the essence of tourism.

In 1910, Hermann Van Schullard, an Austrian economist has tried to clarify few points in his definition particularly for operation, sum of operation, related activities and defined tourism as "The sum total of operations mainly of an economic nature, which directly relate the entry, stay, and movement of foreigners inside and outside a certain country, city or region." In 1937 the League of Nations proposed a definition of "tourist as one who travels for a period of 24 hours or more in a country other than that in which he usually resides" (Karma and Chand, 2004: 34 and Bhatia, 2002: 86). The definition obviously considers the purpose of visit including the individuals traveling for pleasure and or for other reasons.

Similarly, in 1942 two Swiss Professors Walter Hunziker and Kurt Krapf of Berne University defined Tourism as "the sum of the phenomena and relationships arising from the travel and stay of non-residents, in so far as they do not lead to permanent residence and are not connected with any earning activity" (Karma and Chand, 2004: 34; Sharma, 2004: 14). This definition is some how broader and incorporates both travel and stay with clear description of tourism, migration, earning activity and pleasures. International Association of Scientific Experts in Tourism (AIEST) later adopted it.

In 1963, International Union of Official Travel Organization (IUOTO) now the World Tourism Organization, issued various definitions and recommendations during the auspicious occasion of UN Conference on International Travel and Tourism held at Rome Italy. It introduced the terms like 'visitor" to describe any person visiting a country other than in which he has his usual place of residence (Kunwar, 1997: 8 and Bhatia, 2002: 88).

In 1976, Tourism Society of England defined tourism, as "Tourism is the temporary short term movement of people to destinations outside the places where they normally live and work and their activities during the stay at these destinations. It includes movement of people for all purpose as well as day visits or excursions" (Ghimire, 2002: 13).

Mathieson and Wall had defined tourism incorporating the basics of tourism as a temporary movement to destinations outside the normal home and workplace as well as the activities undertaken during the stay including the facilities created to cater for the needs of tourists (Karma and Chand, 2004: 34). Burkart and Medlik also provided similar definition of tourism as temporary, short-term movement of people to destinations outside the place where they normally live and work including their activities during their stay at these destinations (Sharma, 2004: 15)

Tourism is based on the desire for the pursuit of happiness (Enzensberger, 1996: 135). It is essentially a pleasure activity in which traveling from one place to another, country to country and region to region is involved. Similarly, it also involves money for the services and time for that. It basically, includes much travel. It is distinct with related concepts of leisure, recreation, travel and or migration. Therefore, tourism is the result of temporary movement of people from their normal places of residence and work. The activities undertaken during their stay in those places and the facilities provided to satisfy their needs results on tourism activity.

Tourism, in fact comprises the activities of persons traveling to and staying in places outside their usual environment. The period of visit should not be more than one year for leisure, business and other purposes and the exercise of an activity should not be remunerated from the place visited. The words like visitor, traveler, wanderlust and tourist contain the instinct meaning describing a person traveling to a place other than his/her usual environment. The main purpose of the trip may differ with an activity carried out in the place visited.

Tourism is an ever increasing and expanding service industry both at national and international level. Nowadays it has become one of the crucial concerns not only of the nations but also of international community as a whole. It has come up as a decisive link in gearing up the pace of socio economic development world over (See McIntosh et at., 1995: 3). It is the temporary movement of people to destination(s) away from their usual habitat, the activities entered upon during their stay and the facilities developed to provide for their requirements. Tourism has intrigued many scholars, economic theorists, financial analysts and many others to probe into the various facets of tourism thus enabled the experts to be indulged deeper in the subject.

1.3 CONCEPT AND SCOPE OF TOURISM FINANCING

There are various sources of financing for the tourism business. In the first part, the discussion is focused on the sources of financing in terms of supply whereas in the second part the discussion continues in terms of demand for financing.

The development of any sector in the economy needs more and more investment. Tourism sector is not an exception; it certainly needs continuous and huge investment. Nepal being a developing country with limited infrastructure and lack of accumulated capital seriously requires huge investment in most of its socio economic sectors. Such investment is not an easy task, thus announces for the alternative sources and mechanisms of financing. Further, tourism being capital-intensive industry also requires huge amount of capital for the infrastructure and superstructure. In addition to this, more investment and financing is necessary for support services and for the promotion of related industries. Therefore, the investment financing is not necessary only for tourism infrastructure and superstructure but also for every facets of tourism industry.

The availability of finance to develop and promote the tourism industry is critically important for further growth and development of tourism industry and economy (Government of South Africa: 1996).

The establishment, nursing and growth of the trade, industry and commerce owes to the finance. Finance is rightly said to be the lifeblood of the business. Funds are required to commence and carry on the business. It is also required for the expansion, growth and sustaining (Siddiqui and Siddiqui, 2005: 273). Therefore, every business enterprise whether large or small needs finance to run the operation. Business enterprises require capital in various forms comprising a number of assets and of various types both fixed (permanent) and current nature (Mahat, 1981:1).

A firm secures whatever capital it needs and employs it in activities such as production, marketing and finance. It requires real assets and financial assets to carry on its business. Real assets include tangible assets (plant, machinery, office, factory, furniture and building) and intangible assets (technical expertise, technological collaborations, patents and copyrights) whereas financial assets include securities or financial instruments (shares and debentures), lease obligations and borrowing from banks or financial institutions (Pandey, 2004: 3-4).

Business finance includes money funds and capital. It includes both owned capital and borrowed capital. It is a wider term concerned with planning, acquisition, utilization and management of funds (Siddiqui and Siddiqui, 2005: 273). Though finance is must for the productive operation, the requirement or its magnitude basically, depends upon the nature and size of the enterprise.

The types of financing can be various based on purpose of financing, methods and time duration. It simply means that it can be classified as internal and external, formal and informal as well as domestic and foreign.

I. M. Pandey (2004: 442) viewed ordinary shares, preference share and debentures as important types of securities that the firms generally use to raise funds to finance their activities whereas Whitehouse and Tille (1993: 122) viewed the equity and borrowings as the main types of business finance in addition to the raising finance from internal sources. Similarly, Lawrence Gitman (2004: 522) viewed the total capital as composed of debt capital and equity capital.

Further, Whitehouse and Tilley (1993: 122, 135) have discussed the sources and types of finance dividing them in two broad categories of commercial and non-commercial sources of finance. Again, they have divided commercial finance in short and mid-term finance as equity, borrowing, debt factoring, invoice discounting leasing, hire purchase and bills of exchange) as well as medium and long-term finance such as venture capital, long-term borrowing (share issue, debenture).

Another classification of financing in internal and external source is based on the flow of funds. The internal source comprises the retained earning, reserves, surplus and depreciation whereas the external source comprises issuance of shares, debentures, borrowings from banks and financial institution as well as trade credits.

Financing policy, in simple words means to design the capital structure with appropriate proportions of debt and equity. Every business firm aims at maximizing the firm value by minimizing the overall cost of capital. In fact, the cost of capital is useful in deciding about the methods of financing at a point of time (Pandey, 2004: 168).

In such broader view, the central issue of financial policy is the wise use of funds and the central process involved is a rational matching of advantages of potential uses against the cost of alternative sources so as to achieve the broad financial goals, which an enterprise sets for itself (Soloman, 1969: 3).

The mix of debt and equity is called capital structure of the organization. As such, the financing policy of an organization has an important bearing upon the survival of the organization because it influences the flexibility in the operations of the business. Too much of debt in the organization means high fixed cost or interest obligations, which may even endanger the survival of the organization (Singh, 2001: 126). The importance of financial management in tourism industry can be hardly overemphasized (Singh, 2001: 124). Financing decisions are more crucial because it has an impact on profitability (Witt and et al, 1997: 103). Financing policy and system includes all activities pertaining to planning, acquisition and management and evaluation of the funding in the organization.

1.4 OVERVIEW OF THE NEPALESE ECONOMY

Nepal is a small country with majority of its people engaged in agricultural (about 81 percent) activities. However, the agricultural sector contributes only 55 percent on the gross domestic product and 50 percent on the total export. It has received the top priority in every periodical plan and has enjoyed the large amount of budget allocations over the years. The productivity has remained low because of various problems ranging from some structural problems to difficult topographical condition, lack of irrigation facility, traditional practice and lack of commercialization.

Similarly, manufacturing sector is also small providing the employment for 10 percent population and contributing about 20 percent in the gross domestic product. Many efforts are directed for the development of the industrial sector with priority and resources but the achievement has been embarrassing over the years.

Water and forest resources are the endurable resources of the country in contrast to the mineral resources. However, the deforestation problem over the last three decades raises concerns and cautions for conservation and utilization pattern. Notwithstanding, utilization of water resources requires huge investment. The foreign trade is characterized by an export of primary goods, lack of diversification and large trade deficit. Despite of large trade deficits, Nepal's external accounts have been partly offset by invisible surpluses. There are three major sources of convertible foreign exchanges in Nepal, foreign aid, merchandise exports and tourist expenditures (Shrestha, 1999: 6).

Tourism industry seems to be an endurable industry because of its vast potential. Some people may like to call Nepal as the unique museum in the world. It is one of the richest countries in the world in terms of bio-diversity. The elevation of the country ranges from 60 meter above from the sea level to the highest peak on the earth - Mt. Everest at 8848 meter, all within a distance of 150 km. With climatic conditions ranging from sub-tropical to arctic, this wild variation fosters the variety of ecosystem, tropical jungles, and wild life. Further, this spectacular geography is also one of the richest cultural landscapes anywhere. The country is a potpourri of ethnic groups and sub-groups who speak over 70 languages and dialects. It also offers an astonishing diversity of sightseeing attractions and adventure opportunities found nowhere else on the earth (Nepal Guidebook: 2002).

Moreover, the country offers numerous annual festivals that are celebrated throughout the year in traditional style highlighting various customs and beliefs (Nepal Guidebook: 2002). Hence, Nepal has a comparative advantage in the development of tourism because of its natural topography such as mountains, rich valleys, lovely landscapes and rich cultural heritage and so on.

With such vast potentials of the tourism, many countries around the world have enlisted it as a major destination. The "Observer" and the "Guardians" the famous British publications had rightly described Nepal as a second tourist state after the New Zealand in world tourism perspective.

Tourism industry has been considered as a major industry in Nepalese economy. More than 1.50 million people are employed directly or indirectly in this industry. This sector contributes more than 3 percent in GDP. Likewise, this sector earns more than 15 percent of total foreign currency and 30 percent of total revenue (NTB, 2005). With the perspective of foreign currency earning, employment generation, promotion of art and culture, conservation of heritage, promotion of cottage and small industry, increment in per capita income and transfer of know-how and awareness, the importance of tourism is over whelming.

The present status of tourism industry shows a slowdown, though it was remarkably important in Nepalese economy. With the recession in world economy, Nepalese economy is also facing some recessional symptoms. The Maoist insurgency inside the country during the last 10 years and its consequences in law and order situation has an adverse impact in the tourism industry. As the rate of tourist arrival sharply decreased, some of the prominent effects started to prevail automatically drawing overall slackness and vulnerability in related business and other economic sectors.

Nepal has been paying an increased attention for the development of tourism from the very beginning since it welcomed foreign visitors after the advent of democracy in 1951. Therefore, tourism has a belated start in Nepal compared to other countries. Despite having enormous potentialities for tourism development, Nepal has not been able develop it in a desirable manner (Shrestha, 1999: 3). The major reason behind this should be the lack of financing sources and mechanism.

1.5 RATIONALE OF THE STUDY

Tourism has emerged as an important industry almost everywhere in the world. It has occupied a significant position and enjoyed the priority over the years.

Nepal is basically, a developing country. Landlocked in between two giant economies of the world, India and China, Nepal has very small agrarian economy, lacks industrialization and possesses few natural resources. There are only two natural resources with comparative advantages and clear prospects namely water and tourism (ADB and MOTCA, 1990: 88). However, both of them are challenging because of resource constraints and geographical difficulties. The development of hydropower requires a huge amount of investment on one hand and prospective buyer on the other. India may be a potential buyer given that the cost of production is minimum and the selling price comparatively cheaper, along-with long-term arrangements through mutual understanding. In other words, the exploitation of water resources requires huge financing and vast market which is not an easy task.

In contrast, tourism does not suffer from such problems and dependency and thus appears to be a potential sector for the economic growth and development of the country (ADB and MOTCA, 1990: 89). However, it is not out of challenges because it is delicate and depends mostly on others for the growth and development.

Tourism is a vital sector of Nepalese economy as it contributes to correct the adverse trade balance and to generate the employment opportunities. The earning from tourism as percentage of GDP is 2.6 in July 2003, which has gradually increased from 1% in 1975. Though the contribution is negligible in comparison to other countries, there is still enough possibility to increase it considering the huge prospects. However, it has been suffering continuously in terms of management and proper funding.

Similarly, tourism is an activity generating a number of economic and social benefits in the country. It not only augments foreign exchange earning, the scarce resources of the country but also creates employment opportunities such as direct, indirect and induced, through backward and forward linkages with other sectors of the economy such as agriculture, industry and other service sectors. Tourism being a labour intensive activity generates employment opportunities to the vast number of underemployed and unemployed people of the country.

The time has come to study the direct investment in the tourism sector and to analyze it in terms of requirement. Likewise, to account the lending in tourism sector from various commercial banks and other financial institutions and to perform the corresponding analysis research is must. Obviously, tourism sector is broad in its characteristics, includes various sub-sectors and activities such as hotel and resorts, travels and trekking and mountaineering, transportation and production industries, and thus requires proper analysis.

Therefore, the study provides various results, draws some conclusions and attempts to answer the questions regarding sources of financing, the need of borrowing and prospects of tourism financing. Similarly, it provides the elaborative discussions about the trend of financing, the effectiveness of financing and impact of tourism as well as of tourism financing on the economic growth and development of the nation.

However, there have been some studies and research in tourism to open up its broad arena, further studies are lacking. Thus, the proposed research particularly concentrating on the financing policy, pattern, structure and assessment is new and urgent justifying the need of the study. It is also in line with the requirement for the development of tourism at desired level.

1.6 OBJECTIVES OF THE STUDY

Despite the abundant potentialities for the development of tourism in Nepal, the country is not yet fully able to achieve the benefits from tourism industry. Realizing the high prospects of tourism development, the study is confined, mainly for the assessment of tourism financing from both side demand and supply.

The primary objective of the present study is to inquire about the demand for and supply of tourism financing; existing status, structure, pattern and composition of tourism financing as well as to assess the impact and effectiveness of the tourism financing. Precisely, the objectives of the present study can be put as follows:

1. To inquire about the scope and inter-linkage of tourism and tourism financing as well as the economic impact of tourism and tourism financing through the review of relevant literature.

2. To present the profile of tourism industry in Nepal. For this purpose, the study reviews the evolution of tourism, plans, policies and programmes related to this industry and undertakes the descriptive analysis for the data related to the industry and tourists' arrival. It lists out the tourism products and infrastructure, distribution of tourism business and the organizational structure of tourism in Nepal.

3. To inquire about the supply of tourism financing from various sources such as the budget allocation of the government, foreign aid and loan disbursement, the lending of banks and financial institutions as well as the foreign direct investment from the secondary sources of data.

4. To inquire into the role of tourism and tourism financing on the economic growth of the country.

5. To inquire about the role and impact of foreign exchange earning from tourism, total number of tourists' arrival, total no. of tourism business, total no. of trained human resources and total no. of hotel beds on the economic growth of Nepal.

6. To inquire about the role and impact of various sources of tourism financing such as the banks and financial institutions, the government, and foreign aid and loan disbursement on the economic growth of Nepal.

7. To inquire about the pattern and structure of financing of TBE.
8. To examine the variations in the structure of financing between various tourism businesses.
9. To examine the operating performance of the surveyed TBE.
10. To assess the effectiveness of the financing on TBE.
11. To inquire about the borrowing need of the TBE and prospects of tourism financing.
12. To examine the experience of the BFIs for lending to tourism industry.
13. To inquire about the practice of loan processing and credit disbursement.
14. To understand the credit appraisal process and to assess the relative importance assigned by the BFIs for the business and financial aspects of the borrowing company.
15. To examine the association, if any between the importance assigned to various business and financial aspects as well as to undertake the cross verification of the importance assigned between the business and financial aspects.
16. To inquire about the quality of tourism sector loan in the portfolio of the banks and financial institutions.
17. To inquire about the perception of the lending institutions and analyze the data related to the effectiveness of tourism financing.

1.7 RESEARCH METHODOLOGY AND DATA SOURCES

A. RESEARCH DESIGN AND SOURCES OF DATA

Data forms the basis of analysis. The secondary data, published by various authorities and agencies are important for forming a base, as well as to analyze the macro economic scenario. For the purpose of this study, data published by Nepal Rastra Bank, Ministry of Finance, Ministry of Tourism and Civil Aviation, Nepal Tourism Board and Central Bureau of Statistics are used. To carry out analysis at micro level, and to understand the finer aspects of tourism financing and tourism investment firm level data were gathered through questionnaires addressed to different types of units of tourism business (Appendix: A.1) and banks and financial institutions (Appendix: A. 2).

B. PRELIMINARY SURVEY, INTERVIEW AND QUESTIONNAIRES

In the beginning, the general information related to the tourists' arrival, foreign exchange earning from tourism as well as the distribution of the tourism business enterprises and bank/financial institutions was collected in June 2005. Later, particularly during October - November 2005, some informal interviews were conducted. The pilot survey was also conducted through the use of the questionnaire. The questionnaires were fine-tuned based on feedback received during pilot survey.

Two sets of questionnaires were designed one for tourism business enterprises and another for banks and financial institutions. The questionnaire for the tourism business enterprises has four parts viz. introduction, existing financial structure, effectiveness of financing and business prospects and borrowing need. The second part is particularly designed to inquire about structure, pattern and magnitude of financing. It contains the figures for six years from Fiscal Year 1999/2000 to 2004/2005. The third and fourth part largely contain the questions to inquire about the perception of the tourism business enterprises regarding the effectiveness and prospects of financing.

The questionnaire for commercial banks and financial institutions has four parts viz. introduction, loan processing, analysis and effectiveness. The first part attempts to collect the data for 14 years, i.e. from Fiscal Year 1991/1992 to 2004/2005 about loan disbursement and loan outstanding total as well as for tourism sector. The questionnaire further attempts to inquire the perception about effectiveness of finance. Moreover, the information is also gathered about the quality of loan finance and the loan restructuring.

C. POPULATION AND SAMPLE

In order to assess the status, funding sources, patterns and effectiveness of tourism financing; the study enquires it from both demand and supply side. In July 2005, there were 948 travel agencies, 740 trekking agencies, 92 rafting agencies, and 1006 hotels, comprising both star and non-star (MOCTCA, 2005: 78). The exhaustive population of the tourism business enterprises (in the demand side) thus comes to 2,786. Based on discussion with information supplier, it was observed that the details were not updated about the continuity of the organization.

In order to determine the population size, the study employed three simple but deliberate criteria. These criteria are related to (i) the registration of the business as a tourist service provider in the tourism industry division, Ministry of Tourism, (ii) operation of the business at least for three years and (iii) the subscription of the membership in related tourism trade association. Further, these enterprises are expected to be legally updated and renew their license of operation and membership in respective department and trade associations respectively. With the application of these criteria, the population size comes down to 925. In addition to this, the study intended to include some of those tourism business enterprises dealing their business largely with the tourists such as restaurant, curio and gift shops, handicraft, airlines[1] and so on accounting 255. Thus, the potential population of the study (after the adjustment), in demand side (of finance) is 1180 tourism business enterprises as on July 2005. Table: 1.1 presents the population and selected sample of tourism business enterprises.

---

[1] Some Airlines operate most of their flights considering the demand of the tourists.

Table 1.1

Population and Sample of Tourism Business Enterprises

Type of tourism business	Exhaustive Population *	Adjusted Population #	Sample	
			Number	Percent
Travel Agency	948	223	28	12.6
Adventure	832	480	38	7.9
Trekking	740	432	30	
Rafting	92	48	8	
Accommodation	1,006	222	48	21.6
Total	2,786	925	114	12.3
Other business	-	255	16	6.3
Grand Total	2,780	1,180	130	11.0

Source: Nepal Tourism Statistics, 2005

Please refer Appendix: A.3

In July 2005, there were 17 commercial banks, 26 development banks (including 5 regional rural development banks) and 59 finance companies. Though there were other financial institutions comprising 20 financial cooperatives, 47 financial non-government organizations as well as non-bank financial institutions comprising 17 insurance companies, one Employees Provident Fund, one Citizen Investment Trust and another one Deposit Insurance and Credit Guarantee Corporation the study did not find them to be much relevant as potential population and sample for the tourism financing. Thus, the potential population of the study, in supply side (of finance) is 102 banks and financial institutions as of July 2005. Table 1.2 summarizes the distribution of the population and sample in the supply side of tourism financing.

Table 1.2

Population and Sample of Banks and Financial Institutions

Financing Institutions	Population		Sample	
	Number	Percentage on Total	Number	Percentage on Population
Commercial Banks	17	16.7	17	100.0
Development Banks	26	25.5	4	15.4
Finance Companies	59	57.8	13	22.0
Total	102	100.0	34	33.3

In the process of selection of samples, the population details, which were made available according to the clusters by various administrative offices and trade association, were used as a base. From amongst this the selection of the sample was based on convenience. Thus, this is the convenience sampling within the clusters.

On examining representativeness of sample, it is found to be representative (Chapter – V, paragraph 5.2).

D. DATA COLLECTION PROCEDURE

The data for the tourism business enterprises are collected from primary survey undertaken during the period February - April 2006. Similarly, the data from Ministry of Finance, Nepal Rastra Bank, Ministry of Tourism, Nepal Tourism board, and respective banks and financial institutions as well as from tourism business enterprises were collected and used extensively in the study.

The study employs the data comprising both published and unpublished as well as other information related to the study.

1.8 METHODS OF ANALYSIS AND MODEL

The data collected from the primary survey during February – April 2006 as well as from secondary sources were tabulated. The analysis has been performed on microcomputer using the software like, Microsoft Office Excel, SPSS for windows and E-Views. In order to achieve the first objective, the study reviews the earlier research works with descriptive analysis whereas for the second one it computes annual rate of change in percentage and proportion in addition to the descriptive analysis.

For the objective number 3, the study analyses the secondary data along with the computations of ratio and rate of change in percent. Further, for objective no. 4, 5, and 6; it runs the regression using Ordinary Least Square (OLS) method in simple and log linear or in both the forms based upon the selection of the better model of analysis. Different variables are used for different equations and in different combinations (including jointly) in order to find out the determinants and to reach the representative model. In addition, the study inquires about the presence or absence of autocorrelation and initiates the remedial measures to correct the model of analysis.

Objectives 7 to 11 relates to tourism business enterprises. For objective 7, the study employs the data from the primary survey to discuss the pattern of financing and computes the absolute figures in common size statements to study the structure of financing. In order to check the variability (difference) between the distributions among the various types of business and ownership pattern (objective no. 8), it performs one way ANOVA and t-Test for two sample means.

The study employs ANOVA using direct method. Here, one needs to undertake the calculation in following four steps (Aryal and Gautam, 2001):

Step 1: Calculate the variance between the samples (SSC)
$$SSC = \sum_{i=1}^{k} n_i (\bar{x}_1 - \mu)^2$$
Step 2: Calculate the variance within samples (SSE)
$$SSE = \sum_{i=1}^{k} \sum_{j=1}^{n_1} n_i (\bar{x}_{ij} - \bar{X}_i)^2$$
Step 3: Calculate total sum of square (TSS) i.e. TSS = SSC + TSS   or
$$TSS = \sum_{i=1}^{k} \sum_{j=1}^{n_i} (X_{ij} - \mu)^2$$

Step 4: Make the ANOVA table and make decision comparing calculated and tabulated F-value. If the calculated F-value is greater than the table F-value at decide level, here 5 percent, then the result is significant and leads for the conclusion of the variation in the distribution.

In addition, for the comparative analysis of the financial structure of tourism business enterprises, t-Test has been used. Here, again the calculated t-value is compared with the tabulated t-value at 5 percent level of significance. The formula for t-Test is as follows (Gupta, 1987: 16.34):

$$t = \frac{\overline{X}_1 - \overline{X}_2}{S} * \sqrt{\frac{n_1 n_2}{n_1 + n_2}}$$

where, $\overline{X}_1$ = mean of the first sample, $\overline{X}_2$ = mean of the second sample, n_1 = number of observations in the first sample, n_2 = number of observations in the second sample and S = combined standard deviation, which can be calculated by the following formula (Gupta, 1987: 16.34):

$$S = \sqrt{\frac{\sum(X_1 - \overline{X}_1)^2 + \sum(X_2 - \overline{X}_2)^2}{n_1 + n_2 - 2}}$$

To examine the operating performance of the various tourism businesses (objective no. 9), various ratios are computed and the discussion are undertaken. In addition, for the purpose of linking up the duration of business operation and capital structure of the surveyed tourism enterprises and to find out the relationship between these two variables, Karl Pearson's coefficient of correlation is used. The formula for the calculation is as follows (Gupta, 1987: 8.10-11):

$$r = \frac{\sum xy}{N\sigma_x \sigma_y} \quad \text{or } r^* = \frac{\sum xy}{\sqrt{\sum x^2 \sum y^2}}$$

where, x = (X- $\overline{X}$); y = (Y- $\overline{Y}$) ; σ_x = standard deviation of series X; σ_y = standard deviation of series Y; N = Number of pairs of observations r = the (product moment) correlation coefficient and r^* = transformed form of r.

Further, to assess the effectiveness of financing and to inquire the borrowing need as well as for the prospects of tourism financing (objective no. 10 and 11), the study enumerates the perception of tourism business enterprises and compares the respective data. In addition, to find out the association between the existence of trade union and labour relation as well as to map out the intensity of hindering factors, Phi-Coefficient and Chi-square (χ^2) Test are calculated respectively. Here, the methodology for the calculation of the Phi-Coefficient (r_ϕ) is as follows:

$$r_\phi = \frac{(X_1 Y_1)(X_0 Y_0) - (X_0 Y_1)(X_1 Y_0)}{\sqrt{(X_0 Y_1 + X_0 Y_0)(X_1 Y_1 + X_1 Y_0)(X_1 Y_1 + X_0 Y_1)(X_1 Y_0 + X_0 Y_0)}}$$

where r_ϕ = Phi-Coefficient, X and Y represent two responses (aspects) in which the relationship is being examined and 1 and 0 suffix to X and Y represent the 'yes' or the 'no' i.e. application or otherwise of the techniques (aspects).

It is to be mentioned here that the 'yes' for one factor is compared with 'yes' or 'no' for another factor and the 'no' for one factor with the 'no' or the 'yes' for another factor. Thus, the combination of the responses will be (i) Yes, Yes (ii) Yes, No (iii) No, Yes (iv) No, No. Further, to examine whether the value of r_ϕ (Phi-Coefficient) represents significant degree of association between the attributes or not, the test of χ^2 is applied. This χ^2 is given by $n r_\phi^2$. In the case of Phi-Coefficient as the possibility is only 'Yes' or 'No', the degree of freedom (d.f.) will be 1 and if the calculated value of χ^2 is higher than the table value of χ^2 one has to reject the null hypothesis i.e. two variables (techniques) are independent (refer Edwards, 1958: 162-163 and the discussion in the respective paragraphs, for details).

Similarly, a non-parametric test, Chi-square (χ^2) test for goodness of fit is used to find out the difference between the distribution and population. It, in fact inquires about the chance that is operative in bringing about the differences between the expectation and observation (Gupta, 1987: 17.2-3). The formula for the calculation is as: $\chi^2 = \sum (O-E)^2 / E$. The greater the value of discrepancy between the observed and expected frequencies, the greater shall be the value of χ^2. The calculated value of χ^2 is compared with the table value of χ^2 at 5 percent level of significance.

To understand the practices related to the loan processing, credit appraisal, experience of lending and loan disbursement method (objective no. 12, 13, 14, 16 and 17), the study enumerates the perception of BFIs, analyses respective data collected from the primary survey and examines the various aspects.

For objective no. 15, the study estimates the extent of relationship between the responses, examines the association and undertakes the cross verification between the importance assigned to various business and financial aspects using Phi-Coefficient (r_ϕ). It is intended to understand the application of one technique in conjunction with the application of another technique during proposal analysis and credit appraisal.

1.9 POSSIBLE SOURCES OF BIAS

At the outset, it was expected that there would not be any biasness in the selection of the sample and collection of the data. However, it is found that two types of bias can occur during the selection of the sample, conduction of the survey, collection of the data and analysis of the data. First, the possibility of the bias may occur from the criteria used to determine the size of the population and selection of the sampling method during the study.

The second bias may arise from the fact that no organization is ready to disclose complete financial information because of growing business competition and recent slackness in tourism business. Even the listed public limited companies do not want to supply all the information. In fact, tourism business enterprises are either small or family owned or most of them are private limited companies. Proprietorship and partnership firms usually deny supplying the financial information because there is no legal compulsion for them to maintain records on one hand and they are afraid of information leakage on the other.

With these possible sources of bias in mind, the study employs necessary remedies to make the sample more representative and population as appropriate as possible. In order to determine the right size of population, three deliberate criteria are used (mentioned earlier). These criteria comprising (i) registration of the business in the concerned government department and (ii) operation of the business at least for three years and (iii) membership in the trade association related to the tourism business provide with the adjustment in the population size, on one hand and consider the legal compliance of the enterprises on the other. Here, the legal compliance is referred only for the renewal of the license of operation and membership subscription in respective government departments and trade associations. Similarly, to get rid of the second bias, the promise was to be made repeatedly with each and every business enterprises not to disclose the individual name and its financial information in any manner.

1.10 CHAPTER SCHEME OF THE STUDY

The present study is divided into seven chapters. The broad outline of the chapters is as follows:

Chapter 1 is an introductory chapter. It presents the background of the study, concept of tourism and tourism financing. In addition, it deals with the significance of the study, objectives of the study, research design, sources of data and methods of analysis to be adopted.

Chapter 2 presents a theoretical underpinning for the tourism and tourism financing. It also carries out the survey and review of existing literature in tourism in Nepalese perspectives.

Chapter 3 presents the profile of the Nepalese tourism industry. An attempt is made to assess the evolution of the tourism, to account the tourism products and infrastructure to enumerate tourism business enterprises and finally to discuss about the contribution of tourism.

Chapter 4 is designed to examine the existing status of tourism financing in the first part and examine the role of tourism and tourism financing in the economic growth of the country, in the second part. It basically, discusses the data in terms of supply of financing. It presents the analysis with reference to the impact of tourism, in general and tourism financing, in particular from various sources on economic growth measured in terms of Gross Domestic Product etc.

Chapter 5 incorporates the tourism financing of tourism business enterprises from demand side. The chapter discusses the composition and structure of financing. In addition, it also examines the effectiveness and prospects of financing along-with the operating performance and borrowing need of tourism business enterprises. It further goes on to examine the variations in the structure of financing between various tourism businesses.

Chapter 6 discusses the perception of bankers about lending to tourism sector. It enumerates the practices of loan processing and credit appraisal of banks and financial institutions related to the lending in tourism business. It also discusses about the relative importance assigned by the BFIs for the business and financial aspects of borrowing company. It further examines the indicators for the effectiveness of tourism financing based on the response of BFIs.

Finally, Chapter 7 presents the summary of findings and conclusions of the research. It also includes the policy implications and suggestions.

REFERENCES

ADB and MOTCA (1990). **Nepal Tourism Development Program, 1990**. A Report Prepared by Touche Ross Consultancy.

Aryal, Jeetendra Prakash and Arun Gautam (2001). Quantitative Techniques. Kathmandu: New Hira Books Enterprises.

Bernstein, L.A. (1993). **Financial Statements Analysis**. USA: IRWIN

Bhatia, A. K. (2002). **Tourism Development: Principles and Practices**. New Delhi: Sterling Publishers Private Limited.

Burkart, A. J. and Medlik, S. (1974). **Tourism: Past, Present and Future**. London: Heinemann.

Diamond, J. (1977). Tourism's Role in Economic Development: The Case Reexamined. Economic Development and Cultural Change, 25 (3): 539-553 Source: http://www.jstor.org/ accessed on 17/07/2006

Emanual de Kadt ed. (1979). **Tourism: Passport to Development?** Oxford: Oxford University Press.

Enzensberger, Hans Magnus (1996). A Theory of Tourism. **New German Critique.** 68: 117-135. Source: http://www.jstor.org/ accessed on 30/03/2005

Frechtling Douglas C. (1987). Assessing the Impacts of Travel and Tourism –Measuring Economic Benefits in Tisdell, Clem (ed) (2000) **The Economics of Tourism Volume II**. Cheltenham: An Elgar Reference Collection.

Ghali, Moheb A. (1976). Tourism and Economic Growth; An Empirical Study. **Economic Development and Cultural Change**, Vol. 24, No. 3 pp. 527-538.

Ghimire, Ananda (2002). **Travel and Tourism: An Introduction.** Kathmandu: Ekta Books.

Gitman, Lawrence J. (2004). **Principles of Managerial Finance**. 10th Edition. Pearson Education, Inc.

Government of South Africa (1996). **White Paper on Tourism**. Source: http://www.google.com accessed on 25/03/2006

Gupta, S. P. (1987). **Statistical Methods**. New Delhi: Sultan Chand and Company.

Jamieson, Walter and Tazim Jamal (1997). Contributions of Tourism in to Economic Development...... in UN ESCAP (2001). **Promotion of Investment in Tourism Infrastructure**. New York: UN ESCAP

Karma, Krishan. K. and Mohinder Chand (2004). **Basics of Tourism: theory, Operation and Practice**. New Delhi: Kaniska Publishers, Distributors

Kunwar, Ramesh Raj. (1997). **Tourism and Development, Science and Industry Interface**. Kathmandu: Published by Laxmi Kunwar.

Manjit Singh (2001). **Financial Organization and Working of State Tourism Development Corporations**: A Study of Punjab, Haryana and Himanchal Pradesh. A Ph. D. thesis submitted to the Faculty of Commerce and Business Management of Kuruchhetra University

McIntosh, Robert W., Goeldner, Charles R. (1990). **Tourism Principles, Practices, Philosophies**. New York: John Wiley & Sons Inc.

MOCTCA (2005). **Nepal Tourism Statistics**. Kathmandu: Ministry of Culture, Tourism and Civil Aviation, Government of Nepal.

Pandey, I. M. (1999). **Financial Management.** New Delhi: Vikas Publishing House Private Limited.

Pandey, I. M. (2004). **Financial Management** 9th edition. New Delhi: Vikas Publishing House Private Limited.

Pearce Douglas (1981). **Tourist Development**. Essex UK: Longman Group Limited.

Pearce Douglas (1989). **Tourist Development**. Essex UK: Longman Group Limited.

Ritchie, J. R. Brent and Charles R. Goeldner (eds), **Travel Tourism and Hospitality Research: A Handbook for Managers and Researchers**. New York: John Wiley and Sons, Inc.

Seaton, A. V. and et al. (eds.) (1994). **Tourism: The State of the Art. England**: John Wiley and Sons.

Sharma, Shashi Prabha (2004) **Tourism Education: Principles, Theories and Practices.** New Delhi: Kaniska Publishers, Distributors

Siddiqui, S. A. and A. S. Siddiqui (2005). **Managerial Economics and Financial Analysis**. New Delhi: New Age International (P) Limited, Publishers.

Smith, Stephen L. J. (1989). **Tourism Analysis: A Handbook**. Singapore: Longman Group Limited.

Soloman, Ezra (1969). **The Theory of Financial Management**. Columbia University Press.

Tribe, John (1999). **The Economics of Leisure and Tourism**. Oxford: Butterworth Heinemann.

UN ESCAP (2001). **Promotion of Investment in Tourism Infrastructure**. New York: UN ESCAP

Vanhobe, Norbert (2005). **The Economics of Tourism Destinations**. Elsevier Butterworth Heinemann.

Whitehouse, Jan and Colin Tilley (1993). **Finance and Leisure: Leisure Management Series**. London: Financial Times, Pitman Publishing.

Witt, S. F.Y.; M. Z. Brooke; and P. Busklay (1997). **Finance and Control: The Management of International Tourism**. New York: Rutledge.

II

CHAPTER

REVIEW OF LITERATURE ON TOURISM AND TOURISM FINANCING

2.1 INTRODUCTION

2.2 TOURISM LITERATURE IN NEPALESE PERSPECTIVE
- Special Studies and Reports
- Research Articles and Doctoral Thesis

2.3 LITERATURE REVIEW ON TOURISM FINANCING AND INVESTMENT
- Special Studies and Reports
- Research Articles and Doctoral Thesis

2.4 THE ECONOMIC IMPACT OF TOURISM
- Measuring the Economic Impact of Tourism
- Studies in Economic Impact of Tourism

2.5 IMPACT OF TOURISM FINANCING AND INVESTMENT
- Tourism Financing Regime
- Demand for and Supply of Tourism Financing
- Impact of Financing in the Economy
- Studies in the Economic Impact of Investment (bank lending)

2.6 SUMMARY OF THE LITERATURE REVIEW

2.7 APPROACH OF THIS STUDY

CHAPTER II
REVIEW OF RELEVANT LITERATURE ON TOURISM AND TOURISM FINANCING

2.1 INTRODUCTION

This chapter initially attempts to inquire about the scope and inter-linkages of tourism and tourism financing through the review of relevant literature. Therefore, it includes six sections - two for the reviews on relevant literature, two for the economic linkage or impact of tourism and tourism financing and the rest two for the summary and conclusion. In fact, it attempts to build up the theoretical underpinnings particularly in Nepalese perspectives incorporating tourism research in doctoral theses and research as well as in other perspectives incorporating contemporary studies in tourism and tourism financing. Finally, it summarizes the discussion and review to justify the present endeavor through its instinct approach of study.

2.2 TOURISM LITERATURE IN NEPALESE PERSPECTIVE

Tourism has gradually emerged as one of the major industries in Nepal. Though, it is still in its initial stage of development, it is striving to be a benign agent of development and endurable medium to create various contributions. In fact, tourism can contribute as channel for the socio-economic development of the country, as a massive foreign exchange earner, as a big generator of employment through its labour-intensive nature, as an endurable medium of infrastructure development and poverty alleviation as well as a genuine promoter of cultural harmony and peace (Dixit, 1997: 49 and Bahuguna, 2005: 137).

Despite of increasing importance, tourism has attracted relatively little attention in the literature in Nepalese perspective. Couple of articles on tourism are available such as Anand and Bajracharya (1985), Zurick (1992), Paudyal (1998), Ranadhe (1999), Sparrowhawk and Holden (1999), Nepal (2000), Simmons and Koirala (2000), Hepburn (2002), Stevens (2003), Bhattarai, Conway and Shrestha (2005). However, the coverage of such articles was either sector specific, relatively narrow or simply different than of present study.

Various books, such as Ghimire (2000), Satyal (2000; 2004), Kunwar (1997), Chand (2000) present detail and often quite critical discussions on the subject matter. Likewise Singh (1995), Pradhnanga (2000), Shrestha (2000) concentrate their discussions in specific sectors, rather at the single aspect of tourism industry whereas ESCAP (1991, 1995 and 2001), UN ESCAP (2001), Ives (2004) and IUCN (2005) focused in regional perspective. Thus, the literature survey did not provide much reviews and discussions relevant for the present subject matter. In fact, such studies rarely appeared in the contemporary tourism literature. Therefore, it is not to exaggerate that a limited number of studies have been conducted in Nepalese perspective comparing with that of neighboring countries and other developed countries.

Despite of limited literature on tourism in Nepalese perspective, present section attempts to incorporate the instincts of most relevant literature those available during the literature survey. However, it attempts to review most of doctoral research incorporating the objectives of the study, data sources and methodology and research findings. The review is organized in chronological order as far as practicable.

A. SPECIAL STUDIES AND REPORTS

It was only in 1959 that a French national, Georges Lebrec had prepared "General Plan for the Organization of Tourism in Nepal" with the help of the French Government[1]. Lebrec recommended to make promotional materials such as brochures, posters, postage stamps depicting the Himalayan peaks and Flora and Fauna and to use films, documentaries prepared by mountaineering expeditions for the promotion tourism in Nepal. He also suggested establishing Nepal Tourism Office.

Later, Lebrec visited Nepal twice in 1964 and 1966 and prepared other two reports entitled "Report on the Development Tourism" and "Report on Tourism in Nepal" respectively. Both the reports are not available for the review (Shrestha, 1998; Shrestha, 1999; Sharma, 2001 and Satyal, 2004).

National Promotional Committee Report, 1983

In 1981, His Majesty's Government of Nepal had formed National Tourism Promotion Committee. The committee had prepared a report entitled 'National Promotional Committee Report, 1983 emphasizing the promotion of 'Nepal Style" tourism in line with the suggestions forwarded by Nepal Tourism Master Plan, 1972. However, the report suggested for the development of resorts in the mid mountains, promotion of tourism in India and to Europe. The basic thrust was to create premises to encourage the people in organizing the pilgrimage package to both Buddhist and Hindus from Asian countries and particularly from India. It has given stress to start and organize the convention tourism. It has also opted to open up a door for the visits of Indians particularly during hot summer season.

In addition to this, it had recommended for the deputation of a separate person in Nepalese Embassies and otherwise assigning the honorary consuls to look after the affairs of tourism promotion. Likewise, it had recommended for the establishment of a revolving fund for the promotion of tourism and for the participation in international trade fairs (Shrestha, 1999).

Income and Employment Generation from Tourism in Nepal

Nepal Rastra Bank, the central bank of Nepal had conducted a special study entitled 'Income and Employment Generation from Tourism in Nepal' in 1989. The study was comprehensive and had covered

---

[1] Mr. Lebrec had been an advisor under the bilateral cooperation program of French Ministry of Foreign Affairs during 1958-59.

various sectors of the economy in general and particularly about the income and employment from tourism. The study was enriched with vast data coverage and econometric analysis.

"Tourism is an activity generating a number of economic and social benefits. It not only augments foreign exchange earning, the scarce resource of the country, but also creates employment opportunities - direct and indirect and induced employments, through backward and forward linkages with other sectors of the economy; such as agriculture, industry, other service sector etc. It provides a vast spectrum of employment ranging from highly skilled persons to unskilled workers. It also opens up new horizons of employment for employed and partially employed people from different walks of life" (NRB, 1989: 20).

The objectives of the study were to estimate the level and patterns of tourist expenditure in Nepal, to estimate the value added and imports contents and thereby foreign exchange earning from tourism in Nepal, to estimate the income and employment generation in the tourism sector of Nepal. In this study regressions were run on the time series data as well as cross-sectional data for the period 1974 - 1987.

The major findings of the study among others were as follows.

1. The demand for tourism is found to be income inelastic in dependent variables such as tourist expenditure and number of tourists during the period 1974 -1987.

2. Tourist expenditure was found to be highly sensitive with respect to exchange rates, but the sensitivity of tourist arrivals to this variable was less.

3. Altogether 11,176 persons were found directly employed in the tourism sector. Out of this, hotel shared 52.9 percent, airlines 24.5 percent, travel agencies 13.8 percent and trekking agencies 8.8 percent.

Among tourism sub sectors (when direct, indirect and induced effects were combined), the ratio of import content for hotel was estimated at 53.45 percent, travel agencies 74.51 percent, trekking agencies 54.04 percent and airlines 67.05 percent. The ratio of direct import content when the indirect and induced effects were taken out was estimated at 35.45 percent for hotels, 15.12 for travel agencies, 10.79 percent for trekking agencies and 57.60 for airlines.

The value added for the tourism sector i.e. total payment to domestic factors including payments to intermediate and final inputs (when direct, indirect and induced effects were combined) was estimated at 37.6 percent as compared to 37.8 percent for tourism related sector and 37.7 percent for the overall sector.

Further the study concluded that tourism has an immense potential with virtually unlimited scope, has been an important sector for Nepal for its much needed foreign currency earnings and has been generating a sizeable number of employment. The study suggested liberalizing foreign exchange, to emphasize trekking tourism, to do aggressive marketing, to expand both international and national air service, to develop integrated tourism development policy and to establish a full-fledged apex body to look after the affairs.

Role of Private Sector in South Asian Regional Cooperation in Tourism

Binod K. Karmacharya[2] had undertaken the study entitled "Role of Private Sector in South Asian Regional Cooperation in Tourism. The report was submitted in July 1991 to Centre for Economic Development and Administration (CEDA), Tribhuvan University Kathmandu Nepal. The study was carried out with the background of private sector's emerging role in South Asian Countries, as a part of the broad theme of "The role of Private Sector in South Asian Cooperation". The study therefore, was confined to identify the role of private sector in promoting South Asian Cooperation in Tourism with special reference to Bangladesh, India, Nepal, Pakistan and Sri Lanka.

The study initially dealt the tourism and its growth in the South Asian region, supply side of tourism industry, status, problems and prospects of regional cooperation in tourism using data from respective countries. It has also dealt among others, some issues related to human resource development, investment and incentives, and project financing.

The study has attempted to analyze existing status, problems/constraints and prospects for supply side of tourism industry and asked for the leading role of private sector in this growing and challenging industry. The study included the comprehensive data for the period of 6 years in average (Varying 3 - 9 years). The study was therefore descriptive, designed to present the glimpse on the participation and role of both public and private sectors' involvement in tourism industry.

The study has gathered data on number of hotel, number of rooms available, occupancy rate, available mode and status of tour and travel services, strength of trained human resources and various problems remained /inherited in this sector. It has enumerated various problems such as lack of planning, skilled human resources, promotion and marketing activities, investment and financing, transportation, aviation and in country network services. Likewise, it has enlisted lack of tourism information centre, lengthy and cumbersome frontier formalities and wastage and littering problems.

The study has concluded that the prospect of South Asian regional cooperation in tourism is high and increasing day by day and pleaded for the timely implementation of the plan/policy with due priority.

B. RESEARCH ARTICLES AND DOCTORAL THESIS

The study entitled "Tourism as Foreign Exchange Earner: A Study of Tourism in Nepal." by **Ranade** (1999) aimed at analyzing the trend of foreign exchange earnings in Nepal from tourism, the effect of tourism on the Nepalese economy and the trends of tourists' arrivals in Nepal – both Indians and non-Indians during the last two decades (1975 -1995).

The study appeared to be descriptive one thus incorporated facts and figures to illustrate Nepal as a dreamland of tourists along with the discussion on socio-economic conditions. Similarly, it had discussed about the various features to show the growth of tourism. In addition, it strived to conclude the readily quantifiable and positive effects of tourism on the development of GDP.

---

[2] The study "Role of Private Sector in South Asian Regional Cooperation in Tourism, is available for the review in CEDA Library however, its condition appeared to be critical.

Further, the study largely assumed that tourism can bring the general benefits for the economy as a whole. Therefore, the study employed the data on such items, such as number of tourists, foreign exchange earning through tourism, increased revenue to the government and revealed that tourism has been playing an important role in the country. It concluded that the tourism is an important sector in the Nepalese economy because the foreign exchange earnings from tourism has been significant, accounting to 18 percent of total foreign exchange earnings and about 4.3 percent of GDP.

Mr. Viet Burger (1978) has carried out a doctoral study on "The Economic Impacts of Tourism in Nepal: An Input-Output Analysis". At the outset, the study has been considered as the first and important academic research work in the field of Nepalese Tourism. The underlying theme of the study was to define the importance of tourism and its various economic benefits for the country.

The study had two broad objectives (goals). The first objective was to present a case study of the effects of the international tourism in Nepal based on the objectives of the periodical plans. The second objective was to provide the Nepalese policy planners with a set of information necessary for the political decision-making process. In addition, the study had some specific objectives such as to designate meaningful categories of tourist and to measure their respective impacts on the national income and employment, personal and regional income distribution, the balance of payment and trade position and finally on the present and potential impact on agricultural production.

In order to analyze the economic impact of tourism, Mr. Burger has illustrated the theoretical framework and evaluated two widely used methods viz. cost-benefit analysis and inter-industry analysis. He has modified them considering their applicability. He has collected four general sets of data viz. data on input structure of all industries directly or indirectly linked to tourism; information on the origin of inputs (goods and services) and on the distribution of payroll over income classes and nationality of employees and finally the data on expenditure pattern of tourists

In addition, some other data required for the study were collected including inflows of tourist, government provision of goods and services for the infrastructure investment in private and public sector as well as foreign exchange earning from tourism. He has used both primary and secondary data.

The major findings of his study were as follows:

1. **Employment and Capital:** Tourism is generally believed to be labour-intensive activity thus offering employment opportunity and income. It was found that tourism plays an important role in the Nepalese economy. The increase in the volume of tourist flow has direct as well as indirect impacts on the development process of Nepal. However, tourism was found to be more capital intensive roughly three times and similar to that of manufacturing sector.

2. **Income Distribution:** Tourism provides relatively few jobs and offers limited scope for the improvement of personal and regional income distribution. The people living in remote areas and in off-site of tourist areas or routes could not reap the benefits of tourism as they have very limited things to offer.

3. **Foreign exchange Earning:** Tourism had been effective and promising instrument for earning foreign exchange. In 1974-75 the gross foreign exchange earned from tourism totaled to Rs. 156 million i.e. 30 percent of total convertible foreign exchange earning. A larger than

expected proportion of a tourist dollar remains in Nepal as national income. In 1974-75 it was 64 percent for all tourism categories combined.

4. **Salient Features of Tourism:** Seasonality factor was found to be the most prominent factor in Nepalese tourism. In addition, air travel has been dominant as well as the tourists visiting Nepal for pleasure trips.

5. **Tourist Expenditure Pattern:** The per capita gross tourist expenditure was found to be increasing rapidly from NRs. 127 in 1962-63 to NRs. 3339 in 1978-79 and further NRs. 5659 in 1981. However, the average per capita tourist expenditure per day was found to be varying too much.

6. **Government Incentive for Tourism:** The Government was found to be involved in tourism in three ways viz. providing loans to tourism enterprises particularly through Nepal Industrial Development Corporation, providing incentives for tourism particularly income tax holiday, preferential allocation of foreign exchange and lowered customs tariffs and finally the public investment in infrastructure.

7. **Government Tourism Policy:** It was found that government policies on tourism appeared to favor the fairly small group of enterprises and entrepreneurs. Though the government policy seemed favourable to tourism development, it has been handicapped due to the multitudes of bureaucratic procedures.

8. **Investment:** Tourism is capital-intensive industry and requires high investments both from public and private sector. The share of public investment in infrastructure related to tourism was estimated at approximately Rs. 150 million. The public expenditure on tourism was reckoned to be some Rs. 9 million. However, the subsidy of tourism on account of budget revenues and expenditures was found to be relatively small.

9. **Future Direction of Tourism Development:** It is advisable to develop tourism to the extent that foreign exchange is needed for development purposes. It was found necessary to concentrate society's resources in other fields where benefits of the development are shared more widely.

Though Nepal faces many problems in its quest for social and economic development those policies that assure the participation of largest number of people will prove the most successful in overcoming these problems.

The study of **Krishna Ram Khadka** (1993)[3] entitled "Tourism and Economic Development in Nepal" was mainly confined in two important areas of tourism viz. the performance and efficiency of the hotel investment and economic impacts of tourism. Major objectives of the study were concerned with the impact of tourism and development in Nepal. Two specific hypotheses were formulated viz. hotel

---

[3] The review is based on the executive summary and other reviews undertaken by various scholars. The personal visit could not be fruitful enough.

investments have been an efficient means of generating foreign exchange and developing tourism capacity of the economic sectors affects the impact of tourism.

Using both primary and secondary data and input - output model, he attempted to discuss linkages between tourism and economy and estimate the economic efficiency of hotels in generating foreign exchange. He had performed some modifications in the existing models to explain the impacts of tourism under limited supplying capacity of the domestic sector.

The Major findings of his research were as follows:

- There are important factors for the performance of hotel industries such as the hotel bed occupancy rate, double bed room price and marketing activities.
- Among various categories of hotel industry, quality hotels and safari hotels were found to be more efficient generator foreign exchange than others.
- The role of tourism in economic development was found to be significant.
- The net earnings from tourism were greater than that of the other sectors of the economy.
- The promotion of standard hotel serving high paying tourist could enhance the economic impact of tourism.
- Marketing was found to be a major factor in increasing occupancy rate and thus contributing on the performance of the hotels.
- The seasonality factor in Nepalese Tourism was found to be significant.

In fact, Mr. Khadka pleads for the promotion of the Nepalese Tourism to high paying quality tourists, particularly regional tourists from Japan, India and Thailand and other in summer season thus capturing the market of growing economies. Similarly, he pleads for the development of import substitution industries and in ensuring the proper supply for the tourism industry.

Surendra B. Pradhananga (1993) has attempted to explore the answers for some fundamental questions related to tourism such as, the impact of tourism expenditures on government revenue, employment, exports and imports; role of tourism as an engine of economic growth in Nepal and the weaknesses and strengths of existing tourism policy. Similarly, he attempted to identify consumption pattern of tourism or tourism expenditure, to analyze the use of local resources in the tourism consumption and their effects on employment, to probe into capacity utilization of hotels in relations to the tourists' length of stay and finally to examine the change in government revenue resulting from the tourism export and so on.

Using both primary and secondary data, the study inquired about the tourists' consumption pattern and its economic impact on employment, export and national revenue. It has analyzed the direct, indirect and induced effects of tourist expenditure along with the backward and forward linkages of tourism. In addition, it has examined the impact of import and export of goods and services and generation of employment.

The study found that the direct employment opportunities generated were 12.4% in tourism sector, 32.8% in tourism related and 54.7% non-tourism sector. The local resources used by tourists were found to be relatively important in the tourism consumption pattern. The expenditure on the local product was found to be concentrated mainly on three items viz. carpets, garments and handicrafts.

The major weaknesses of the tourism industry were found to be the leakage of foreign exchange. Similarly, high import contents, seasonal fluctuations in demand and over dependence on seasonality factor have also been found as other impediments for the tourism industry. Most of travel agencies and hotels of Nepal were under-financed, under staffed, under utilized and found to be unproductive.

The study has suggested in framing a tourism development strategy and policy of foreign direct investment. Similarly, the study asked the government to come up with a new thrust, strategy and policy to generate more revenue from tourism through planned efforts.

Hari Prasad Shrestha (1998) had undertaken a doctoral research on "Tourism Marketing in Nepal" to inquire and assess the tourism marketing efforts initiated by Nepal as well as to examine the market potential of tourism, existing marketing policy and practices vis-à-vis tourism products and infrastructures and their contribution in Nepalese economy.

Using both primary and secondary data through field survey and interviews, he has tested various hypotheses (24) ranging from the estimation of influencing factors of tourist arrival to the assessment of difference between the importance accorded and actual experience gained by the tourists.

The Major findings of the research were as follows:

Nepal is extremely rich in tourism products because of natural, cultural and historical heritage wealth and products. It equally possesses tremendous diversities to develop it as a major tourist destination.

Tourism has recorded a sound growth rate of 18.5 percent during last 25 years (1962-1997).

Nepalese tourism has some specific features such as the major flow of tourists in autumn and spring seasons, the purpose of trip as holiday/pleasure, source of their information as friends/relatives and the largest numbers of visitors from India.

Tourists were found highly satisfied with their visits as they had realized their expected goals indicating the potential for further tourism development in Nepal.

Majority of tourists (55%) have felt the dearth of publicity materials and support infrastructure related to tourism.

Tourists were found to be generally satisfied with weather, natural scenery, wild animals, people's behaviors, sense of remoteness and authenticity, religious customs, fulfillment of sense of adventure, historical sites, culture, entertainment, language communication, agency services and guide services vis-à-vis importance accorded to them. However, they were found to be less satisfied with immigration, transportation, airlines services, lodging, sightseeing tours, shopping facilities, tourist information services and food and drinks in Nepal.

They rated tourism services as highly satisfactory particularly for accommodation, sightseeing tours, shopping facilities, food and drinks, language communication, customs, agency services and guide services. The single most important experience satisfying the tourists visiting Nepal was the hospitality, friendliness, helpfulness, humbleness, honest and welcoming attitude of the people.

The tourism experts viewed that tourism marketing was unorganized, unprofessional and the total marketing effort was poor. It equally has lacked the adequate professionalism and sufficient budget allocation.

The empirical analysis showed that tourist arrival in Nepal has been significantly influenced by world tourist flow, tourist arrival in South Asia, promotional expenses made by Nepal, income level in originating markets and the lagged variable. The log-linear model had best explained the tourist arrival in Nepal.

Finally, the study has raised some questions such as how the country realizes its tourism potential, how it can market in tourism generating markets and what strategies should be followed to market the comparative advantage. It argued whether these questions are important or not. It finally concluded that these questions need to be answered in order to develop the ways to exploit the potentials and make it as a vehicle of growth and engine of equitable development.

Puspa Shrestha (1999) has undertaken a doctoral research on "Tourism in Nepal: Problems and Prospects" to discuss about the tourism development over the period.

The main objective of the study (Shrestha, 1999: 8-9) was concerned with the problems and prospects of tourism in Nepal. The specific objectives were to assess the trend in tourism development, to assess the role of tourism in the economy, to review tourism plans and policies, to inquire into the current problems, to highlight the prospects and finally to recommend measures and appropriate strategy for tourism development in Nepal.

The study was based on primary as well as secondary data. The primary data and other information were derived from questionnaires (2 sets) one for tourists and other for the personnel and experts related to tourism industry. Similarly, secondary data were collected from various national and international publications. The data collected from both the sources were analyzed to find out the demand for tourism on the basis of tourist arrivals, their length of stay and amount of their expenditure.

The Major findings of the research were as follows:

Tourists were found to be quite satisfied with their visit to Nepal and had shown intention of revisit. However, they have highlighted some crucial problems such as pollution and environmental degradation, lack of tourism products, services and infrastructure. They also pointed out about some other problems such as, lack of medical facilities in remote areas, public toilets, security and political disturbances.

Tourism experts were agreed about the immense potentiality of tourism in Nepal. However, they had issued some concerns about the crucial role of tourism with due consideration of resource constraints and landlocked situation of the country. They were not happy with the present condition of tourism development and asked for the earliest attention particularly on air accessibility, marketing and promotion activities, environment pollution, service infrastructure, competition, political situation and quality of tourism product.

Tourism industry had lacked the proper planning, efficient and sound policies and timely implementation and hence has been suffering. Tourism being a multi-sector industry asks for a comprehensive and concrete policy to cater the changing demand.

The comparative analysis of the problems of tourism industry as visualized by the tourists and experts in tourism sector vis-à-vis the actual situation of tourism sector revealed that the problems should be perceived from various angles for developing and promoting tourism industry in Nepal. No doubt, there are a lot of problems. Finally, the study concluded that Nepal has immense potentiality for tourism development.

Om Prakash Sharma (2001) has conducted research on "Tourism Development and Planning in Nepal" considering the empirical and cross sectional approaches. Though the topic is a major concern for both developed and developing countries, has not received adequate attention in Nepal. Thus, his study is intended in contributing better understanding and successful implementation of the policies.

The study is concerned on two premium aspects of tourism. The first aspect deals with the extent of tourism development in true sense of the term. The other aspect intends to provide policy planners with a set of information related to the appropriate policies for tourism development in periodical plans. It has been essential to understand tourist expenditure behaviour for detecting the policy variables to analyze and to determine the relationship between tourism and the macro economic variables.

The major objective of the study was to examine the extent of tourism development and policy planning in Nepalese Perspective followed by some specific objectives as:

- To analyze in brief the growth pattern of tourism;
- To examine the effects of tourism on the economic development process;
- To study the expenditure pattern of tourist to assess the demand structure;
- To assess the institutional role for tourism development;
- To formulate tourism planning to suggest an effective and reliable policy.

The study has used both secondary and primary data to evaluate tourism development and policy formulation for planning purposes. It has adopted desk research in analyzing growth trends regarding total tourists arrival, earning, hotel accommodation, employment generation, and economic effects and to predict the variables. It has also analyzed various variables concerning the purpose to find the trend using linear, quadratic and exponential functions.

Besides in order to measure the concentration and seasonality he has used Hirschman-Gini concentration index and for the employment used simple regression model. Similarly, for economic impact analysis the ordinary least square (OLS) method has been applied to the single linear, log linear and first difference form using government internal revenue, tax revenue and per capita income. Almon Polynominal lag model has also been tested to find the response of lagged variables. Further the Granger Causality Test has been applied to find out lead and lag relationship with trade volume of the country.

The Major findings of the research were as follows:

The study on growth pattern of tourism demonstrates remarkable growth of tourist arrival, earning from tourism and consistent increasing trend in share of tourism earning to merchandise exports and GDP. Moreover, travel receipts have been antidote in providing the resources required exterminating a significant part of the exchange gap and trade deficits during the period (1974-1996).

An impressive growth has been witnessed in hotel sector, followed by its rooms and beds. However the average guest night per tourist has virtually remained stagnant and the hotel occupancy rate for Kathmandu has gone down.

Though, the royalty is inversely related to foreign exchange earning from tourism, the majority of mountaineers expressed positive views about the relationship between royalty and mountaineering employment.

The case study concerning the trekking employment confers that the western development region alone generates 56% followed by eastern development region as 36%. Similarly in terms of destination, Kanchanjungha and Manaslu have created highest rate of employment per trekker 3.7 and 2.8 persons respectively (pp218-220).

Tourism earning is one of the factors, which has its effects on the development indices like tax revenue, government internal revenue and real GDP. However the impact of tourism earning on per capita income remains insignificant. The gross saving of the country is found as increasing as an increase in tourism earning (pp 220-221).

The expenditure elasticity is a proper tool in analyzing expenditure pattern. The expenditure on accommodation, transport and the miscellaneous items has been found most elastic while that on food, communication, tax and fees seem to be inelastic.

Concerning the marginal budget share of tourist expenditures, the results disclosed that a major part of the expenditures as a result of every incremental US $ 100 is still shared by the basic necessities of tourism viz. accommodation, food and transport.

Finally the study concluded that despite of considerable extent of tourism development, a plethora of problems were inherited in the economy as a whole as well as the tourism sector in Nepal. The problems such as the domination of seasonality, tourism an import increasing factor and more or less a stagnant average length of stay seemed to be difficult to correct in a short duration. The problems like successive increase in royalty for mountaineering, much weaker trekking rules and regulations, administrative inefficiency and absence of its coordination with related Institutions are supposed to be controlled.

Rudra Prasad Upadhyaya (2003) has conducted study on "Tourism as a Leading Sector in Economic Development in Nepal" considering the empirical and cross sectional approaches. Though the topic is a major concern for both developed and developing countries, has not received adequate attention in Nepal. Thus, the study was expected to contribute for better understanding and successful implementation of the policies. In addition it was intended to find out whether the impact of tourism has been beneficial in true sense.

The major objective of the study was to examine the extent of tourism development and policy planning in Nepalese Perspective followed by some other specific objectives such as to analyze the growth pattern of tourism, to examine the effects of tourism on the economic development process, to study the expenditure pattern of tourist, to assess the institutional role for tourism development and to formulate tourism planning.

The study was an empirical in nature. It had mainly used secondary data both published and unpublished and statistical techniques like regression analysis; and correlation analysis. Major findings of the study were as follows:

1. To cope with higher tourist inflow more and more star and non-star hotels were coming up in Nepal along with increased bed capacity. There has been structural shift in the sense that the share of beds in star hotels declined from 62 percent in 1984 to 26 percent in 2001 whereas that in non-star hotel increased from 38 percent to 74 percent in the respective years.

2. Higher inflow of tourist also necessitated more trained manpower and increasing travel and trekking agencies. Thus, it has been found that the impact of tourist inflow has its positive bearing on hotels, air transport, and travel, trekking and rafting agencies besides more trained manpower.

3. The analysis of sectoral behaviour of the economy of Nepal has shown that higher inflow of tourists also necessitated more trained manpower and increasing travel and trekking agencies. Thus, it has been found that the impact of tourists' inflow has its positive bearings on hotels, air transport, and travel, trekking, rafting agencies besides more trained manpower.

4. The analysis of sectoral behaviour of the economy of Nepal has shown that the trend growth rate of the primary sector came down to 2.6 percent per year during 1990-99 from 4.1 percent in the period of 1984-90. However, secondary and tertiary sector registered growth and went up to 6.3 and 6.0 percent per year from 6.0 and 5.5 percent in respective period.

5. Regression analysis applied to three sectors (primary, secondary and tertiary) of the economy showed that all the three sectors have positive and significant effects.

6. The farm sector had low growth potential as well as inducement effect in the economy whereas the tertiary and secondary sectors had high growth potential in the economy.

7. The available patterns of tourist expenditure suggested that they spent mainly on accommodation, foods, sight seeing, beverages and trekking. These sectors shared 64 percent of total tourist expenditure in 1987-88. Tourist expenditure had a strong effect on government expenditure. The regression analysis showed a strong and significant inducement effect on government regular as well as on development expenditure.

8. Foreign direct investment had been an important source of capital inflow in Nepal. It was found that after manufacturing the tourism sector had the largest number of approved projects

9. The constitution of the country guarantees the fundamental and human rights, provides freedom of residence and movement from one place to another which is directly related to tourism. In fact, Nepalese laws related to tourists are very soft, liberal and tourist friendly.

Mr. Narayan P. Maharjan (2005) has carried out research on "Tourism Planning in Nepal." In this study he has assessed the planning practices in terms of number of tourists and stagnant growth rate thus concluding it as an inadequacy of existing planning resulting from improper and myopic planning.

The basic objective of the study was to inquire and assess the tourism planning efforts initiated by tourism institutions in Nepal. Other specific objectives were to examine tourism planning practices in Nepal and to evaluate the effectiveness of the tourism plans and programmes.

The study was a descriptive cum survey research. It included both primary and secondary data gathered from the survey and from different interviews with officials, executives, executive members and experts involved in tourism industry.

Major findings of the study were as follows:

- Most of these institutions have been found practicing short term planning and generally lacking long-term vision and strategic thinking. Majority did not consult expert in planning, did not use information feedback, and neither gave inputs nor paid attention for macro plans. Bureaucracy had dominated planning practices. It lacked research and was highly politicized and was based on adhocism.

- Most of these institutions opined that political strikes (Bandhs) and inadequate budgets were major blocking factors. In addition, other factors were lack of competent human resources, weak infrastructure, rigid bureaucracy and appropriate legal environment.

- Tourism plans lacked integration with macro plans, relationship with overall national tourism plan, did not provide for the collaborative and integrated efforts in local level tourism programs and generally lacked clear cut direction.

- Micro level tourism institutions expected the government support for appreciation and rewards, participation of workshop especially in planning, consultancy and financial assistance. Equally they asked for the support of macro public sector organizations for reducing constraints, creating tax incentive, improving information service and establishing tourism area.

- National microenvironment has been found to be the major basis of tourism planning followed by product, destination, resources, international scenario and national policy. Relevant information has been major aspect in decision-making followed by research base and recent model. The planners and policy makers felt that physical and natural resources are most potential resources for tourism planning followed by social and cultural resources, settlement pattern and social and cultural traits.

- The political decision- making was found to be most dominant factor in planning whereas other factors were alternative strategy development, defined goals, clear objectives, and market analysis.

- The major goal of tourism planning was found to be improved economical viability of tourism followed by increased cooperation among all sectors. The planners gave due importance for promotional and marketing activities. In addition, they perceived that almost all goals of tourism were inadequately considered in tourism planning.

- The tourism experts have opined that tourism planning has not been strategic and it has suffered form adhocism. Government tourism planning practice was found to be below the satisfactory level.

- Lack of tourism program has been the major obstacle for successful tourism planning followed by inadequate budget, improper planning, poor communication, lack of integration and support from private sector.

The major finding of the research was that the tourism planning of Nepal is symbolized as myopic planning. There is no planning relationship with any institutions whether related or not in tourism.

2.3 LITERATURE REVIEW ON TOURISM FINANCING AND INVESTMENT

Despite increasing importance, tourism has attracted relatively little attention in the literature on tourism financing and investment. Thus, the reviews and discussions on such aspects have rarely appeared in the contemporary tourism literature. Apparently no one provides the journal article specifically treating the topic, and focusing on either demand for or supply of tourism financing. Couple of articles on tourism investment is available such as Bodlender (1984), Bull (1990), Franck (1990), Wen (1991), Forsyth (1994) and Schmidgall (1999). However, the coverage of such articles was either country specific or relatively narrow. Various books, such as Burkart and Medlik (1981), Chand (2000), Seth (2001), Raina and Lodha (2004) present brief and often quite critical discussions on the subject matter whereas Whitehouse and Tille (1995), Massenger and Shaw (1993); Nagi (1997); and Releigh and Roginsky (1999) concentrate the discussion particularly in hotel and lodging sector, rather at the single aspect of tourism industry.

In addition to these literatures on investment and finance, some UN agencies like WTO, UNDP, UNCTAD and ESCAP have carried out some studies, organized seminars and published reports and thus created certain premises and inspiration for the emerging subject matter.

"On the other hand, 'grey literature' sources, such as EC (1998), Roldán (no date), and WTO (1995), typically treat the topic in greater detail" (Lindberg; Molstad; Hawkins; and Jamieson, 2001: 508-511).

In order to raise the awareness of tourism researches regarding financing and investment, present study intends to review the related literature and also to provide a brief summary of issues, trends and practices.

A. SPECIAL STUDIES AND REPORTS

IUOTO (1971) A Study on Sources of and Conditions of Financing

In 1971, International Union of Official Travel Organization (IUOTO) had undertaken the "Study on Sources of and Conditions of Financing for Tourist Development Projects". This report was prepared in persuasion of the resolution adopted by IUOTO. It contains a list of public and private banks, commercial companies, international organization and other agencies already financing tourism projects or prepared to do so. And in addition, the financing terms and conditions were included in the report. One of the findings of this study was that the traditional distinction between private and public financing tends to disappear gradually. Most tourism projects are of a scope requiring both private and public participation. This can also be said about the pooling of international sources with local capital both private and public.

The purpose of the study was in two folds.

To provide the comprehensive list of banks, commercial companies, international organizations and other institutions which have already contributed financing or are prepared to provide financing.

To indicate the terms and conditions for the financing along with time duration, rate of interest, collateral requirement or guarantee and so on.

The preparation of the study was undertaken in three stages comprising collection of information, analysis of information and consolidation and conclusions. The report had provided a general picture of the capital market for the promotion of tourism. Major findings of the survey were as follows:

There were three types of institutions that likely to supply the tourism financing viz. public and private institutions that finance the projects within the country, institution situated in a country but engaging in international operations and international sources of financing.

"The most common forms of financing are of the traditional kind: mortgage loans for the financing of buildings and loan secured by pledges for the financing of the equipment. However, the capital made available in this way rarely covers more than 50 percent cost of the work or the guarantees offered. The balance is covered by novel supplementary types of financing, such as leasing or franchising."

The study indicated that the traditional dividing line between public and private funds is becoming considerably blurred. Indeed, public funds (financing or infrastructural investments which are not immediately profitable) and private funds (buildings) are very often combined in one in the same project. Moreover, there are many cases of states acting as ordinary private investors through public institutions.

There were three types of financing sources available for tourism development projects as Financing Sources of National Projects such as public institutions, semi public bodies, commercial undertaking (Banks, insurance companies. commercial companies), National sources of financing International projects such as public and semi-public institutions entrusted to grant credits usually to developing countries and International Sources of financing such as multinational companies and international organizations.

Oliver, Bennett (1991)

Bennett Oliver's (1991) study was based on the draft final report carried out for Asian Development Bank and the World Tourism Organization (ESCAP, 1991). The paper aimed at providing a framework and guidelines for financing policies and strategies for tourism development. The study also contains case studies for three countries - Fiji, Indonesia and Nepal.

The objective of the study was to produce a practical framework and guidelines for formulating policies and strategies for financing tourism development in developing countries.

Major findings of the survey related to Nepal were as follows:

Nepal has a very similar number of visitors to Fiji. Its visitor total now exceeds that of Sri Lanka but it is well below the number recorded by larger neighboring countries particularly India.

- Domestic tourism in Nepal is dominated by pilgrimages and visits to friends and relatives and has little impacts on the demand for hotel accommodation.
- There has been very little private foreign investment in tourism and in hotels. Government has a very limited involvement in hotels and leaves travel agency operation to the private sector. The government owned Nepal Industrial Development Corporation has been providing multilateral funding particularly for hotels.
- Nepal welcomes foreign investment. The constitution of the country ensures for the foreign investment. But there have been many hindrances for obtaining relevant permission.

- The department of tourism is regulating the hotels and travel agencies through licensing, classifying and so on. The department is also responsible for marketing with a tiny budget. However, it has opened up the doors for joint promotion initiatives.

- The department has tended to act as a controlling agency for tourism development rather acting as a supporting body for prospective investors. It has no project implementation capacity of its own, nor had any projects available for submission to prospective funding agencies.

- Though Master Plan for Tourism was designed in 1972 many of its proposals have not been implemented.

- The key components in assessing the tourism financing to the tourism sector among others are the scale and extent of the public sector in tourism, importance of the development aid in the economy, role of foreign investment, mobilizing domestic capital for tourism development and providing a mechanism for effective management of loans.

- Nepal is highly dependent on foreign aid and multilateral or bilateral donors' finance virtually in all-significant infrastructures. The Ministry of Tourism has had very limited influence on investment priorities. The basic stress was on the poverty alleviation and providing basic infrastructures.

- Nepal has signally failed to attract significant foreign investment in the tourism sector. There are for main reasons such as projects may not highly attractive in financial terms: for hotel this results from relatively low revenue in relation to high initial cost, particularly for land. The failure to pursue debts owed by existing hotels exacerbates the difficulty of establishing new ones.

The second reason is the lack of active promotion of investment opportunities in the tourism sector. Worse than that, there is little professional marketing of Nepal as destination with the result that prospective investors do not even consider the country.

The third reason is related to the government rules and regulations. These rules are difficult for the outside investors to understand. There is no single agency for the prospective investor to deal with and the whole approval procedure can take a substantial amount of time.

Likewise, the forth reason is related to the foreign exchange regime. It is strict and inflexible as well as it requires a considerable time to obtain permissions. While many existing organizations in the travel industry evade the restrictions easily, it is not an environment, which encourages foreign investors.

- There is confusion for the responsibilities in the government bodies and overlapping of roles and functions. A foreign investor might find it difficult to see where to start. The staff can be transferred to and from other Departments of Government and are not always sufficiently well versed in the peculiarities of the tourism industry or of the modus operandi for the outside investor.

- Nepal is also weak in mobilizing domestic capital particularly for major projects. Almost all businesses are family owned, including the majority of hotels. The shortage of investment opportunities has led to an emphasis on property as an investment, particularly in the

Kathmandu Valley. As a result land prices are extremely high. This in turn discourages investment.

- The larger single source of long-term finance has been the Nepal Industrial Development Corporation. Commercial banks tend to lend for a maximum of five to seven years at a commercial rate of interest.
- Nepal lacks a strong independent accounting profession and mechanisms for calling in loans where management is poor and weak.
- The development banks in particular have a poor record of loan management. As customers have not been repaying loans this tends to result in commercial environment where hotels are able to charge low prices in turn discouraging new investment including foreign investment.

Similarly the findings of the survey related to incentives for the financing were as follows:

- Nepal provides the investment incentives for hotels. It consists of such measures as investment allowances, duty exemptions or concessions and tax holidays.
- It does not provide grant finance to the private sector. Similarly, there is a common complaint about the incentives only focused on the hotels not in other travel sector.
- The most justifiable complaint was the penal taxation on tourist coaches in Nepal, originally 200 percent and later to 100 percent. This level of tax makes it difficult to justify the purchase of new vehicles, as it is difficult to charge more in operating customers.

In addition to above findings some other findings include funding sources, investment incentives, taxation and other regulatory mechanisms. The key objectives in financing are to achieve a good return and to minimize the project risks. Allied to this is the need for a recovery mechanism if things go wrong. Nepal is weak in this.

ESCAP (1991)

ESCAP has organized a seminar on "Investment and Economic Cooperation in the Tourism Sector in Developing Asian Countries" of the region in Tokyo and Sendai Japan from Oct.15 to 21, 1991. The purpose of the seminar was to strengthen national capabilities to create a favorable investment climate for the development of tourism and to promote economic and technical cooperation for tourism development.

Participants from the countries including Nepal have presented the country reports covering subjects such as current situation in tourism development, foreign investment in the tourism sector and economic technical cooperation in the field of tourism.

Major findings and recommendations of the seminar were as follows:

Present status of investment in the industry in this region was far from being satisfactory. Investment in the tourism sector, both domestic and foreign, was found to be generally low, except in certain members of ASEAN.

It was not possible to determine precisely the share of foreign Investment in each country's total tourism – related investments.

There were however, indications that Foreign Direct Investment in tourism services was virtually absent in most ESCAP Economies with exceptions of HK, Indonesia, Malaysia, the Philippines, the Republic of Korea, Singapore and Thailand. Rules and regulations to attract FDI were inflexible and difficult to comply with. In most countries, there was no single agency for the perspective investor to deal with, and approval of the project could be time consuming.

Transnational hotels corporations were involved though some forms of non–equality arrangement such as management contract, franchises and technical services agreements. The extent of such involvement was not known. Such non-equity participation was useful but the need for Foreign Direct Investment remained paramount.

While many socio-political factors were responsible for the lack of investment, the most serious constraint was the inability of the government to accord appropriate priority.

Certain features of the tourism industry could also be blamed for the lack of private investment. The industry was basically land and labour intensive and possesses the projects with longer gestation period and depends heavily upon infrastructure development.

Moreover land prices had soared virtually everywhere, further dampening the spirits of investors. Investors being profit motivated certainly prefer to invest in projects yielding quick returns.

In many countries the promotion of tourism investment had been constrained by the absence of well defined tourism policy. In the absence of clear defined directions and guidelines, tourism projects were implemented in an unplanned manner.

Foreign Exchange regimes were strict and inflexible leading to inordinate delays in obtaining necessary promotions.

Sub regional efforts were considered crucial for the development of tourism in the ESCAP region. ASEAN and SAARC members were jointly promoting tourism in their respective areas. It might be excellent to step up the cooperation and promote tourism as a package.

Tourism should be accorded a high priority by governments. In order to determine its true significance, government should consider its long-term positive effects on society rather than judging it solely by narrow economic criteria. It should be borne in mind that the tourism was not a mere luxurious development exclusively for tourists. It was as important as other industrial sectors.

For the systemic development of tourism sectors, governments should formulate comprehensive tourism policies including socio-economic objectives for tourism development, the role of government, the boundaries of public and private sector involvement, investment policy and other regulations for tourists and tourism.

B. RESEARCH ARTICLES AND DOCTORAL THESIS

Despite the increasing importance of tourism at various levels for the varied economic reasons, there are apparently, not many studies undertaken on tourism financing and investment. In addition the case with the foreign direct investment and financing in tourism did not appear to be much different. However, in this section, an attempt is undertaken to review the studies and research related to tourism financing and investment.

Clem TisdellJie Wen (1991: 175-193) has undertaken a study on Investment in China's Tourism Industry incorporating its scale, nature and policy issues. It provided an overview of tourism investment in China during the period 1979 to 1988. The study includes the discussion about the foreign investment, its nature and impact.

The study found that such investment has played a vital role in the expansion of the tourism and has been a leading industry in China. Very often the economic interdependence of tourism with other sectors of the economy was ignored by policy-makers related to the tourism industry. Thus, it argues that the lack of attention to these inter-Sectoral interdependencies has resulted in unbalanced tourism industry. Investment in the tourism industry in China has tended to be concentrated in the building of hotels.

The study concluded that the investment has been dominated by foreign capital and there appears to have been over concentration on the building of high-class hotels. A top-heavy structure has emerged which is not well-suited to customer demands. In general, the building of hotels appears to have proceeded more on the basis of preconceptions by officials and suppliers than on the basis of market or economic analysis. Thus, the current location and pattern of supply has been such as to make many hotels uneconomic.

Adrian Bull (1990: 325-331) has studied about the effects of foreign investment in Australia. The article explored about existing theories of overseas investment in manufacturing in relation to the tourism industry.

The study found that throughout the 1980s the Australian tourism industry has received an increasingly large proportion of its financing from abroad. Foreign investment has been mainly through the capital which is supplied from abroad. The study included a policy model that necessitated the Australian tourism to compete aggressively to reap the benefits from overseas investment.

Similarly, the study of **Larry Dwyer Peter Forsyth** (1994: 512-537) provides an overview of foreign investment in Australian tourism focusing on its levels and patterns. The study proceeds to clarify some of the impacts for foreign investment in tourism. He employed widely accepted Eclectic Paradigm of international production to explain. He found that the foreign investment has played an important role in the development of tourism worldwide. However, such type of analysis has been neglected over the years. After distinguishing between illusory and real impacts in Australia, the paper attempts to discuss about the benefits and costs of additional foreign investment in tourism for both developed and developing nations.

However, the study of **Christian Franck** (1990: 333-338) is different as it studied about the tourism investment in regional perspective. He inquired about the potential rather untapped tourism markets of the Central and Eastern Europe. In fact, these countries were trying to convert from socialist planned economies to the free-market system and gradually opening the doors for the foreign tourism.

To take advantage of the potential for wealth creation offered by the development of a Western-style tourist industry, the study pleaded for the careful planning and investment. It argued that the finance is not easy to obtain. However, it stressed for the western support that appears to be forthcoming in the form of joint ventures, equity swaps and leasing agreements.

Further, **Jonathan Bodlender** (1984) in his article on tourism investment inquired about the increasing potential of tourism to create jobs and wealth. He argued that such potential of tourism unfortunately, could not be matched by government and private sector realization of what the industry has to offer. It argued that unless investment from these two sectors is forthcoming, potential will be lost all round. Tourism jobs are cheap to create compared to other industrial sectors and the high tourism multiplier effect ensures a good return on investment for government, private industry and therefore for the national economy as a whole.

Mr. Manjit Singh (2001) had undertaken Ph. D. research on "Financial Organization and Working of State Tourism Development Corporations of Punjab, Haryana and Himanchal Pradesh State".

In this study, he had presented the profile of state tourism development corporations and discussed about their financing pattern and operating performance. In addition, he had discussed about the project planning management in these corporations and tried to throw light on areas where further improvements were felt necessary.

The specific objectives of the study were:

1. To examine that requisite project planning and economic viability study precede the establishment of various complexes,
2. To appraise the existing financial structure of these corporations,
3. To evaluate the operating performance of these corporations and
4. To suggest necessary measures to improve the performance of the corporations under study.

The study was empirical one. It had largely used secondary data collected from the concerned corporations and state tourism departments through various annual reports, feasibility reports and other official documents. In addition, some primary data were collected particularly with respect to project planning through the interviews conducted with the staffs in these corporations.

To analyze the data various statistical tools had been used. Since many ratios had been used to understand the financial structure and to review the operating performance of these corporations a longitudinal analysis of these ratios had been made to analyze the growth pattern during the period. Thus the analysis included the techniques like Growth Rates comprising simple, compound and trend growth; Co-efficient of Variation: t-statistics for comparison of means and ANOVA.

Major findings of the study were as follows:

The study had revealed that during the last 3 decades, both the central and state governments have shown slightly more concern for developing tourism infrastructures. Likewise, these three corporations have made efforts to create necessary infrastructure for healthy growth of tourism in their respective states. Tourists' clientele had increased followed by the average occupancy rate of the hotels and lodges. Sales were increased considerably providing a marginal increase in profit. However, the prohibition policy of the state government in Haryana had been a major set back for the tourism in state incurring heavy loss in turnover and profitability.

The study argued that all the corporations under study had been reflecting mess-up in project planning practices, though the degree varied. It starts from a weak project organization accompanied by indiscriminate political interference during the selection of the project. The feasibility studies conducted were superficial, carrying no relevance. Project financing was without realistic assessment and project implementation was marred by time and cost overruns. Project reviews were never undertaken. It was coupled with minimal technical and market expertise but with unlimited political interference.

It was found that corporations under study were too much depending either on central or state government assistance for financing the projects instead of generating internal surplus. These corporations had by and large conservative capital structure. In addition, they were found to be playing safe without using loan capital from the banks and financial institutions. In fact, it was because of either they got too much assistance from the government or were unable to get loans from the financial institutions. These corporations had developed a tendency to rely more on short-term borrowing including the central financial assistance. Thus, they have failed to follow a suitable financing policy.

The examination of the performance indicated that operating efficiency was far from being satisfactory. For instance, Haryana Tourism Corporation, which is considered slightly better among all the three corporations, had average Return on Assets just 0.7 percent while the others have shown negative ROA during the period under study.

Return on Shareholders equity of these corporations was fluctuating and inadequate over the period. Likewise, the Return on Capital Employed also indicated very gloomy picture of these corporations. The average return was very low or even negative over the period. The growth analysis also indicated high degree of variations in the ratio of all the three corporations under study. However, Punjab Tourism Development Corporation was on the verge of bankruptcy, suffering losses almost during entire period under study.

Capital Intensity Ratio had shown a positive signs in all the corporations under study, though at its minimum in Himachal Pradesh indicating seasonal business. Inventory Turnover Ratio appeared to be satisfactory. Thus, assets utilization scenario in the corporations under study presented a mixed picture. Net Profit Margin and operating profit in these corporations were found to be negative except in Haryana. Though the situation was improving slowly along with high fluctuations, it was not encouraging yet because of the nature of earning i.e. profit was the result of interest received on Fixed Deposit.

Various ratios such as Material consumed to Sales, Employees benefit to sales and business promotion expenses to sales had great bearing on the investigation of the expenditure side of the corporations. The analysis clearly indicated a gloomy picture in the above aspects and ultimately did not produce any healthy signs.

2.4 THE ECONOMIC IMPACT OF TOURISM

Tourism businesses depend extensively on each other as well as on other businesses, government and residents of the local community. Economic benefits and costs of tourism reach virtually everyone in the region in one way or another. Economic impact analysis provides tangible estimates of these economic interdependencies and a better understanding of the role and importance of tourism in economy (Stynes, No date: 1).

"The generation on foreign currencies and the economic growth based on 'new sector' (with the consequently creation of new jobs) are the two most important potential effects of the tourism sector development in an economy (Gibson, 1993; Morley, 1992; Brohman, 1996)" (Jimenez and Ortuno, No date: 2).

A. MEASURING ECONOMIC IMPACTS OF TOURISM

As such, there are a number of concepts and concerns associated with expanding the economic benefits of tourism (UN ESCAP, 2001: 3). Various scholars, among others, Douglas (1981, 1989) provided the theoretical framework to measure the economic impact of the tourism activity. Similarly, Ghali (1976), Diamond (1977) and Jamieson and Jamal (1997) among others, attempted to measure the economic impact of tourism as well as the generation of employment opportunity through tourism considering various direct and indirect effects.

In fact, there have been various techniques or methods to measure the economic impact of tourism in this or that way, sometime even creating the confusion in the choosing an appropriate method for the specific study. Here, an attempt has been undertaken to briefly review the methods in assessing the economic impact of tourism[4].

Supply-Demand and Price Elasticity

The economic contribution of tourism activity to a community or region is primarily influenced by a diverse number of factors within and outside the destination. In fact, it is difficult to calculate impacts because of varied effects of tourism, the diverse number of participants, and the complex interrelationships between various sectors. The economic impact of tourism can be explained using economic concept of supply and demand.

The law of demand and supply is applicable because tourism is also an economic activity. A number of variables influence the demand and supply of a tourism product or service. For example, if the price of a hotel room increases, demand may decrease, as visitors seek other locations or accommodation sources, and the supply of available hotel rooms therefore increases. The supply-demand relationship of tourism is influenced by factors such as the price elasticity of demand for tourism. When demand is price elastic, a lower price could generate a higher demand and hence higher revenues. Similarly, if demand is price inelastic, a lower price could result in lower overall revenues (for detail discussion, see Lundberg, Krishnamoorthy and Stavenga (1995)[5].

Direct and Indirect Effects of Tourism Earnings

Tourism has a variety of economic impacts. Tourists contribute to sales, profits, jobs, tax revenues, and income in an area. The most direct effects occur within the primary tourism sectors - lodging, restaurants, transportation, amusements, and retail trade. Through secondary effects, tourism affects most sectors of the economy. An economic impact analysis of tourism activity normally focuses on changes in sales, income, and employment in a region resulting from tourism activity (Stynes, No date: 4).

---

[4] Much of the discussion in this section is primarily based on UN ESCAP (2001: 4-13)

[5] A good discussion of the subject can be found in Lundberg, Krishnamoorthy and Stavenga (1995).

The economic benefits of tourism can be direct or indirect. The primary effect is direct that results from direct tourist expenditures for goods and services whereas the indirect benefits are generated by the circulation of tourism expenditures in the destination through inter-business transactions. "The direct effects are the easiest to understand because they result from the visitor spending money in tourist enterprises and providing a living for the owners and managers and creating jobs for employees" (Goeldner; Ritchie and McIntosh, 2000: 426). For example, indirect benefits can be generated from the investment and spending by the businesses that benefit directly from tourism expenditures. The direct business receipts, when re-funneled as investments or used to purchase other goods and services from domestic suppliers (who, in turn, purchase goods and services from other domestic suppliers), stimulate income and employment in other sectors (UN ESCAP, 2001: 7).

"In addition, tourism spending within the destination area can create induced benefits. As income levels rise due to the direct and indirect effects of change in the level of tourism expenditure, some of the additional personal income (related to the change in tourism expenditures) is spent within the destination. This results in induced benefits, such as local income and jobs in the local goods and service sector. Hence, the spending by tourists at the destination can create direct benefits in tourism-related services and sectors such as accommodation, hospitality, attractions, events and transportation. This spending can also create a significant amount of indirect and induced benefits in other sectors such as agriculture, construction and manufacturing. Indirect and induced benefits are also referred to as the secondary effect" (UN ESCAP, 2001: 7).

Multiplier Model of Tourism Revenue Turnover

Multipliers measure the effect of expenditures introduced into an economy. Tourism multipliers are used to determine changes in output, income, employment, business and government receipts, and balance of payments due to a change in the level of tourism expenditures in an area. In fact, multipliers capture the secondary economic effects (indirect and induced of tourism activity.

For example, if tourism expenditures is increased due to a special event in the destination, some of this added revenue (first round of expenditures) may be used by the event to purchase food and other goods from the local economy, as well as on payment of wages, salaries, government taxes etc., (second round of expenditures). The suppliers to the event may then spend the money received from the event on other goods, services, taxes etc., thus generating yet another round of Expenditures. Employees from the events and local suppliers to the events may use the additional personal income, derived from the direct and indirect effects of the increase in tourism expenditures. Some of the added revenues from the increase in tourism expenditures may, however, undergo leakage.

"The net effect of the successive rounds of spending of added tourism expenditure is the multiplier effect. In essence, tourism multipliers attempt to describe the relationship between direct tourism expenditure in the economy and the secondary effect of that expenditure upon the economy. Some of the factors that affect the multiplier are the size of the local economy, the propensity of tourists and residents to buy imported goods or services, as well as the propensity of residents to save rather than spend (where saving reflects money kept out of circulation, i.e., not reinvested)" (UN ESCAP, 2001: 7-8).

In mathematical terms, the multiplier effect can be calculated as:

$$\text{Multiplier} = 1 / (1 - C + M)$$

Where, C = Marginal propensity to consume (i.e., the proportion of any increase in income spent on consumption of goods and services), and

M = Marginal propensity to imports (i.e., the proportion of any increase in income spent on imported goods and services).

There are some common multipliers such as the income multiplier, which measures the extra domestic income (primary and secondary) generated by an extra unit of tourism expenditure; the employment multiplier, which measures the increased number of primary and secondary jobs created by an extra unit of tourism expenditure; the government multiplier, which measures the extra government revenue created by an extra unit of tourism expenditure.

Multipliers can be calculated for a country, region or community. However, the information provided by tourism multipliers has to be very carefully evaluated. Factors such as the size of the destination can significantly affect the multiplier. A smaller economy may have a much smaller multiplier than a larger one since more goods and services might be imported to meet the tourists' needs, resulting in a greater leakage of revenues out of the destination.

Input-Output Analysis

An input-output model (I-O model) is a mathematical model that describes the flows of money between sectors within a region's economy. Flows are predicted by knowing what each industry must buy from every other industry to produce certain output. Using each industry's production function, I-O models also determine the proportions of sales that go to wage and salary income, proprietor's income, and taxes. Multipliers can be estimated from input-output models based on the estimated re-circulation of spending within the region (Stynes, No date: 6).

The analysis commences with the development of a table that illustrates, in matrix form, how transactions flow through the economy over a time period. The rows of the matrix show the sales of the total output by each sector to every other sector. The columns demonstrate the inputs required by every sector from the other sectors. When assessing tourism accommodation, the rows in the table would demonstrate the output, i.e., the revenues generated by each industry from the sale of products or services, including accommodation, meals, tour guides and related services such as laundry, medical services etc. The columns would allow us to see the inputs (goods, services, labour and capital) that go into the output of the accommodation sector, including food, utilities, paper products, advertising and promotion services, wage and salary levels etc. Using a combination of matrix manipulations, multipliers can be calculated to provide an assessment of the effects of different sectors on each other. While input-output tables are helpful in understanding the linkages of the sectors in the economy, it must be remembered that the information obtained provides a snapshot of inter-industry economic actions at only one point in time (UN ESCAP, 2001: 9-10).

Tourism Satellite Accounts

Satellite accounts provide comprehensive information on a field of economic activity, and are generally tied to the economic accounts of a nation or region. The Tourism Satellite Account is a relatively new phenomenon. For example, the British Columbia Ministry of Development, Trade and Tourism (in the province of British Columbia, Canada), has developed a Tourism Satellite Account as a separate input-output model designed to display tourism's contributions to the province related to the overall input-output model of the province. A Tourism Satellite Account has also been developed by Statistics Canada in order to assess the significance of tourism to Canada (e.g., its size, structure and economic importance).

The account uses concise definitions of tourism and attempts to provide a clear and real measure of tourism-related economic activity. Both direct and indirect tourism activities are accounted for in areas such as, but not limited to, demand, supply, employment, taxes etc. Such a tool is crucial in determining the complex spending patterns of visitors as well as the goods and services that cater to their needs (UN ESCAP, 2001: 10).

Tourism Satellite Accounts determine the value of tourism to the economy and identify the amount of benefit and the employment, income, taxes and other benefits that flow from those sectors. In addition, they provide a comprehensive picture of the size and scale of tourism in a country, and can help to gather support for ensuring adherence to the principles of sustainable tourism development.

Cost-Benefit Evaluation

It is also known as Benefit Cost Analysis (B/C). It simply answers to the question that which alternative policy generates the highest benefit to the society? The B/C analysis estimates the relative economic efficiency of alternative policies by comparing benefits and costs over time. It also identifies the most efficient policies from the perspective of societal welfare, generally including both monetary and non-monetary values. It makes use of a wide range of methods for estimating values of non-market goods and services, such as the travel cost method and contingent valuation method (Stokey and Zeckhauser 1978; Sudgen and Williams 1978).

In assessing such information, it needs to determine not just whether jobs and wealth are created, but also how the benefits are distributed, what costs result from the development process, and whether the benefits of tourism outweigh the economic, social and cultural costs. It is clear that economic analysis needs to be integrated with other data (environmental, social, cultural etc.) in order to provide a reasonable indication of whether tourism is a good strategy for the destination.

Cost-benefit analysis is an important activity to perform, but is also difficult to carry out, since a number of the costs are very difficult to quantify. How does one measure the "sense of place" or "spiritual happiness" of a population? How does one quantify the loss value of habitat fragmentation to ecological integrity? While strides are being taken to develop full-cost, environmentally-based accounting, some measures may need to remain qualitative rather than quantitative.

B. STUDIES IN ECONOMIC IMPACT OF TOURISM

Travel has been a feature of all human societies since the beginnings of civilization but it has only been in the last half of the present century that mass tourism has emerged as a major world industry (Ayres, 2000: 114). In line with the development of related activities, it has attracted a considerable discussions and researches about various aspects of tourism, and the economic aspects of the tourism stood as fundamental. Imminent writers like Emanual de Kadt (1978), Pearce Douglas (1981, 1989), Goeldner, Ritchie and McIntosh (2000), Smith (1989), Douglas Frechtling (1987), Seaton and et al. (1994), John Tribe (1999), Clem Tisdell (ed) (2000) and Norbert Vanhobe (2005) have discussed about the economic aspects of tourism and its role in the economic growth and development of the country. These studies have definitely created the base for the further study and even for the further empirical analysis. In addition, Ghose, Siddique and Gabbay (eds) (2004); Anand Ballabh (2004); Mak James (2004); Sunil Kabia (2005) and Anil Sharma (2006) have also discussed about the economic impact of tourism in their respective publication.

In fact, there have been considerable mentions about the economic impact of tourism in varied publications. Most of them concentrate their analysis on theoretical aspects and provide only descriptive discussions. However, in this section of the chapter an attempt has been made to review some studies (research articles) that are considered most relevant for the current study because they provide the instincts for the theoretical underpinning and empirical frameworks for the economic impact of the tourism. Therefore, present section of the chapter contains a brief discussion and review for the study such as Ghali (1976), Diamond (1977), Sathiendrakumar and Tisdel (1989), Jie Zhang (2001), Jimenez and Ortuno (no date), Stynes (no date) and UN ESCAP (2001).

Moheb A. Ghali (1976: 527-538) has undertaken a study to empirically examine the role of tourism in the economic growth. The purpose of the study was to evaluate the contribution of one of Hawaii's major exports – tourism – to the rate of economic growth and the stability of this growth.

The study used a slightly expanded version of the growth equation. It used the variables such as rate of growth of personal income (y) as a linear function of the rate of growth of exports (x), the rate of growth of private investment (i) and the rate of growth of state and local government expenditures (g) with their weighted share in personal income in the preceding year. The study had used the following growth model:

$$y = \alpha_0 + \alpha_1 x \left(\frac{X}{Y}\right)_{t-1} + \alpha_2 i \left(\frac{I}{Y}\right)_{t-1} + \alpha_3 g \left(\frac{G}{Y}\right)_{t-1}$$

where, capital letters denote levels and lowercase letters denote percentage rate of change in the variables.

Further, it had used three other models, the first two to determine the level of investment (either in hotel construction or in other construction) and the third to find the rate of change in state and local government expenditures.

$$I_{1t} = \beta_0 + \beta_1 (\Delta T)_{t-1} + u_t$$
$$I_{2t} = \gamma_0 + \gamma_1 Y_{t-1} + e_t$$
$$G_t = \delta_0 + \delta_1 Y_{t-1} + v_t$$

The study concluded that the contribution of tourism in Hawaiian economy has been significant during the period 1953 - 1970. It equally cautioned that the analysis was on the contribution of tourism to the total output and should not be taken to welfare because the study had only addressed about the answer to the question of "How much the tourism had contributed."

Similarly, J. Diamond (1977: 539-553) has empirically analyzed the role of tourism in the economic development of the developing country in general and Turkey in particular. The major objective of the paper was to concentrate on tourism's economic rationale as well as to analyze the causes and difficulties associated with promoting tourism in developing countries.

The study concludes that the tourism has been a great help for some underdeveloped countries. It equally questions about two aspects determining the export performance of less advanced countries: "first the world demand conditions they face, and second, often overlooked, the capacity of these countries to supply commodities in the amount and proportions dictated by international trading conditions."

The developing countries generally face considerable difficulties on both the demand and the supply side because the industry requires considerable amounts of imported inputs. The study argued that the tourists' receipts greatly overstate the industry's actual contribution to the foreign account. "Moreover, while the industry is fairly labor intensive in operation, the expansion of productive capacity is rather capital intensive. Thus tourism is not a very efficient means of creating employment. Further, not only tourism require types of labor in short supply, but the work tends to be seasonal and low paid and creates social tensions"

The study of Sathiendrakumar and Tisdel (1989) attempted to analyze the role of tourism in the economic development of the Maldives. The study considered the economic and related consequences of international tourism for the Maldives. The objective of the paper was to consider the contribution of tourism in terms of foreign exchange earnings, government revenue, national output, and local employment as well as to examine tourism's potential to employ persons displaced from fishing.

The study found out that the tourism is the Maldives's largest earner (gross) of foreign exchange. It appeared less important as an earner of foreign exchange than fisheries because of import leakages. It is capital intensive and employs less than one seventh of the number employed in fisheries.

Tourist development has been strongly concentrated on male which received the lion's share of economic benefits. It has promoted centralization and brought small impact on local poverty and disguised unemployment. The study even doubts about the employment creating potential of tourism. However, isolated tourist development has reduced the social cost of tourism to a great extent though it has created small positive contribution in the employment and economic welfare in the Maldives.

Jie Zhang (2001)[6] had undertaken a study on Tourism Impact Analysis in Danish Regions. The major purposes of the study were to introduce the general equilibrium model (tool) called 'LINE' and to apply the model for the tourism economic impact analysis in regional perspective. The study argued that the model is more flexible and complete as it combines both Keynesian demand model and Leontief's input-output model and claimed it as better than other previous models. The model gives a large number of regional economic indicators for analyses.

The study has presented the key economic indicators following the real circle, i.e. from place of residence by group and household, then further to place of demand by component and by commodity. The key economic indicators are reflected by the changes in regional output, income, employment, taxes, consumption and trade.

---

[6] It was a paper presented to the 41st Congress of the ERSA held in Zagreb, Croatia during 29 August – 1st September 16, 2001.

Jimenez and Ortuno (no date) examined the role of the tourism sector in economic development in Spanish perspective. The objective of the study was to assess the real role of the foreign currencies receipts from tourism in the Spanish economy. The study has used two variables such as earnings from international tourism and imports of produced goods. It considered annual data for the Spanish case from 1960 to 2002.

The empirical analysis found that the foreign currency receipts from tourism affects the imports of manufactured products. However, the main contribution of the study was that the relationship was not a transitional situation from 1960 to around the eighties but it was a long-run stable relationship and not casual but causal. International tourism has the advantage of providing considerable amounts of foreign currency to support the growth of manufacturing activities and appropriately planned spatial expansion can ensure that the development of the two sectors is complementary. However it also asks for the awareness of some dangers arising from the destruction of natural and socio-cultural resources and or from the construction of hotels without limit.

The study of Daniel J. Stynes (no date) appeared to be informative because it has incorporated most of the questions expected to arise during the economic impact analysis of tourism. In fact, a variety of methods, ranging from pure guesswork to complex mathematical models, can be found to be estimating economic impacts of the tourism. Therefore, the study incorporates the meaning of the economic impact, its use, the details of tourism economic impact, multiplier effects, measurement techniques, approaches of assessment, steps in conducting the impact study of tourism, interpretation of the impact study and finally about the cost of impact analysis.

Economic and Social Commission for Asia and the Pacific, in its study (UN ESCAP, 2001) has identified some of the major issues related to investment in tourism infrastructure and economic benefits of tourism. The study was primarily confined on the Economic impact/effects of tourism.

In fact, the tourism expenditures have both primary and secondary effects. The economic impact of tourism can be measured as the difference in economic well being between the income levels that would have existed without tourism activity and the income levels after tourism activity. There are a number of tangible and less tangible economic benefits and costs, such as increased resources for the protection and conservation of natural and cultural heritage; income and standard of living from tourist expenditures; induced income from tourism expenditures; new employment opportunities; and increased community visibility leading to other economic development opportunities. Further, other economic benefits include new induced employment opportunities; increased tax base; improved infrastructure and facilities; and development of local handicrafts.

Similarly, the potential costs include "seasonal employment; low status/paying jobs; inflation; increased costs (land, housing, food and services); pollution; increased traffic/congestion; negative impacts on cultural and natural heritage resources (which could affect tourism revenue over time); increased crime; increased taxes; leakage of revenues and external domination; over-dependence on tourism as a prime economic activity" (UN ESCAP, 2001).

In addition to the economic costs discussed above, there are other costs that may have an indirect or long-term impact on the economic contributions of tourism. For example, land values may change as high-priced projects replace traditional and less profitable land uses.

Other studies such as Burger (1978) Pradhananga (1993), Sharma (2001) and Upadhyay (2003) had focused on the economic impact of tourism in Nepalese perspective and provided the elaborative discussion and empirical analysis. As these studies have already reviewed in earlier section of this chapter it is not desirable to repeat the discussion.

In fact, there has been considerable discussion about the role of tourism as a force for economic change both in developed and developing countries. The economic benefits and costs of tourism reach virtually everyone in the region in one way or another (Stynes, no data: 1). The tourism industry increases foreign exchange earnings, employment generation and income distribution (NRB, 1989: i.; Diamond, 1977: 539). Tourism contributes to national income, foreign exchange earning and state revenue as well as creates employment opportunities (Sharma, 2001: 2). Economic benefits extend directly and indirectly to a whole area and to the whole population. It also strengthens balance of payment and motivates various productive and income generating activities ultimately creating direct, indirect and induced effects on overall economic growth and development. Therefore, the increase in foreign exchange earnings through the growth of tourists arrival, total number of tourism business and supplies have a distinct influence on the overall growth in the economy.

It has been clear that tourism plays a catalyst role in the process of economic development of developing countries (Shaw and Williams, 1994; Sharma, 2001: 2). Therefore, tourism has been one of the prominent sectors of the economy in general, a key piece for many developing countries as a strategy of development of other sectors (Jimenez and Ortuno, no date) and a leading sector of Nepalese economy (Upadhyay, 2001: 245) in particular.

2.5 IMPACT OF TOURISM FINANCING AND INVESTMENT

A. TOURISM FINANCING REGIME

Nepal has been paying an increased attention for the development of tourism from the very beginning since it welcomed foreign visitors after the advent of democracy in 1951. Therefore, tourism has a belated start in Nepal compared to other countries. Despite of enormous potentialities for tourism development, Nepal has not been able to develop it in a desirable manner (Shrestha, 1999: 3). The major reason behind this should be the lack of investment and financing.

In Nepal, Tourism Master Plan, 1972 has been a strong basis for the beginning of tourism activities. The master plan has provided with details to carry out the various activities and programmes. The major objectives of the plan were to provide growth of international tourism to and within Nepal in an optimum manner, to provide a planned development of the tourism sector, to induce economic activities and to assist in the development of other economic sectors and to develop tourism in a manner which will preserve and enhance the social, cultural and historic values of Nepal (HMG, 1972: 2).

Tourism plans and programmes were always aimed at contributing to the promotion of tourism industry, bringing about a favourable tourism environment, developing tourism resources and providing support for tourism businesses. Unfortunately, sufficient planning could be seen for the overall and planned development of the tourism industry. Further, there was nothing as a deliberate arrangement, neither a fund for the promotion and development nor the sustainable financing source for the tourism industry. Therefore, there has been a dearth of arrangement; appropriate source and proper mechanism for the financing of tourism industry/sector.

In simple words, financing means the act of providing money for a project or activity whereas the investment means placing of money so that it will earn interest and increase in value (Dictionary of Banking and Finance). As tourism financing is expected to cover both the investment and financing function, it is essential to frame out the financing regime. Therefore, not only the availability of finance to develop and promote the tourism industry but also the system of financing is critically important for further growth and development of tourism industry and economy (Government of South Africa: 1996). Tourism financing and investment has assumed a significant place in some countries.

In South Korea, the Tourism Promotion and Development Fund supports the construction of tourism facilities, the renovation and construction of basic facilities, accommodation and resort businesses, and the undertaking of research activities. The money thus provided from the fund will be utilized in encouraging investment of the private sector, expanding relatively inexpensive public resort facilities and improving tourist information systems and public welfare (ESCAP, 2001: 4-5).

Similarly, in India, Tourism Finance Corporation of India provides financial assistance to enterprises for setting up and/or development of tourism-related projects, facilities and services. In addition, it considers corporate/short term loans, financing of working capital, take over of projects and advances against credit card receivables. Besides, it also coordinates and formulates guidelines and policies related to financing of such projects (Tourism Finance Corporation of India, 2006).

The main objective of the tourism development should be to increase its contribution to the economy and society. It deserves proper management of tourism industry as one of the important sectors of the economy. Mismanaged or unmanaged development of tourism brings more undesirable consequences rather than benefits. Therefore, proper tourism policies and their effective implementation are highly desirable to develop the tourism industry. Every government includes tourism in their development agenda because of its potentiality in earning foreign exchange, creating employment opportunities and generating revenues. But the development of tourism has not been an easy task and most probably will remain at least for the near future. The basic reason behind this is crystal clear because most of the countries have limited resources to create and maintain development infrastructure and have to face many hindrances for its development.

Tourism financing is very much similar with the financing of other economic sectors. If tourism is considered as an industry then the financing component will be clear and self explanatory. The concept, scope, sources and status of industrial finance has been found to be discussed extensively. The basics of financing are similar if not same. Therefore, financing in tourism as in other cases comprises a mix of the various funding sources (ESCAP, 2001: 4-5)[7].

The capital requirement for major tourism investments is such that foreign investment will often be required. Government can do a great deal to facilitate foreign investment by making it as easy as possible

---

[7] The details about the sources of financing is presented in third section of the forth chapter.

for the foreign investor. This does not preclude national control or protection of the environment. There is a need for improved mechanisms for mobilizing domestic capital and for encouraging local investment in tourism. This simply requires easy and clear frameworks (ESCAP, 1991).

Nowadays, with the liberalization and globalization tourism is spreading beyond the limited boundaries of society and community. It is well versed in national, greater regional and international arena. Public sector and private sector as well as the international communities are interested to develop tourism in its fullest extent. Thus, the scope of tourism financing and investment is increasing day by day attracting greater personal, societal national and international attention.

B. DEMAND FOR AND SUPPLY OF TOURISM FINANCING

It is already mentioned that every business enterprises need financial resources to undertake the profitable investments. They require investments either in the form of current assets and fixed assets or combination of both. In other words, business firms undertake investments to add on their stock of capital and to replace existing capital goods. The quantity of investment goods demanded depends on the interest rate, which measures the cost of funds used to finance investment (Mankiw, 2003: 54). In fact, the demand for investment financing depends on marginal product of capital and expectation of future growth. In addition, in a country like Nepal, it also depends on investment climate and tax regime because the government generally provides incentives to induce economic activities and growth.

Similarly, the supply of financing also depends on the rate of interest. In addition, money supply determines the availability of total credit and interest rate conditions the size of the credit supply in economy along with regulatory frameworks of the central bank related to directed credit, reserve requirement and credit creation. However, the investments made in the facilities and equipments provide with the magnitude of financing for the specific sector over a period. Therefore, the interest rate either to determine the demand for financing or to forecast the supply of financing assumes prominent role. However, in order to determine primary and secondary variables that determine the demand and supply of tourism financing an empirical analysis seems to be desirable.

C. IMPACT OF FINANCING IN THE ECONOMY

"In a world of balanced budgets, each spending unit's current and capital expenditures would be financed entirely from its current income" (Gurley and Shaw, 1956: 259). Though, self-finance continued to be important for several reasons, could not cater the growing demand for deficit financing. As such, the trend has changed significantly over the decades and made the government, business enterprises and even consumers to lean more heavily on external finance (Gurley and Shaw, 1955: 518). Therefore, they can either mobilize internal finance through saving for example, reserves and profits or external resources (for example, loan, trade credit and foreign capital). In fact, they use both the sources establishing a proper composition of sources considering the business opportunities and growth potential.

Every business enterprises need financial resources to undertake the profitable investments. They require investments either in the form of current assets and fixed assets or combination of both. In other words, business firms undertake investments to add on their stock of capital and to replace existing capital goods. The quantity of investment goods demanded depends on the interest rate, which measures the cost of funds used to finance the investment (Mankiw, 2003: 54). In fact, the demand for investment financing depends on marginal product of capital and expectation of future growth.

Tourism industry is so crucial because it brings various multiplier effects in the economy including income and employment. Thus, it has become as a prominent sector in the economy and assumed the distinct place in most of the developing countries including in Nepal. The tourism industry is multidisciplinary and multi-sectoral (ESCAP, 2001). It embraces various activities both in service and production sector generally requiring high doses of capital investment with long gestation periods (Chib, 1989: 163; Chand, 2000: 267). The growth of tourism industry generally increases the demand for tourism product and services. In order to cater such demand, business enterprises come up in the market, human resources respond with enhanced skills and knowledge the government provides with policy framework and infrastructures. The availability of tourism products and services highly depends upon the production capacity, natural resources and attractiveness as well as in other supply conditions (Goeldner, Ritchie and McIntosh 2000). Nevertheless, the other fold of the story is related with actual practice comprised business enterprnuership, investment climate, financing and conducive government policies and financing mechanism for the growth and development.

Finance plays a life sustaining role in the industrial development. It acts as a lubricant in the process of economic growth and is an essential element for every economic activity. Thus, adequate supply of financing increases the overall growth and development (Chand, 2000: 267-293). Similarly, the investment made by various institutions on accommodation, products and services triggers the tourism earning and employment along with economic and social transformation (Sharma, 2001: 224). Tourism financing sources ranging from direct government financing and multilateral and bilateral grants to banks and financial institutions as well as foreign investment encourage the investment. Nevertheless, the mobilization of domestic capital and firm's internal sources can also be the enduring supply (Seaton et al., 1994). Thus, tourism financing comprising the government investment in civil aviation, annual development expenditure in tourism and loan supplied by banks and financial institutions is the significant factor to increase income (Sharma, 2001: 224) and to exert pressure to operate the business activities more effectively ultimately creating the lubricant (Chand, 2000: 268) for the overall economic growth.

D. STUDIES IN ECONOMIC IMPACT OF INVESTMENT (BANK LENDING)

The impact of loan and investment on the economic activity, i.e. the national income is measured by the money supply they create in the economy. With the increase in money supply, the economic activities increase. This leads to higher savings by the public leading to an increase in investment amount and the national income. William Silber (1969) in his study has tried to find the answer of question like, Does it matter in evaluating the impact of monetary policy whether an expansion (contraction) in money supply occurs through the banking system's purchase (sale) of securities from (to) the public or whether it increases (decreases) loans? If so, then what will be the impact of purchase of securities by the banks on money supply for that matter on National income? Further is it important to distinguish between different types of loans?

The researchers such as Paul S. Andersen (1969), William Silber (1969), and Tim S. Campbell (1978) have compared the impact of loans and advances with that of investment in securities to find out their respective contribution on the national income. They assumed that the increase in loans and advances increases the money supply more than that of the investment. Further, the increase in money supply enhances the economic activities thus leading to economic growth. This happens simply because in case of a loan, the borrower spends money quickly on real goods and services, whereas the seller of the security may not spend on real goods and securities immediately and may purchase rather another financial security. Thus, the marginal propensity to spend loan money on real goods and services may be greater than that of the investments (Shrestha, 1995).

In this context, the study of Sunity Shrestha (1995)[8] appears to be relevant as it empirically examines the impact of lending from the commercial banks in various sectors of the economy. Using both primary and secondary data, the study has critically analyzed the behaviour of the commercial banks.

The major objectives of the study were to evaluate the financial performance of commercial banks of Nepal, to examine investment of commercial banks of Nepal with reference to securities, loans and advances, to establish the relationship of banks portfolio variables with national income and interest rates and finally to provide a suggestive package based on the analysis of the data.

The Major findings of the study inter-alia were as follows:

The commercial banks have played a catalystic role in the economic growth of the country.

The reserve level of the banks was in excess and still growing just increasing the size of idle money and loss of opportunity.

Debt equity ratio for all the commercial banks was very high, greater than 100 percent.

The performance level of the foreign banks was better than that of the domestic banks.

The investment of commercial banks in securities show that maximum investment was made in development bonds and least in shares of government owned corporations. The shares of non-government companies were insignificant in volume of investment in comparison to the government securities.

The industrial sector lending was getting more loans from the banks as compared to the commercial sector.

The highest marginal elasticity is due to agriculture sector, where as least combination is measured by CSI sector.

Demand for deposit of commercial banks in Nepal is positively affected by the GDP from non-agriculture, and the deposit rate and lending rate of interest.

Supply of bank credit has been observed to be related to total deposit, lending rate and bank rate. The important variable, the lending rate, has been found to be insignificant which led us to conclude that the change in lending rate does not affect the supply of bank credit.

Demand of bank credit has been found to be affected by the national income (GDP) and lending and Treasury bill rate.

The study has employed the diagnostic approach of research to test various hypotheses. In fact, the study has empirically examined the impact of lending for the economic growth and development. In addition, it has examined the growth of commercial bank branches and their asset holdings. Some

---

[8] The publication in a book form is a revised version form of her Ph. D. Thesis entitled "Investment planning of Commercial Banks in Nepal" submitted to Faculty of Management Studies, Delhi University.

structural ratios of the commercial banks were also computed to evaluate the contribution. Finally the profit performance chart and total management achievement index was computed for all the banks.

2.6 SUMMARY OF THE LITERATURE REVIEW

This section summarizes the review of literature. It is designed neither to repeat the review nor to explain the theory and practices, but to summarize the review of previous studies and research to frame out a corresponding reference required for the current study.

A. LITERATURE IN TOURISM GENERAL

The brief review undertaken on concept and scope of tourism and tourism financing in previous chapter (Chapter – I) has revealed that tourism became an indispensable activity and subject. Tourism assumed significant position due to its strong impacts on socio-cultural and economic dimensions. It also proved that financing is a life blood for the organizations, including tourism business enterprises.

Similarly, the review undertaken in earlier section of this chapter provided the premises for further discussion. The review of literature in Nepalese perspective pictured the early initiations of tourism development and promotions (please refer in Shrestha, 1998; Shrestha, 1999; Sharma, 2001 and Satyal, 2004).

B. LITERATURE IN NEPALESE PERSPECTIVE

Other studies, such as Ranade (1999) proved tourism as foreign exchange earner and NRB (1989) had estimated the level and patterns of tourist expenditure; the value added and imports contents; thus concluded tourism as an activity generating a number of economic and social benefits as well as a generator of income and employment. However, the study of Karmacharya (1991) was confined in regional perspective that found a high prospect of South Asian regional cooperation in tourism.

Mr. Khadka's study (1993) has widened the understanding of the issues relating to the measurement of surplus capacity of the domestic sectors, economic impact in tourism under limited and unlimited supplying capacity of the economy and planning for tourism industries. It also provided the guidelines for the efficient allocation of resources and various categories of hotel in Nepalese tourism industry.

Meanwhile, the study of Pradhananga (1993) has inquired about the tourists' consumption pattern and its economic impact on employment, export and national revenue. It has analyzed the direct, indirect and induced effects of tourist expenditure along with the backward and forward linkages of tourism. In addition, it has examined the impact of import and export of goods and services and generation of employment thus found to be detail for the economic impact analysis.

Similarly, the study of Shrestha (1998) was confined mainly in tourism marketing. It has focused and enlisted some marketing activities that were either in practice or felt necessary for the overall development of the tourism industry. It has explored the problem through the discussion of potential role of tourism in the economic development along with the assessment of marketing efforts, target market, strategies and professionalism.

The study of Shrestha (1999) has attempted to identity the problems of tourism on the basis of its contribution to the national economy, the status of tourism infrastructure, the review of planning and policies of the government and the responses of the tourists and experts. Besides this, it has highlighted the prospects of tourism in Nepal.

The study of Sharma (2001) has argued about the role of institutional factors and found their catalyst role for the tourism development. It also inquired about the investment made by institutions in triggering tourism earning and employment along with the economic development and social transformation. The analysis has found out a significant role of investment on civil aviation, government expenditure for tourism promotion and loan issued by banks and financial institutions. It also indicated that other investment factors except the supply of trained manpower have high degree of association in increasing gross earning and the total tourist arrival.

Likewise, the study of Upadhyay (2003) was concerned on two premium aspects of tourism. The first aspect was related to the tourism development from the development of required infrastructure in reaping its growth potential and impact on the economic development. Another aspect of the study was related to provide policy planners with a set of information and appropriate policies in developing tourism. It has concluded that tourism has been a leading sector of the Nepalese economy.

However, Maharjan's study (2005) was confined on the planning aspect of tourism. The study found that Nepal lacked integrated tourism planning and sufficient budget allocation. It has inquired about the role of private investors and lauded for the leading initiatives. It has recognized the role of tourism sector in producing some unique product concepts and ultimately in creating a model for world tourism. In addition, it has stated, "tourism industry has lacked farsighted and focused leadership as a result of secular business interests of a few in powers, instability in political leadership and resultant lack of continuity of government and bureaucracy."

C. LITERATURE IN TOURISM FINANCING AND INVESTMENT

The study, IUOTO (1971) has enquired the details about the public and private banks, commercial companies, international organization and other agencies that were already financing tourism projects or prepared to do so. In addition, it has prepared the list of financing terms and conditions.

Similarly, the study of Bennett (1991) was confined on tourism financing. It inquired about the investment financing and pleaded for the commercial considerations rather than political. It elucidated for the proper investment legislations, which are simple and easily communicable with an approach designed to protect the investor. The paper has lauded about the one window policy as an appropriate policy for the investment. It equally asked for straightforward and clear, fair and quickly applicable foreign exchange control regulations. Notwithstanding to above, the study asked for developing capital market and creating a healthy business atmosphere to promote domestic investments in tourism.

The study of ESCAP (1991) examined about the investment and economic cooperation in tourism. It found the existing status of investment in the industry and concluded it as far from being satisfactory. Investment in the tourism sector, both domestic and foreign, was found to be generally low. However, the study could not determine precisely about the share of foreign Investment in each country's total tourism – related investments because there had been an indication of virtual absence in Foreign Direct Investment in tourism services in most ESCAP Economies.

In addition, it has dealt about the important factors for the promotion of tourism investment in the tourism sector including political stability, economic growth, price stability, essential infrastructure, skilled human resources, fiscal incentives, marketing and promotional activities, immigration rules and the overall image of the country in the outside world.

The study of Singh (2001) was somehow different. It has discussed about the financing of State Tourism Development Corporations. It has inquired about the project planning management of these corporations. In addition, it has examined the feasibility reports of some of the complexes established by these corporations and status reports of the various ongoing projects.

It has reviewed the financing pattern through the common size liability schedules of these corporations and compared among them through various ratios comprising Debt Equity Ratio, Interest coverage ratio, funded debt to net working capital ratio, net sales to net worth ratio and current liability to net worth ratio. Similarly, it investigated the performance of these corporations again using different ratios.

D. OTHER STUDIES IN ECONOMIC IMPACT OF TOURISM AND FINANCING AND INVESTMENT

Other studies about the tourism financing and investment provided with preliminary discussions and enlisting of various factors related to the investment. Such studies were confined either in the context of developed countries, Asian and other developing countries or in the specific aspect of tourism. The literature review certainly gave some guidelines for the understanding of the possible factors and concept of investment in tourism however; it failed to provide a comprehensive analysis of tourism financing.

The studies of Ghali (1976) and Jimenez and Ortuno (2005) though were based on country specific analysis, definitely provided frameworks and ingredients for the economic impact analysis for similar cases ranging from developed to developing countries. The study of Diamond (1977) has analyzed the demand for services and the supply of services for Turkish tourism. In fact, the study reexamined the role of tourism raising some vital questions both on positive and negative effects of tourism.

The study of Sathiendrakumar and Tisdel (1989) considered the variability of the tourist demand and limitations posed by the environmental factors for the expansion of the industry and along with the social cost of tourism, competition and opportunity cost. In fact, it had argued for the ability of tourism industry to provide alternative employment opportunities for the local inhabitants (fisherman) displaced by technological change. Similarly it paid attention for the possible consequences for the balance of payments and public finance; and competition and opportunity cost considerations.

The tourism impact analysis presented in the Zhang's (2001) paper gives the demonstration of how regional analysis can be carried out by using an economic model. The purpose of any well-specified model is to offer decision-makers and regional analyst a useful tool for a wide variety of policy-oriented issues. The model presented in the study can be applied in several other policy-oriented projects, such as agriculture, transport and taxation policy and all kinds of regional analysis. Thus, such analysis can be suitable and as well as applicable for similar type of impact analysis.

Stynes's (no date) and UN ESCAP's (2001) study provided elaborative discussion for the economic impact of tourism. Similarly, the study of Shrestha (1995) appeared to be relevant for the impact analysis of bank lending in different sectors of the economy. It has incorporated the contribution of the credit lending in the economic growth of the country.

The study attempted to explore the answers for some vital questions related to the behaviour of the commercial banks such as, what is the policy strength of central bank, what is the performance of the commercial banks, whether the investment decision of the banks remaining under the regulations, are contributing for the performance of commercial banks, do the investment of commercial banks on securities and loans verify the objectives of maximization of profit, and whether the recovery of the loans is satisfactory or not ?

It appears from the survey of literatures that though there have been many studies to analyze the various aspects and role of tourism, the financial aspect in tourism and its role for the development of the country was found to be neglected. Similarly, very few studies have been undertaken in Nepalese perspective thus providing limited scope for the detail review about the tourism industry. Further, the status of the literatures particularly in tourism financing and investment in Nepalese perspective is almost non-existing.

2.7 APPROACH OF THIS STUDY

The review, as undertaken in the current chapter provides a strong basis for the present study in two ways. The first base is related with the concept and where-about of the tourism and has provided a clear path for the study whereas the second is related with the availability of existing works to indicate the requirement for the fresh discussions and analysis.

Therefore, this study is supposed to assess the trend and practice of tourism financing and investment in Nepal. It attempts to identify the various aspects of financing digging through the theoretical underpinnings and practice of that by tourism business enterprises over the period. It enumerates the required primary data from the field research and summarizes the secondary data related to the financing and investment of tourism, establishes the relationship and analyzes them to achieve the conclusion.

The study is quite different from those mentioned above in various forms. The difference is assessed in two dimensions viz. what is extra matter that present study attempts and what is matter that it does not cover. In fact, the difference thus gained is the premises of the present study as it incorporates the justification of the present study.

It is different from the studies and research articles enumerated through the literature in Nepalese perspective in three ways. The first difference is that unlike those studies, present study deals particularly about the financing pattern of the tourism business enterprises. The second is concerned with the scope of the study because it inquires vigorously about the policy environment and inter-sectoral relationship. The third is most explicit, thus simply raises the question about the emerging concept in and around the academic arena for the further research.

Similarly, it is also different from the doctoral thesis reviewed in earlier sections. Because, these studies either confined in the particular aspect of the tourism or attempted to incorporate too much details about the tourism. In fact, most of the studies have concentrated to find out the various dimensions of tourism and to prove it as an endurable resource for the development and growth of the economy but none of them strived to analyze details about the tourism financing and investment.

Moreover, it is different than some of studies that were related to past periods or used different evaluating criterion and focused on developed country where the prices and quantity variables are determined by demand and supply forces in the market. It could have benefited from the studies undertaken particularly of the developing country like Nepal because of the similar economic characteristics such as lack of competition, fragmented market, structural bottlenecks, etc. In fact, financing activity/function is critical enough and thus requires the systematic analysis to find out the relationship with other economic variables and to get at the conclusion.

REFERENCES

Anand Ballabh (2004). **Fundamentals of Travel and Tourism**. New Delhi: Akansha Publishing House.

Anand, M. M. and Puskar Bajracharya (1985). Strategies for the Development of Tourism in Nepal. **"Gurans"** Annual Magazine of Nepalese Students in Delhi University. Delhi: Nepalese Students Association

Anderson (1969) in Shrestha, Sunity (1995). **Portfolio Behaviour of Commercial Banks in Nepal**. Kathmandu: Mandala Book Point.

Anil Sharma (2006). **Tourism for Economic Development**. New Delhi: Maxford Books.

Ayres, Ron (2000). Tourism as a Passport to Development in Small States: Reflections on Cyprus. **International Journal of Social Economics** 27: 114-133.

Bahuguna, Anjali (2005). Tourism in India: Development Perspective. **The Indian Economic Journal**. Vol.39 No. pp. 138-141.

Bennet, Oliver (1991). Tourism financing in ESCAP (1991) **Investment and Economic Cooperation in the Tourism Sector in Developing Asian Countries**. Report of a Seminar Organized by ESCAP Bangkok, 5-21 October 1991 Tokyo and Sendai Japan.

Bhattarai, Keshav; Dennis Conway and Nanda Shrestha (2005). Tourism, Terrorism and Turmoil in Nepal. **Annals of Tourism Research**, 32 (3): 669-688

Bodlender, Jonathan (1984). Tourism Investment for the Future. **Tourism Management**, Volume 5, Issue 2, Pages 150-152. Source: **http://www.sciencedirect.com/science/articles/Accessed on 30/06/2005.**

Bull, Adrian (1990). Australian Tourism: Effects of Foreign Investment **Tourism Management**, Volume 11, Issue 4, Pages 325-331. Source: **http://www.sciencedirect.com/science/articles/Accessed on 31/12/2005.**

Burger, Veit (1978). **The Economic Impact of Tourism in Nepal: An Input Output Analysis**. A Ph. D. Thesis Submitted to Faculty of the Graduate School, Cornell University, Austria

Burkart, A. J. and S. Medlik (1981). **Tourism: Past, Present and Future**. London: Heinemann Professional Publishing.

Cai, Junning; PingSun Leung; and James Mak (no date). **Tourism's Forward and Backward Linkages**. University of Hawaii at Manoa. Source: **http://www.searchepnet.com/articles/tourism/ Accessed on 30/06/2006.**

Campbell (1978) in Shrestha, Sunity (1995). **Portfolio Behaviour of Commercial Banks in Nepal**. Kathmandu: Mandala Book Point.

Chand, Diwaker (2000). **Nepal's Tourism: Uncensored Facts**. Varanasi: Pilgrims Publishing.

Chand, Mohindar (2000). **Travel Agency Management; An Introductory Text**. New Delhi: Anmol Publications.

Copeland, R. Brian (1991). Tourism, Welfare and De-industrialization in a Small Open Economy. **Economica, New Series**, Vol. 58 No. 232. pp. 515-529.

Diamond, J. (1977). Tourism's Role in Economic Development: The Case Reexamined. Economic Development and Cultural Change, 25 (3): 539-553 Source: http://www.jstor.org/ accessed on 17/07/2006

Dixit, Kanak Mani (1997). Tourism Trends and Issues Across The Himalaya. **Journal of Travel and Tourism**, 1 (1): 45-59

Emanual de Kadt ed. (1979). **Tourism: Passport to Development?** Oxford: Oxford University Press.

ESCAP (1991). **Investment and Economic Cooperation in the Tourism Sector in Developing Asian Countries**. Report of a Seminar Organized by ESCAP Bangkok, 5-21 October 1991 Tokyo and Sendai Japan

ESCAP (2001). **Opportunities and Challenges for Tourism Investment**, ESCAP Tourism Review No. 21. New York: United Nations

Forsyth, Larry Dwyer Peter (1994). Foreign Tourism Investment: Motivation and Impact. **Annals of Tourism Research**, Volume 21, Issue 3, Pages 512-537. Source: http://www.sciencedirect.com/science/articles/ Accessed on 30/06/2005.

Franck, Christian (1990). Tourism investment in central and eastern Europe: Preconditions and opportunities. **Tourism Management**, Volume 11, Issue 4, Pages 333-338. Source: http://www.sciencedirect.com/articles/Accessed on 30/06/2005

Frechtling Douglas C. (1987). Assessing the Impacts of Travel and Tourism –Measuring Economic Benefits in Tisdell, Clem (ed) (2000) **The Economics of Tourism Volume II**. Cheltenham: An Elgar Reference Collection.

Ghali, Moheb A. (1976). Tourism and Economic Growth; An Empirical Study. **Economic Development and Cultural Change**, Vol. 24, No. 3 pp. 527-538.

Ghimire (2000). **Travel and Tourism: An Introduction**. Kathmandu: Ekta Books Distributors.

Ghose, R. N.; M. A. B. Siddique and R. Gabbay (eds) (2004). **Tourism and Economic Development**. US; England: Ashgate Publishing Limited

Goeldner, Charles R.; J. R. Brent Ritchie and Robert W. McIntosh (2000). **Tourism: Principles, Practices and Philosophies**. New York: John Wiley and Sons.

Government of South Africa (1996). **White Paper on Tourism**. Accessed from web site: http://www.google.com on March 25, 2006

Hepburn, Sharon J. (2002). Touristic Forms of Life in Nepal. **Annals of Tourism Research**, 29 (3): 611-630

IUCN (2005). **Rural Tourism: Makalu Barun Conservation Project**. Kathmandu: International Union for Conservation of Nature and Natural Resources

IUOTO (1971). **A Study on Sources of and Conditions of Financing**. Geneva: International Union of Official Travel Organization.

Ives, Jack D. (2004). **Himalayan Perceptions: Environmental Change and the well-being of mountain peoples**. London: Rutledge

James, Mak (2004). **Tourism and the Economy: Understanding the Economic of Tourism**. Honolulu: University of Hawaii Press.

Jamieson, Walter and Tazim Jamal (1997). Contributions of Tourism in to Economic Development...... in UN ESCAP (2001). **Promotion of Investment in Tourism Infrastructure**. New York: UN ESCAP

Jimenez, Isabel Cortez and Manuel Artis Ortuno (2005). **The Role of Tourism Sector in Economic Development**: Lessons from the Spanish Experience. Source: **http://www.searchepnet.com/fulltextarticles/tourism/ Accessed on 30/06/2006**.

Khadka, Krishna Ram (1993) **Tourism and Economic Development in Nepal**. A Ph. D. Thesis Submitted to Development and Project Planning Department, University of Bradford, United Kingdom.

Kunwar, Ramesh Raj. (1997). **Tourism and Development, Science and Industry Interface**. Kathmandu: Published by Laxmi Kunwar.

Lindberg, Kreg; Arild Molstad; Donald Hawkins and Water Jamieson (2001). International Development Assistance in Tourism. **Annals of Tourism Research**. Vol. 28 No. 2. pp. 508-511.

Lundberg, Donald E.; M. Krishnamoorthy and Mink H. Stavenga (1995). *Tourism Economics*, New York, John Wiley and Sons.

Maharjan, Narayan P. (2004). **Tourism Planning in Nepal**. A Ph. D. Thesis submitted to Faculty of Management, Tribhuvan University Kathmandu, Nepal

NATA (1990). **Investment Opportunities in Tourism in Nepal** - Silver Jubilee Souvenir. Kathmandu: Nepal Association of Travel Agents

Nepal, S. K. (2000) Tourism in protected areas: The Nepalese Himalayas. **Annals of Tourism Research** 27, (3) 661–681.

NRB (1989). **Income and Employment Generation from Tourism in Nepal**. Kathmandu: Nepal Rastra Bank.

Pearce Douglas (1981). **Tourist Development**. Essex UK: Longman Group Limited.

Pearce Douglas (1989). **Tourist Development**. Essex UK: Longman Group Limited.

Poudyal, Shoor Bir (1998). International Demand for Tourism in Nepal, **Economic Review,** No. 10. (pp.)

Pradhananga, S. B. (1993). **Tourist Consumption Pattern and Its Economic Impact in Nepal** Ph. D. Thesis submitted to Central Development of Economic Tribhuvan University, Kathmandu Nepal

Pradhnanga (2000). **Tourists' Consumption Pattern and Its Economic Impact in Nepal**. Delhi: Adroit Publishers.

Raina, A. K. and R. C. Lodha (2004). **Fundamentals of Tourism System**. New Delhi: Kaniska Publishers, Distributors.

Ranade, Prabha Shastri (1999). Tourism as Foreign exchange Earner: A Study of Tourism in Nepal. **Foreign Trade Review, Vol.** 33, No.3-4: 103-118

Releigh, Lori E. and Rachel J. Roginsky (eds.) (1999). **Hotel Investments: Issues and Perspectives**. Education Institute American Hotel and Motel Institute.

Ritchie, J. R. Brent and Charles R. Goeldner (eds), **Travel Tourism and Hospitality Research: A Handbook for Managers and Researchers**. New York: John Wiley and Sons, Inc.

Roldan, Jorge (1994). Investing in Eco-tourism Projects. **Inter-American Investment Corporation**. GD 33.046

Roldan, Jorge (No date). **The Financing Requirements of Nature and Heritage Tourism in the Caribbean**. Washington D. C. Department of Regional Development and Environment.

Sathiendrakumar, Rajasundram and Clem Tisdell (1989). Tourism and the Economic Development of the Maldives. **Annals of Tourism Research**, 16, 254-269.

Satyal, Yagna Raj (2000). **Tourism Monograph of Nepal**. Delhi: Adroit Publishers.

Satyal, Yagna Raj (2004). **Tourism in Nepal: A Profile**. Delhi: Adroit Publishers.

Schmidgall, Raymond S. (1999). Investment Analysis Tools. In Releigh, Lori E. and Rachel J. Roginsky eds. (1999). **Hotel Investments: Issues and Perspectives**. Education Institute American Hotel and Motel Institute.

Seaton, A. V. and et al. (eds.) (1994). **Tourism: The State of the Art. England**: John Wiley and Sons.

Seth, Pran Nath (2001). **Successful Tourism Management: Tourism Practices. Volume II**. New Delhi: Sterling publishers. Pvt. Ltd.

Sharma, Om Prakash (2001). **Tourism Development and Planning in Nepal**. A Ph. D. Thesis presented to Faculty of Social Sciences, Banaras Hindu University India.

Shaw, Gareth and Allan Williams (1994). **Critical Issues in Tourism: A Geographical Perspective**. Oxford: Blackwell Publishers.

Shrestha, Hari Prasad (1998). **Tourism Marketing in Nepal**. A Ph. D. Thesis Submitted to Faculty of Management Tribhuvan University Kathmandu Nepal

Shrestha, Hari Prasad (2000). **Challenges of Tourism Marketing in Nepal**. Delhi: Adroit Publishers.

Shrestha, Puspa (1999) **Tourism in Nepal: Problems and Prospects**. A Ph. D. Thesis Submitted to Department of Economics, Banaras Hindu University, Varanasi, India

Shrestha, Sunity (1995). **Portfolio Behaviour of Commercial Banks in Nepal**. Kathmandu: Mandala Book Point.

Silber, Willium (1969) in Shrestha, Sunity (1995). **Portfolio Behaviour of Commercial Banks in Nepal**. Kathmandu: Mandala Book Point.

Simmons, D. G. and Koirala, S. (2000) **Tourism in Nepal, Bhutan and Tibet**: Contrast in Facilitation, Constraining and Control of Tourism in the Himalayas. In C. M. Hall and S. Page (ed.) **Tourism in South and South East Asia – Issues and Cases** (pp. 256–67). Oxford: Butterworth-Heinemann.

Singh, Bali Ram (1995). **Glimpses of Tourism, Airlines and Management in Nepal**. New Delhi and Jaipur: Nirala Publications.

Singh, Manjit (2001) **Financial Organization and Working of State Tourism Development Corporations: A Study of Punjab, Haryana and Himanchal Pradesh**. A Ph. D. Thesis Submitted to Department of Tourism, Kurukshetra University, Kurukshetra, India

Smith, Stephen L. J. (1989). **Tourism Analysis: A Handbook**. Singapore: Longman Group Limited.

Sparrowhawk, John and Andrew Holden (1999). Human Development: The Role of Tourism Based NGO's in Nepal. **Tourism Recreation Research**, 24 (2): 37-43

Stevens, Stan (2003). Tourism and Deforestation in the Mt. Everest Region of Nepal. **The Geographical Journal**, 169 (3):255-277

Stynes, Daniel J. (no date). **Economic Impacts of Tourism**. Source: http://www.searchepnet.com/fulltextarticles/tourism/ **Accessed on 30/06/2006**.

Sunil Kabia (2005). **Tourism and the Developing Country**. New Delhi: Mohit Publications.

Tisdell, Clem (ed) (2000) **The Economics of Tourism Volume II**. Cheltenham: An Elgar Reference Collection.

Tourism Finance Corporation of India (2006) downloaded from the worldwide website. Source: http://www.tfciltd.com accessed on 20/01/2006

Tribe, John (1999). **The Economics of Leisure and Tourism**. Oxford: Butterworth Heinemann.

UN ESCAP (2001). **Promotion of Investment in Tourism Infrastructure**. New York: UN ESCAP

Upadhyay, Rudra Prasad (2001). **A Study of Tourism as Leading Sector in Economic Development in Nepal**. A Ph. D. Thesis presented to Department of Economics, University of Lucknow India.

Vanhobe, Norbert (2005). **The Economics of Tourism Destinations**. Elsevier Butterworth Heinemann.

Wen, Clem TisdellJie (1991).Investment in China's tourism industry: Its scale, nature, and policy issues. **China Economic Review**, Volume 2, Issue 2, Pages 175-193.

Whitehouse, Jan and Colin Tilley (1993). **Finance and Leisure: Leisure Management Series**. London: Financial Times, Pitman Publishing.

WTO (1995). **Multilateral and Bilateral Sources of Financing for Tourism Development**. Madrid: World Tourism Organization.

Zhang, Jie (2001). Tourism Impact Analysis in the Danish Regions. Paper presented at 41st congress of the ERSA Zagreb, Croatia August – September 2001. Source: http://www.sciencedirect.com/science/articles/**Accessed on 31/12/2005**.

Zurick, D. N. (1992) Adventure travel and sustainable tourism in the peripheral economy of Nepal. **Annals of the Association of American Geographers** 82, 608–628

CHAPTER

TOURISM INDUSTRY IN NEPAL: A PROFILE

3.1 INTRODUCTION

3.2 EVOLUTION OF TOURISM

3.3 TOURISM PRODUCTS AND INFRASTRUCTURE

3.4 TOURISM POLICY AND PLANS
- Initial plans
- Tourism Master Plan, 1972
- Tourism policy, 1995
- Other tourism plans and programs

3.5 INSTITUTIONAL ARRANGEMENT FOR TOURISM

3.6 TOURISM BUSINESS ENTERPRISES

3.7 LEGAL AND REGULATORY FRAMEWORK
- Registration and licensing
- Acts, rules and regulation
- Investment incentives

3.8 CONTRIBUTION OF TOURISM

3.9 CONCLUSION

CHAPTER III

TOURISM INDUSTRY IN NEPAL: A PROFILE

3.1 INTRODUCTION

This chapter contains the brief discussion about the evolution and present status of tourism industry in Nepal. Since, the status of tourism industry can be visualized from the state of tourism products as well as the plans and programmes implemented over the period (Maharjan, 2004: 104); the chapter basically, contains the discussion about the tourism products and infrastructure facilities.

It also includes the description about the tourism business enterprises, legal and regulatory framework, investment incentives available for the tourism investment as well as the contribution of tourism in Nepal. The basic thrust of this chapter is to introduce the Nepalese tourism industry and present it in such a way depicting the whole affairs of the industry.

3.2 EVOLUTION OF TOURISM

Since ancient times Nepal was known as the abode of Gods, many Chinese and Indian people came to Nepal to make a long pilgrimage to the places of venerated worship (Satyal, 2004: 30). In addition to this, there were other forms of journeys particularly some commercial trips for the lure of Nepalese wool, journey routes (crossing points between Tibet and India and exchange of envoys to maintain friendly relation at the political level. Such type of tourism though could not provide much commercial importance over the period, laid milestones for the further development and publicity. Hence, such type of development can be regarded as Ancient Tourism.

The democratic revolution of 1951-52 was a boon for Nepalese tourism. With this, Nepalese people got liberty and the foreigners got an opportunity of visiting the exotic country. Tourism in Nepal is of recent phenomenon. It has a very short history though it has witnessed the visits of various travelers and saints in earlier days of civilization.

Therefore, it is clear that tourism in Nepal in its modern form was started only in the fifties, after the dawn of democracy resulting on an open door policy for the tourists and visitors (ESCAP, 1991: 194 and FNCCI, 1996: 12) from all over the world.

Nepal's expanding friendly and diplomatic relations with many countries, membership in the United Nations Organization and also in other multilateral organizations like International Union of Official Travel Organization (now World Tourism Organization) and other UN agencies has definitely provided far-reaching publicity. In addition to this, the expeditions made by mountaineering teams and pleasure tours by busy and enthusiastic people from different parts of the world have automatically made publicity and provided the concrete space for further promotion. They have also spread the name as the land of Everest, the birthplace of Gautam Buddha, the third pole of the earth and the home of the gallant Gorkhas to each and every corner of the world (Satyal, 2004: 33, FNCCI, 1996: 12).

Nepalese tourism has witnessed some landmarks in its history. It was enriched with the Tourism Master Plan, 1972; enactment of related legislations; promulgation of Tourism Policy, 1995; formation of Nepal Tourism Board as an institutional partnership between public and private sectors and improvement in the tourism infrastructures. Moreover, the sector has been promoted as a prime destination with more systematic and planned approach. In fact, it was ultimately to develop major areas of tourism concern and to facilitate the local participation in the development and conservation of tourism resources.

Gradually, tourism became one of the most important segments of the Nepalese economy (MOTCA, 1998: 9). It is found to be continuously growing over the years. Though it has witnessed some fluctuations during the review period (1966 – 2005), it sustained the growth and became the leading sector of the economy (Upadhyay, 2001: 247). The sustained growth of tourism over the period can be attributed to the involvement of public and private sector in different infrastructure development and promotional activities.

In this section of the chapter, the development of tourism in Nepal is assessed in terms of visitors' arrival (including the arrival from the originating markets on regional basis) and some salient features such as length of stay and purpose of the visit. In addition, it is assessed in terms of foreign exchange earning from tourism.

Table 3.1 depicts the development of tourism in Nepal since 1966. The number of tourists visiting Nepal has gradually been increasing over the period. In Fiscal Year 1965/66, only 9,211 foreign tourists (except Indian tourists) had visited the country. The number reached to 90,431 in F. Y. 1974/75; 164,380 in 1979/80; 246,361 in 1989/90 and 346,180 in 1994/95. As such, the number reached to the maximum at 477,774 in F. Y 1998/99 registering a tremendous growth.

However, the trend showed a major setback in arrival starting from year 2000. In F. Y 1999/2000, the number decreased to 459,350 registering a negative growth of 3.9 percent. It further declined to the lowest of 289,000 in F. Y. 2001/02 registering sharp decline of more than 35 percent. The major reason behind this was the ever-spreading terrorism around the world and Maoist insurgency inside the country. Afterwards, it has shown some improvements, started to increase albeit at slower pace, and reached to 295,679 and 388,043 during F. Y. 2002/03 and 2003/04 respectively. However, during the F. Y. 2004/05 it again witnessed a decline of 23.8 percent and limited only in 295,611.

The composition of the tourist arrival in terms of Indian and foreigners showed a mixed trend. The share of Indian tourist remained to be around 28 percent and that of other foreigners around 72 percent. During the earlier period of the study (1975-1995) the share of Indian tourists remained at around 27 percent and later it slightly went down to 26 percent. It could not show any shifting despite of continuous efforts of promoting tourism in nearest and accessible market. Again, it is astonishing to acknowledge the decline in its share especially after 2000. Nevertheless, in terms of nationality, Indian tourists have surpassed other and stood at the apex position occupying in an average 28 percent over the period. This figure however represents Indian tourists arriving in Nepal by air only. Japanese tourists come in second position holding around 8 percent share followed UK, USA and Germany each holding below 5 percent share on an average.

The average length of stay of the tourist remained to be around 11 days. In fact, there has been wide fluctuation in the duration of visit. Table 3.1 shows both the increase to the maximum of 13.5 days in F. Y. 1995/96, decrease to the minimum of 7.9 days in F. Y. 2001/02. It remained at 13.5 days and 9.1 days in F. Y. 2003/04 and 2004/05 respectively.

Table: 3.1
Growth in Tourism

Fiscal Year	Foreign Tourist	Indian Tourist	Total Tourist Arrival	Percent Change	Length of Stay days*
1965/66	9,211	-	9,211	-	-
1974/75	71,563	18,868	90,431	882	13.1
1979/80	124,221	40,159	164,380	82	11.2
1984/85	107,647	56,899	164,546	0.1	11.3
1989/90	198,128	48,233	246,361	50	12.0
1994/95	230,158	116,022	346,180	41	11.3
1995/96	262,448	117,853	380,301	9.9	13.5
1996/97	273,477	128,809	402,286	5.8	10.5
1997/98	301,636	138,647	440,283	9.4	10.8
1998/99	336,713	141,061	477,774	8.5	12.8
1999/00	359,043	100,307	459,350	-3.9	11.9
2000/01	362,330	86,401	448,731	-2.3	11.9
2001/02	229,873	59,127	289,000	-35.6	7.9
2002/03	218,972	76,707	295,679	2.3	9.6
2003/04	291,733	96,310	388,043	31.2	13.5
2004/05	227,228	68,383	295,611	-23.8	9.1

Source: Nepal Tourism Statistics (Various issues), Ministry of Tourism and Civil Aviation
* The figure for the length of the stay incorporates the period of Gregorian year (Jan. - Dec.)

Table 3.2 summarizes the regional distribution of tourist arrival in Nepal (based on WTO regional classification). It shows slight changes over the period of study. The share of Asia remained to be the major accounting on an average 47.4 percent. It was followed by Western Europe and North America holding around 35.1 percent and 10.7 percent share respectively. Other markets such as Eastern Europe, South and Central America, Australia and Pacific and Africa held minor share of less than 4.0 percent in total.

Table: 3.2

Regional Distribution of the Tourist Arrivals

Year*	Asia	Western Europe	North America	Australia & Pacific	Eastern Europe	Central & S. America	Africa	Others & not specified
1962	250	1980	3724	117	22	54	8	24
1970	3841	22346	15992	2667	440	584	100	0
1980	61916	70363	17817	8081	1597	2192	712	220
1985	78466	62876	22888	10643	3058	1564	559	935
1990	98320	110750	26343	13108	3275	1872	611	606
1995	180377	133809	29702	11499	3860	3049	1073	26
1996	205809	132787	30635	12233	6114	4230	1775	30
1997	222849	137028	36301	13047	6416	4554	1645	17
1998	240460	151070	43038	14643	6741	5937	1795	8
1999	249793	164913	46910	15207	6723	6096	1857	5
2000	224532	159325	49032	15641	6962	6076	2040	8
2001	164989	131661	39120	13036	6201	4634	1596	0
2002	148670	87912	21265	8420	5276	2793	1132	0
2003	200045	95162	22992	9608	6451	2262	1612	0
2004	218387	116505	25505	10947	7661	4373	1161	758
2005	230282	98046	22853	8317	8263	3559	1302	2776
Average	47.4	35.1	10.7	3.7	1.5	1.1	0.4	0.1

Source: Nepal Tourism Statistics (Various issues), Ministry of Tourism and Civil Aviation
* The figure incorporates the period of Gregorian year (Jan. - Dec.)

Similarly, Table: 3.3 is designed to provide the information on tourist arrival by purpose of visit. The major purpose of the visit of the tourists during the review period appeared to be the holiday and pleasure. Another reason for the visit was found to be the trekking and mountaineering in the mountains and hills in the country. Other purposes such as business, official, pilgrimage, convention and conference as well as others found to be holding a share of less than 10.0 percent in total arrival.

Thus, it is clear that largest number of tourists was found to be visiting Nepal only for recreational purposes. Despite of this, the tourists visiting for adventure can be more important because they usually go to far remote places, have a long duration of stay and use various products and services.

Table: 3.3

Tourist Arrivals by Purpose of Visit

Year*	Holiday pleasure	Trekking Mountain-eering	Others	Official	Business	Pilgrim-age	Convention Conference	Total
1970	41881	556	1087	1528	918	0	0	45970
1975	70124	12587	591	4227	4911	0	0	92440
1980	130600	19302	2850	4654	5491	0	0	162897
1985	128217	28707	4419	9230	10416	0	0	180989
1990	161839	39999	5190	26578	11728	6713	2838	254885
1995	183207	84787	42953	20090	21829	5257	5272	363395
1996	209377	88945	39165	20191	25079	4802	6054	393613
1997	249360	91525	19565	24106	27409	4068	5824	421857
1998	261347	112644	21271	22123	24954	16164	5181	463684
1999	290862	107960	19574	24132	23813	19198	5965	491504
2000	255889	118780	17291	20832	29454	15801	5599	463646
2001	187022	100828	22316	18727	18528	13816	0	361237
2002	110143	59279	58907	17783	16990	12366	0	275468
2003	97904	65721	111758	21967	19387	21395	0	338132
2004	167262	69442	71893	18088	13948	45664	0	385297
2005	160259	61488	67179	16859	21992	47621	0	375398
Average	57.6	18.8	9.1	5.3	5.2	3.5	0.6	100.0

* The figure for the year represents the Gregorian year (Jan. - Dec.).
Source: Nepal Tourism Statistics (Various issues), Ministry of Tourism and Civil Aviation

3.3 TOURISM PRODUCTS AND INFRASTRUCTURE [1]

Nepal is a mountainous country. The divergent geographical feature has endowed with various attractions and richness. It is amazing that within a short distance there is so much diversity and variety. The 800 km stretch of the Nepal Himalayan is the greatest in the world with eight peaks that rise above 8,000 meters including the highest in the world, Mt. Everest. The unprecedented distribution of the world heritage sites within short distance (seven sites within the distance of around 20 km.) is also amazing. The famous Royal Bengal Tiger and the One-horned Rhinoceros are also inhabitants of the country. Moreover, friendly people of different cultures are always ready to offer a fascinating glimpse of traditional rural life and to provide lifetime experience for the tourists. The visitors from all over the world experience exotic life style while searching for the Shangri-La (FNCCI, 1996: 9).

A question may arise here, what is tourism product? A tourism product is anything that can be offered to a tourist for attention, acquisition, or consumption; it includes physical objects, services, personalities, places, organizations and ideas (Maharjan, 2004:107). Similarly, Cooper et al. (1993) have defined a tourism product as an amalgamation of what a person receives or experiences. The services he uses and the products he purchases during his trip.

Therefore, a tourism product is an augmented product or the totality of benefits that the person receives or experiences in obtaining the formal product, physical objects, services or combination of both offered to the visitor. For example, some of these elements may be the services of the travel agent, hotel accommodation and catering, transportation, entertainment and other tourist services like gift shops.

Present section of the chapter deals about the tourism products and infrastructure already available for the tourism industry or are in an early stage of development. Exhibit 3.2 presents a welcome note to the tourists whereas Exhibit 3.2 presents a glimpse of the tourism products and infrastructure through the collection of the photographs (http://www.welcomenepal.com).

---

[1] Much of the discussion about the tourism product is in line with (related to) the description provided in a promotional brochure published by Nepal Tourism Board (www.welcomenepal.com)

Exhibit: 3.1
Introduction and Essential Information for Tourists

Welcome to Nepal

Nepal is one of the richest countries in the world in terms of bio-diversity due to its unique geographical position and latitudinal variation. The elevation of the country ranges from 60m above sea level to the highest point on earth, Mt. Everest at 8,848 m. all within a distance of 150 km with climatic conditions ranging from sub-tropical to arctic. This wild variation fosters an incredible variety of ecosystems, the greatest mountain range on earth, thick tropical jungles teeming with a wealth of wildlife, thundering rivers, forested hills and frozen valleys.

Within this spectacular geography is also one of the richest cultural landscapes anywhere. The country is a potpourri of ethnic groups and sub-groups who speak over 70 languages and dialects. Nepal offers an astonishing diversity of sightseeing attractions and adventure opportunities found nowhere else on earth. And you can join in the numerous annual festivals that are celebrated throughout the year in traditional style highlighting enduring customs and beliefs.

We are glad to extend our warm hospitality and hope your stay in Nepal is a memorable one.

Tourists are advised to use the services of registered travel/trekking companies and hotels only. By using the services of government registered service providers, you will be ensuring the most comfortable and reliable holiday possible.

If you have any queries or comments, please feel free to contact us at the following address:

Ministry Culture, Tourism and Civil Aviation, Tourism Industry Division, Bhrikutimandap: Tel; 977-1- 4256232, 4256231, 4256228, 4247037, Fax No. 4227281 Email: tourism@mail.com.np

Location:	Latitude = 26° 22' N to 30° 27' N Longitude =80° 4' E to 88° 12' E
Border:	China's Autonomous Region Tibet in the North India in the South, East & West
Total Area:	147,181 sq. km.
Population:	23,151,423 (2001 Census)
Highest Peak:	Mt. Everest, 8,848 M.
Capital:	Kathmandu
Government:	Parliamentary Democracy with Constitutional Monarchy
Language:	Nepali
Religion:	Hindu
Currency:	Nepalese Rupee

Source: www: mocta.gov.np

Exhibit: 3.2
A Glimpse of Tourism Products and Infrastructure

Source: www.welcomenepal.com

Mountain Climbing

Nepalese Himalayas have in fact become a great theatre for the mountaineering activities and a dream for the climbers. Since the country and its peaks were opened to climbers, the success and failure stories are piled up to provide an impetus to thousands of people to meet the ultimate challenge. The climbing will remain always to be a challenging attraction to many people, irrespective of gender, race, caste, culture, religion and nationality.

Trekking

Trekking is perhaps the best way to experience natural beauty and cultural richness. To realize the unbeatable combination and to feel the greatness it is necessary to walk through them. Again, it is challenging because there is no easy access, thus necessary to walk along either the beaten trails or virgin tracks. It certainly provides a lifetime experience, as claimed by many trekkers during their journey along with forests of rhododendron, isolated hamlets, and small mountain villages, temple, monasteries and breath-taking landscapes.

Rafting

Rafting (including kayaking) is one of the best ways to explore the typical cross section of natural as well as ethno-cultural heritage of the country. There are numerous rivers in Nepal, which offer excellent rafting or canoeing experience. The government has opened only 10 rivers for commercial rafting trips. Among others, Trisuli, Kali Gandaki, Bhote Koshi, Marshyanghi, Sun Koshi and Karnali rivers (class 4-5+) for the continuous white water and the raging of uninterrupted water. Canoeing, one of the extremely popular sports in Europe is also available in Nepal. Canoeing gives the freedom to explore some of the most ruggedly beautiful, yet forbidden places. Visitors get all gears including life jackets, camping and the standard rafting paraphernalia ultimately making excellent tourism product.

Jungle Safari

There are many National Parks and Sanctuaries in Nepal attracting visitors from all over the world. This product is becoming popular as it involves bird watching, nature walk, jungle drive and elephant back. It definitely provides a sight of the one – horned rhino at every elephant safari. Besides the rhinos, wild boars, spotted deer, sloth bear, four-horned antelope are also usually seen. It is no more surprising to expect a majestic appearance of Royal Bengal tiger during the journey.

Bird Watching

Nepal is gradually emerging as a paradise for bird lovers with over 646 species (almost 8% of the world total) of birds, and among them almost 500 hundred species are found in Kathmandu Valley alone. The most popular bird watching spots in Kathmandu are Phulchoki, Godavari, Nagarjun, Bagmati River, Taudaha and so on. Besides Kathmandu, other places and valleys are also becoming popular as they provide with most rewarding experience and ultimate richness of tourism.

Mountain Flight

Flight is most feasible mean to go in far remote places to experience the natural and cultural beauties. Flights are common for various tourism activities such as mountaineering, trekking, rafting and even for jungle safari. In addition, Mountain flights have become a popular tourist attraction most recently. These flights appeal to all category of travelers to encounter the tallest mountains on earth. They also offer the closest possible aerial views of Mt. Everest, Kanchenjunga and the Tibetan Plateau. Such flights offer a panoramic view of the Himalayas in just one hour and even provide alternative option to grasp the breathtaking view of the Himalayas for time constrained, busy scheduled and physically challenged visitors.

It is already mentioned that the tourism products are of various types thus it is not feasible to illustrate all of them and deal in some paragraphs. Just to list some of the wonderful and most adventurous tourism products include Rock Climbing (natural as well as artificial), Hot Air Ballooning, Bungy Jumping, Para Gliding, Ultra-light Aircraft particularly in Pokhara and Mountain Biking in both rural and urban centres. These products provide the visitors with a chance among others to explore the diverse terrain of the exotic country, encounter with living heritage and experience the wildest adventure and feel peace and tranquility.

The tourism products of Nepal seem really unique. The natural beauty coupled with biodiversity and heritage produce unlimited potentiality for new and unprecedented tourism products. Nepalese tourism products are becoming popular though, there is many more to do to explore the potentiality of various products and publicize them appropriately.

Recently, Nepal started to focus in various products, diversify the market, establish a distinct image, manage the industry, and offer it in the tourism generating markets. Some preliminary symptoms are started to be seen in this or that way.

3.4 TOURISM POLICY AND PLANS

Tourism planning in its initial form was initiated only in 1966. It has provided with the systematic classification of tourism. It was followed by Nepal tourism master Plan 1972, designed to cover initially for 10 years. In 1995, Tourism Policy was designed. It has opened up various venues for both government and private sector.

There have been serious efforts to promote the industry in the past. Though the planning was not performed properly and budget was nominal, the sector has been showing an increasing trend in terms of revenue and employment. Tourism is emerging as one of the fastest growing, multifaceted, and diverse and still highly fragmented industry in form all over the world. Therefore, Nepal has to review and redesign vital components of tourism planning (Maharjan, 2004: 2-4). Nevertheless, the major objectives of any tourism planning and development process should be to minimize negative impacts and ensure that the positive benefits are realized in an equitable manner (UN ESCAP, 2001).

Initial Initiatives

It has been already mentioned that modern tourism[2] in Nepal is of recent phenomenon. Just after the dawn of democracy in 1950, the country was opened to the foreigners (FNCCI, 1996: 12). At the outset, there were no plans and policies regarding tourism in Nepal until late 1950's (Shrestha, 1998).

---

[2] Though Nepal was known as a famous destination attracting various people from the globe, authentic records are in scarce to show the presence of tourism industry.

In 1957, Nepal had established 'Tourist Development Board' to look after the tourism matters. It was only in 1959 that a French national, Georges Lebrec has prepared 'General Plan for the Organization of Tourism in Nepal' with the help of the French Government[3]. Lebrec has recommended to make promotional materials such as brochures, posters, postage stamps depicting the Himalayan peaks and Flora and Fauna and to use films, documentaries prepared by mountaineering expeditions for the promotion tourism in Nepal. He has also suggested establishing Nepal Tourism Office.

The status and organization of the board has been altered frequently. The board later had successfully started the tourist guide courses and collection of Tourist Statistics and introduced Hotel Arrival forms (Satyal, 2004: 38).

Nepal Tourism Master Plan, 1972

It was only in 1970's that the initiation to promote and develop tourism in a planned manner started. It was then obvious with the formulation of a high-level 'Nepal Tourism Development Committee' in 1971. As a result, 'Nepal Tourism Master Plan, 1972' was prepared in 1972 with the joint cooperation of Government of Germany and His Majesty's Government of Nepal (HMG/N, 1972 and Satyal, 2004: 38). The master plan has explored and enlisted the natural and cultural attractions and regarded them as great potentials for the development of tourism. It had classified Nepalese tourism as an organized sightseeing, independent 'Nepal Style Tourism', trekking and pilgrimage as well as asked for the proper promotion. It had suggested for preserving and maintaining the natural and cultural heritage sites for the sustainable tourism development in Nepal and in encouraging the private sector for the tourism investment (HMG/N, 1972).

The Master Plan, 1972 was a comprehensive plan and could be termed as a milestone in planning and development of tourism in Nepal. It has envisaged the development plan and program in two phases, viz. first phase (1972 - 1975) and the second phase (1976 - 1980). The plan had recommended the development of physical infrastructure such as roads, airports, hotels, resorts and preservation of cultural and natural tourist resources. It had identified several places like Kathmandu, Pokhara, Tansen, Lumbini and Chitwan as tourist places and suggested for the development of infrastructure. In addition, it had recommended for the establishment of Ministry of Tourism dealing both public matters and promotion activities.

Nepal Tourism Marketing Strategy (1976 - 1981)

In 1975, Joseph Edward Susnik, marketing advisor from Yugoslavia has prepared Nepal Tourism Marketing Strategy 1976-1981.

In his report, Mr. Susnik had suggested for the formation of 'Nepal Tourism Marketing Committee', and 'Nepal Tourism Infrastructure Committee' with the representation of private sector. It has also suggested for the formation of tourist offices in India and Germany. However, his suggestions were similar with that of 'Nepal Tourism Master Plan, 1972' (Shrestha, 1999).

---

[3] Mr. Lebrec was advisor under the bilateral cooperation program of French Ministry of Foreign Affairs in 1958-59.

National Promotional Committee Report, 1983

In 1981, His Majesty's Government of Nepal had formed National Tourism Promotion Committee. The committee had prepared a report entitled 'National Promotional Committee Report, 1983 emphasizing the promotion of 'Nepal Style" tourism, however in line with the suggestions forwarded by Nepal Tourism Master Plan, 1972.

The report particularly has suggested for the development of resorts in the mid mountains, promotion of tourism in India and to Europe. The basic thrust was to create some awareness programs to encourage the people for the pilgrimage tour focusing both Buddhist and Hindus from Asian countries, in general and India in particular. In addition to this, the report has opened up the prospects of the convention tourism. It has also opted to promote special packages for Indian particularly during hot summer season. In addition to this, it had recommended for the deputation of a separate person in Nepalese Embassies and otherwise honorary consuls to look after the affairs of tourism promotion. Likewise, it had recommended for the establishment of a revolving fund for the promotion of tourism and for the participation in international trade fairs.

Nepal Tourism Master Plan Review, 1984

It was only 1984, the assessment of 'Nepal Tourism Master Plan, 1972' was carried out and the report entitled 'Nepal Tourism Master Plan Review, 1984' was published. The report essentially presented a general glimpse of the past performance and pleaded for its further validity. It has suggested action plans for implementation of the plan and for the promotion of tourism in Nepal.

The report further suggested to design various destination oriented marketing programs and to improve the capability of Ministry of Tourism in assuming responsibilities institutionally, administratively and technically.

Nepal Tourism Development Program, 1990

Asian Development Bank has provided a financial assistance to prepare Nepal Tourism Development Program, 1990. The basic purposes of the programme were to review existing plans and policies and suggest modifications providing a long-term strategy for using resources on a sustainable basis. Similarly, other tasks were to prepare tourism development action plans for the development of tourism and to frame a sound organizational structure as well to update institutional capacity.

Nepal Tourism Development Program consists of reports in four volumes entitled Product Development Programme, Marketing Strategy, Environmental Impact and Institutional Framework for the Development of Tourism. The report proposed for tourism development programmes particularly domestic air transport, urban tourism in Kathmandu, infrastructure development in Pokhara, institutional development and tourism manpower development and training. The study has observed that the basic economic strategy of the tourism industry should be to earn foreign exchange, employment generation, income generation and regional distribution. Meanwhile, it has also pleaded for the achievement of proper returns on the capital investment and for mobilization of future investment. Thus, the report had envisaged, particularly for:

- Making Mount Everest and the Himalayas a 'must see' destination on the world tourist map.
- Establishing the Kathmandu Valley as the mystic valley of Shangri-La kingdom,

- Establishing the Pokhara valley as the gateway mountain resort to the Himalayas
- Providing a series of remarkable but short excursions from Kathmandu for ordinary sightseeing travelers
- Increase in budget for promotional programs.

The report recommends that involvement of government in tourism should focus on the provision of infrastructure, the improvement of tourism attraction and establishment of accommodation that is not feasible for the private sector. As there are difficulties for raising capital for the more substantial hotels and tourist attractions, opening of capital market for long-term paper such as shares, bonds, and debentures should be addressed for the development of tourism. The tourism development strategy should be towards quality tourism. The study report has also made recommendations regarding institutional restructuring such as the formation of a National Tourism Commissions and development tourism expertise within the Ministry of Tourism.

Tourism Policy, 1995

After the restoration of democracy through the popular 'Peoples' Movement' in 1990, then the elected government firmly initiated liberalized economic policy and opened up the economy for the private sector and foreign investment. In the light of such economic policy, the government formulated Tourism Policy in 1995. The major objectives of the policy were to develop the tourism industry as a main economic sector through the identification of relationship with other sectors; to increase employment, foreign currency earnings and national income and to correct regional imbalance through the expansion of the industry to rural areas. Similarly, other objectives were to improve natural, cultural and human environments of the nation, to maintain good image in the international community, to develop and promote Nepal as an attractive tourist destination (HMG/N, 1997:2).

The policy has envisioned that 'Nepal will be developed as a centre for adventure tourism with an attractive image. The policy contains 'Policy' and 'Working Policies' for the long-term development of the tourism industry in the country. The "Policies" thus mentioned are quoted as follows (HMG/N, 1997).

1. The private sector participation shall be highly encouraged in the development and expansion of tourist activities and His Majesty's Government's involvement in this field shall mainly focus on the development of the tourism infrastructures and in addition to that HMG shall also play a role as a coordinator as well as a catalyst.
2. Participation of the Nepalese people in the integrated manner will be carried out for environmental conservation programmes, which contribute to sustainable tourism development.
3. Existing tourism infrastructure and facilities will be upgraded. Priority will be given to developing new tourist destinations, particularly in rural areas.
4. Popular religious tourism sites will be improved and promoted in order to develop religious tourism.
5. Nepal will be developed as a centre for adventure tourism.
6. Tourist service and facilities in the kingdom will be encouraged to upgrade in quality. Special efforts will be made to make Nepal a secure place for tourists.

7. Due attention will be paid to improving regional imbalances while developing tourism.

8. Competitive tourism promotion and marketing will be launched in tourist originating markets to establish Nepal as a major tourist destination.

9. Linkages will be established between tourism and agro-based as well as cottage industries. Emphasis will be placed on developing these related sectors simultaneously.

10. Local investment will be encouraged in service-oriented, travel and trekking agency businesses in which local investors have proven capability. Foreign investment, including joint ventures, will be promoted in areas, which transfers skills and technology or in capital-intensive industries like hotels and resorts.

11. The National Civil Aviation Policy will be implemented as an integral part of Tourism Policy.

In addition to the above, the policy has classified tourism industries in seven categories, designed the facilities and incentives to be provided for the tourism industry, formulated the provision for tourism work force, and designed the institutional arrangements comprising Tourism Council, Ministry of Tourism and Civil Aviation and Tourism Development Board).[4]

To be more detail, the policy has classified the tourism industries into seven categories comprising classified hotel industry, resorts, Travel agencies, Rafting agencies, classified restaurants and bar, adventurous/recreational tourism business (Skating, Gliding, Cable Car Complex, Hot Air Ballooning, Gulf Course, Polo, Horse Riding) and manpower training centers related to the tourism industry (HMG/N, 1997).

Hotels and Resorts are classified as industry receiving national priority and enjoying the facilities as well as incentives as per the provision of Industrial Enterprises Act, 1992. Other tourism services are also entitled to receive facilities based on value added, and employment generation. Similarly, they are entitled to get duty concessions on the import of specified products based on working capital and plans and services on priority basis for communication equipment, electricity and water supply. In addition, hotel, restaurant, resorts, and other tourism services would be entitled for the specified facilities and incentives based on their opening and operation in the rural areas specified by the government, (HMG/N, 1997).

Hence, the policy has incorporated various aspects of the economy, provided with the competent policy frameworks and designed the structure to enable the proper functioning of the industry in the long run.

Other Tourism Plans and Programs

In addition to above major policies and plans, some other projects have been carried out for instance **Second Tourism Infrastructure Development Project, 1995** especially designed to provide a detail programmes for infrastructure development and **Tourism Sector Development Programme, 1997** designed for the development tourist hubs such as Kanchenjungha, Jumla, Sukla Phanta, Bardiya,

---

[4] The existing Department of Tourism was dissolved to remove duplication of the functions as per the provision of the Tourism Policy itself.

Lumbini and Chitwan. These programmes were designed to provide with development standards for tourism industry and their implementation strategy, tourism information system and its implementation package.

Similarly, in the year 2004 "The Tourism Marketing Strategy for Nepal 2005–2020' was designed for the Nepal Tourism Board and Nepal's tourism industry to tap the opportunities and develop the tourism industry. In fact, the strategy in itself is the culmination of extensive review and consultation and is the first comprehensive marketing strategy (Travers, 2004: vii). It includes the analysis of every tourist generating markets and uncovers the possibility to exploit the growing market. It also projects the figures. In fact, these figures started to seem ambitious because of instability inside the country and lack of promotional activities outside the country. It is a fact that tourism's potential can only be realized in a climate of peace and stability (Travers, 2004: 2).

However, these programmes and plans did not cover some crucial issues/aspect of Nepalese tourism such as marketing and promotion of the products/services and financing as well as investment in tourism sector. Despite of growing concern over the economic and social aspects of tourism it is really amazing to note the dearth of detail study covering the mission, vision, strategic planning and long-term development of the sector.

3.5 INSTITUTIONAL ARRANGEMENT FOR TOURISM

Tourism reaches into the varied aspects of life. It creates various benefits for most of the economic sectors, directly and indirectly. It generates employment opportunities and helps in the promotion and conservation of the art and culture. It can help in reducing disparities in income and employment within the country (ESCAP, 2001: iii). The tourism industry has been one of the best foreign currency earners in the country and thus provided a significant contribution to the economy.

Nepal is no more a forbidden land. It has been attracting the people from all over the world. However, the travel and tourism itself in its present form, is not so old comparing to that of several European and North American nations. Tourism has received special recognition, priority in national planning and special consideration in government policies. The government is found to be making efforts to encourage and help this trade (FNCCI, 1996:13).

The Government has been actively promoting tourism in Nepal. It has always encouraged the private sector for their involvement and participation. The sector has enjoyed various forms of the government's involvement, allocation of resources and initiation of studies and analysis pertaining to the pros and cons of the industry.

An organization plays a vital role in its planning, development and growth. Organization consists of individuals that work to achieve the organizational goal and objectives. Organization arranges people into working groups, associates them for similar functions and provides the direction for combined action. In addition, a framework, structure or formal setup facilitates the overall operation, deals with issues and finally combines the efforts of various groups and their action to achieve the objectives.

Every institution needs organization to function properly. Tourism may not be an exception. It certainly needs it. Tourism industry not only includes physical resources, infrastructure and services but also requires the active involvement of people. Thus, the basic determinant for the success of tourism organization can be threefold specifically, attractions such as climate, scenery, historical and cultural features; accessibility comprising distance of destination, their location and transportation facilities and amenities; accommodation, catering and entertainment facilities.

An appropriate mix of all the three above (components) is necessary for the success of tourism. Hence, it is the task of organization to ensure the combination of these determinants and their availability in right time.

The organization of tourism can be divided into two parts.

1. Sectors of tourist organization: Providers of the tourism services, hotel and catering services, transport and entertainment
2. Levels of tourist organization: Local, national, regional and international

Likewise, the tourism organization can be horizontal and vertical though it varies from country to country. Almost every country around the globe has tourist organization. The rational behind the establishment of tourist organization is the result of gradual awareness and realization of various benefits from the tourism. To achieve the benefits and to minimize the negative impacts equally, systematic efforts backed by efficient organization is must. In addition, in order to carry out management function properly organization becomes a framework.

The Tourism Policy, 1995 identifies the lines of responsibility between the Tourism Council (issuing general guidelines), Ministry of Tourism and Civil Aviation (policy and regulatory matters) and the Nepal Tourism Board (policy implementation, including tourism planning, product development, marketing and promotion) (MOTCA, 1997 and ESCAP, 2001: 176).

Here in this section, an attempt is made to discuss about the various organizations involved in tourism and particularly about the Tourism Council, Ministry of Culture, Tourism and Civil Aviation, the then Department of Tourism, Nepal Tourism Board and Nepal Academy of Tourism and Hotel Management.

A. TOURISM COUNCIL

A high-level Tourism Council, under the chairmanship of the Prime Minister has been constituted in 1992 with a vast representation of government as well as of private sector. The basic thrust behind the establishment of the council was to develop the tourism industry as a backbone of national economy and to maintain coordination and cooperation among various agencies related to the tourism industry.

The major functions of the council are particularly; to remove the difficulties arising in the tourism sector, to give policy level guidelines to the subordinate executive agencies (Ministry of Tourism and the Nepal Tourism Board) and to review related plans and programmes. The council incorporates the wide representation of ministers, secretaries and private professionals. It is a common forum for both public and private sector and suitable venue to formulate long-term policies in tourism.

Tourism Policy, 1995 under institutional arrangement has provided with some details about the council as "In order to develop the tourism industry as a backbone of national development and to maintain coordination and cooperation among various agencies related with the tourism industry, a high level 'Tourism Council' has already been formed. The council shall perform the functions as to remove difficulties arise in the tourism sector; to give policy level guidelines to the subordinate executive agencies (Ministry of Tourism and the Board) and to review related plans." (MOTCA, 1997)

B. MINISTRY OF CULTURE, TOURISM AND CIVIL AVIATION

Ministry of Tourism was established in 1978 (2035 BS). In 1982, Civil Aviation affairs were merged into this ministry thus; it became the Ministry of Tourism & Civil Aviation. Further, in 2000, Cultural affairs were also integrated in the Ministry and it was called the Ministry of Culture, Tourism & Civil Aviation. Again, after 3 years, the cultural affairs were transferred to Education Ministry and it finally regained the status as Ministry of Tourism & Civil Aviation. Recently a cabinet minister - Minister for Tourism and Civil Aviation, heads the ministry.

The main functions of the ministry are as follows:

1. Formulation of policy and planning as well as their timely implementation
2. Promotion and preservation of natural, cultural and human resources
3. Regulation and Supervision of Travel and Trekking Agency
4. Formulation, implementation, monitoring and evaluations of various policies related to tourism and civil aviation.
5. Establish and maintain proper relation and cooperation with international organizations related to tourism and civil aviation.
6. Ensuring proper representations in various national and international venues, symposium, seminars and conferences
7. Construction, renovation, preservation and advancement of airports and other respective transportation

Recently (July 2005) the ministry has six divisions, two departments (Department of Archaeology and Nepal Copyrights Registrar's Office), one legal section and 140 staffs comprising 56 Officers (gazetted level) and 84 other non-gazetted and classless staffs (MOTCA: 2005).

In addition to the above, the ministry also looks after and plays a catalytic role for the operation and management of special organizations like Nepal Tourism Board and Civil Aviation Authority of Nepal; corporations like Royal Nepal Airlines Corporation and Nepal Tourism Board; development organizations; development committees and some other related institutions.

C. DEPARTMENT OF TOURISM

Department of Tourism had been performing well over the years for the overall management of the tourism industry. It was established in 1962 as full-fledged department. It was a major government organization over the years particularly for the execution of the tourism policy and plans as laid down by the Ministry of Tourism.

Major objectives of Department of Tourism were as under listed:

1. To stimulate travel and tourism in the country
2. To promote and market the tourism in international arena particularly in tourism generating markets.

3. To formulate the appropriate policies and plans

4. To establish joint efforts and perform programmes as laid down by the ministry.

Tourism Policy, 1995 has enlisted some of the major function of the department, as "It shall be the duty of the Department of Tourism to frame, in accordance with the stipulated policy, directions and guidelines given by the Tourism Council and Ministry of Tourism and Civil Aviation, programmes concerning tourism development and to implement the same." (MOTCA, 1997)

The department of Tourism was dissolved and transformed into the Nepal Tourism Board in 1997. It was dissolved as per the provision provided in the Tourism Policy, 1995. Most of functions and responsibilities particularly related to the design and implementation of the tourism plans, tourism promotion, infrastructure development, tourism service, expansion of facilities, manpower development and preservation of ecology have been transferred to Nepal Tourism Board. Likewise, Ministry of Tourism has absorbed some other functions such as registration of tourism industries, regulation as well as arrangement of facilitates to be provided for the tourism industry and enterprises.

D. NEPAL TOURISM BOARD

Nepal Tourism Board was established in 1997. Both the Nepal Tourism Board Act 1997 and Tourism Policy, 1995, facilitated the establishment of the board. The House of the Parliament passed the act in December 1996 and it obtained the Royal Seal in February 1997. The Board replaced the Department of Tourism and started to function as autonomous institution. In fact, the board is designed as a partnership between the HMG/N and the private sector travel industry of Nepal.[5]

The board is highly decorated with the responsibilities like formulation and implementation of tourism programmes, tourism promotion, infrastructure development, extension of tourist service and facilities, human resource development and environment conservation. It is supposed to formulate and implement tourism development programmes in accordance with the policy guidelines and directives set forth by the Tourism Council and Ministry of Tourism and Civil Aviation. Nepal Tourism Board was also entrusted to work as a National Tourist Organization (NTO) of the country commencing December 31, 1998 (NTB, 2003). Thus, it is even empowered to represent the kingdom in various international forums and organizations.

The Tourism policy, 1995 has also proposed Board to be an autonomous and flexible body capable of carrying out all tourism related activities except those, which must be carried out by His Majesty's Government. The board will have a separate seal and fund. The fund as such includes the contribution of HMG/N in the form grants, contributions of the private sector and assistance of the international donor agencies. The board will have full authority to spend money out of this fund. The area of jurisdiction, duties and responsibilities of the board including other operational details will be specified (MOTCA, 1997).

The Tourism policy, 1995 has provided with the details for the composition of the board as follows (MOTCA, 1997):

---

[5] **The Kathmandu Post** December 31, 2004, p. III col. I

His Majesty' Government shall form a Tourism Development Board under the chairmanship of Honorable Minister/State Minister for Tourism consisting 8 to 10 members as nominated by His Majesty's Government from among the concerned agencies and private tourism entrepreneurs.

While nominating members of the Board from among the private tourism entrepreneurs, they shall be selected from among the persons who may give contribution to the development of tourism industry.

His Majesty's Government may designate a member secretary of the Board, from among the members of the Board.

Nepal Tourism Board is statutory institution and thus has some statutory duties and responsibilities. The government has empowered the board. It can work as a professional and dynamic NTO to address the pressing needs by designing specific brand image for Nepal as travel destination and supports the same by the self-sustained promotional campaigns. Here is some more elaboration on the role and responsibility (NTB, 2003: 9; NTB, 2004: 2).

To develop and introduce Nepal as an attractive tourist destination in the international marketplace

To promote the tourism industry in the country while working for the conservation of natural, environmental and cultural resources

To work towards increasing the gross domestic product and foreign exchange income by means of promoting the tourism industry.

To work towards increasing the employment opportunities in the same industry.

To develop Nepal as secure, dependable as well as an attractive travel destination by establishing a respectable travel trade community.

To work towards providing quality service to the tourists visiting Nepal.

To study the bottlenecks against the same by means of conducting research and getting implemented the results of such research in order to do away with these bottlenecks.

To promote and develop institution for the promotion of tourism industry

Nepal Tourism Board has been successfully carrying out its activities despite of challenges and resource constraints. It is making a serious effort to safeguard tourism and upgrade image of the country as a safe and beautiful destination in the world over.

D. NEPAL ACADEMY OF TOURISM AND HOTEL MANAGEMENT

Hotel Management and Tourism Training Centre was established in 1973 by the government to cater the growing need of skilled manpower in tourism. In 2004, it has been renamed as Nepal Academy of Tourism and Hotel Management. Earlier it was the sole authority to produce skilled workforce in tourism. After the restoration of democracy in country and initiation of liberal and open policy in tourism, some institutions were established and started to give training.

The academy has successfully been preparing an array of human resources required for the tourism industry. More recently, it is providing training for more than 1000 persons, in an average. Earlier, the figure was in lower level, for instance it produced only 716 persons in F. Y. 1994/95 compared to 425 in

F. Y. 1989/90. The number of persons getting the tourism training increased remarkably to 1,204 in F. Y. 1995/96.

Table: 3.4

Manpower Trained by Nepal Academy of Tourism and Hotel Management

Fiscal Year	Manpower Trained	Cumulative number	Growth Percent
1984/85	107	107	
1985/86	183	290	71.0
1986/87	300	590	63.9
1987/88	797	1,387	165.7
1988/89	1,018	2,405	27.7
1989/90	425	2,830	-58.3
1990/91	684	3,514	60.9
1991/92	569	4,083	-16.8
1992/93	1,024	5,107	80.0
1993/94	667	5,774	-34.9
1994/95	716	6,490	7.3
1995/96	1,204	7,694	68.2
1996/97	1,495	9,189	24.2
1997/98	1,605	10,794	7.4
1998/99	1,071	11,865	-33.3
1999/00	1,197	13,062	11.8
2000/01	1,127	14,189	-5.8
2001/02	1,033	15,222	-8.3
2002/03	787	16,009	-23.8
2003/04	1,475	17,484	87.4
2004/05	1,386	18,870	-6.0

Source: Economic Survey (Various Issues). Ministry of Finance Nepal.

The figure reached at its highest of 1,605 in F. Y. 1997/98. However, the number started to decrease after F. Y. 1997/98. In F. Y. 1999/00 and 2000/01, only 1,197 and 1,127 persons received the training respectively. The figure decreased and marked the lowest figure (in recent period) of 787 during F. Y. 2002/03. Again, the figure started to improve in following years recording 1,475 and 1,386 in F. Y. 2003/04 and 2004/05 respectively.

The figures over the period indicated the performance of the academy. The academy has given tourism related training to 2,830 persons during the period from F. Y. 1984/85 to 1989/90. It registered a gradual growth until Fiscal Year 1999/00 and provided the training for 13,062 persons in total during the period. Afterwards, it witnessed a minor decline until F. Y. 2002/03. Again, in F. Y. 2003/04 and 2004/05 it took a momentum. Hence, the number of skilled persons during the review period continuously increased and reached to 18,529 at the end of F. Y. 2004/05.

3.6 TOURISM BUSINESS ENTERPRISES

The tourism industry comprises various tourism business enterprises or establishments receiving a significant proportion of their sales revenue from visitor expenditures (OAS, 1997: 3). In other words, it comprises various tourism business enterprises such as hotels and resorts, travel agencies, trekking and mountaineering and restaurants, airlines and transportation.

In order to provide the details about the requisites of a tourism industry, United Nations and World Tourism Organization have developed the Standard Classification of Tourism Activities (SICTA). The SICTA includes and classifies business enterprises that are highly dependent on tourism demand. It does not define the tourism industry, but rather provides a framework for selecting appropriate industry sectors to be included in the supply side tourism activities. It details 185 supply side "economic activities" related to tourism either directly providing goods and services to visitors such as transportation, accommodations, food service, entertainment and recreation or indirectly providing services to tourism businesses such as hotel construction and tourism schools. Further, SICTA classifies the tourism industry in primary, secondary and tertiary sectors depending upon the share of revenue from visitors in total business turnover (WTO, 1996 and OAS, 1997:3).

Tourism industry comprises various tourism business enterprises from accommodation to adventure and entertainment to transportation. Therefore, the industry embraces variety of establishments such as hotels and resorts, travel agencies, trekking and mountaineering, restaurants, airlines and transportation. In addition to these, the industry needs entertainment places and shopping facilities, along with basic infrastructures like airports, air services, road and telecommunication, as well as amenities like electricity, water supply, sewerage and waste disposal systems.

Present study is focused primarily on the primary tourism establishments. It briefly presents the distribution of tourism business enterprises and growth pattern over the period. It is basically designed to enumerate the basics of tourism industry in Nepal.

It is not necessary to repeat that tourism industry of Nepal is young. As the country is small, underdeveloped and landlocked, it also has limited economic activities. Nevertheless, most of tourism business enterprises are operating with active private sector initiatives and performing well over the period. Table: 3.5 provides the size of the tourism business enterprises (directly related to tourism) and its composition for the period from 1980 to 2005.

In F. Y. 1990, there were 469 tourism business comprising 168 hotels, 145 travel agencies, 139 trekking agencies and 17 rafting agencies. The number of tourism business enterprises registered impressive growth since 1990 and reached to 1,283 in F. Y. 1995; 2,109 in 2000; 2,489 in 2003 and 2,786 in 2005.

There were only 73 hotels (classified) and 5109 hotel beds in 1980. The number is continuously increasing over the years. It registered a remarkable growth during the review period and reached to 168 with 10,244 beds in 1990. After 10 years, it reached to 848 with 34,958 beds in 2000 achieving a remarkable growth. In spite of slow down in tourism business and down turn in tourist arrival in the country particularly after 2000, number of hotels and hotel beds produced a steady growth. It reached to 966 with 38,270 beds and 1,006 39,384 with beds in the year 2003 and 2005 respectively.

Table: 3.5
Distribution of Tourism Business

Year	No. Hotel and Resorts	No. of Travels	No. of Trekking	No. of Rafting	No. of Hotels, Travels, Trekking and Rafting	No. Hotel Beds
1980	73	-	-	-	73	5,109
1985	80	-	-	-	80	6,910
1990	168	145	139	17	469	10,244
1995	520	386	310	67	1,283	21,807
2000	848	637	537	87	2,109	34,958
2001	888	691	580	87	2,246	36,163
2002	943	738	611	87	2,379	37,616
2003	966	788	645	90	2,489	38,270
2004	996	877	705	91	2,669	39,107
2005	1,006	948	740	92	2,786	39,384

Source: Economic Survey (various issues).

During the review period, travel, trekking and rafting agencies registered the gradual growth in the number. In 1990, there were only 145 travel agencies, 139 trekking agencies and 17 rafting agencies in the country. In a time span of 15 years, the number of travel agencies increased to 948, trekking agencies increased to 740 and rafting agencies increased to 92. Figure 3.1 presents the distribution of the tourism business enterprises during the review period.

Figure: 3.1
Distribution of the Tourism Business Enterprises

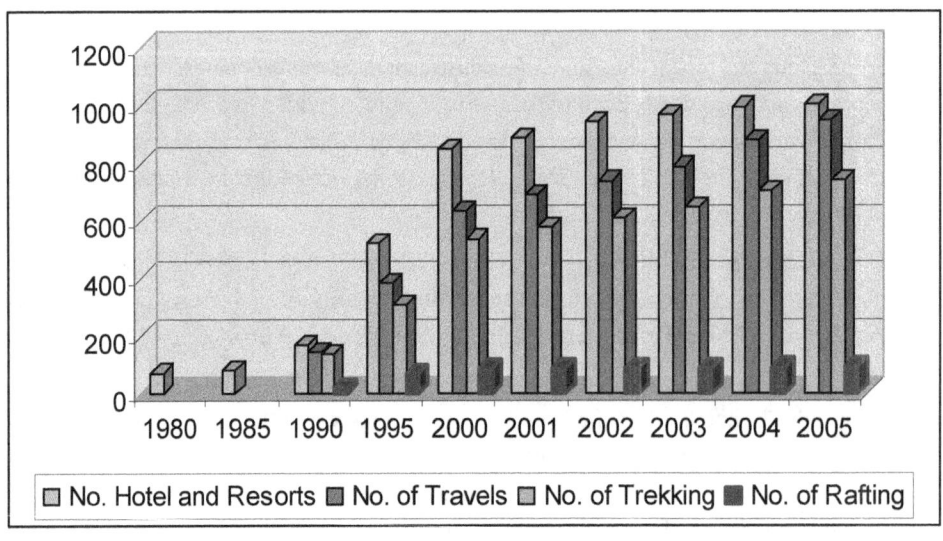

The figure is not exhaustive, thus, does not include cargo agencies, airlines, and some others as they have only a little bit direct relationship with tourism. However, the number is found to be less representative, because it does not adjust the agencies either liquidated or closed their operation because of inability to renew and complete the formal obligations or otherwise collapsed over the years.

3.7 LEGAL AND REGULATORY FRAMEWORK

The legal basis for tourism industry is based on the various laws enacted earlier in order to maintain and regulate the particular segment of the Tourism industry. It was only in 1995 that the "Tourism Policy", was formulated. The main purpose of the policy is to contribute on the enhancement of international friendship, the improvement of the national economy, and the development of a sound domestic tourism industry. Similarly, it was designed particularly in bringing about a favorable tourism environment, developing tourism resources and providing support for tourism businesses.

Every government should in principal, prepare a complete policy on tourism promotion in order to achieve the purpose of that law. The law also prescribes the government's obligations to establish annual and long-term plans for tourism promotion, including the attraction of foreign visitors; improvement of tourist facilities; preservation of tourism resources. It also includes the provision like direction and supervision of tourism industry businesses; education of tourism industry employees; designation and development of tourist sites; promotion of domestic tourism; and establishment of a fund for tourism promotion and development (ESCAP, 2001).

The acts, rules and regulations related to tourism industries are summarized in the Table: 3.6. In addition, some practices are prevalent in the tourism industry and are still valid for the operation of tourism business.

Table: 3.6

Tourism Acts and Regulation

S. N.	Acts and Regulations	Enactment	Amendment
1	Tourism Act	1978	
2	National Aviation Policy	1993	1996
3	Nepal Tourism Board Act	1997	
4	The Immigration Act	1992	
5	Mountaineering Expedition Rules	1978	
6	Climbing Rules	1981	
7	Hotels/Resorts/Restaurants & Bar Rules and Regulation	1981	

In addition to these acts, rules and regulations, there are some other legislations and regulatory norms that have a direct impact on the overall operation of tourism activities. These acts to name some of them are, Foreign Exchange Control Act, Income Tax Act, Industrial Enterprises Act, Foreign Investment and Technology Transfer Act.

The Nepalese government has initiated the liberalized policy in general and tourism in particular. Therefore, the tourism sector has been enjoying the private entrepreneurship and investment. The government has provided legal title for the trade associations such as Hotel Association of Nepal, Travel

Agents Association, and Trekking Agents Association etc. along-with certain powers and regulatory mechanisms. Therefore, tourism industries are equipped and empowered with various activities to run the business even in the challenging environment.

Investment incentives

Most of the developing countries have been providing investment incentives to motivate the business entrepreneurs particularly for productive activities. Earlier most of the incentives were designed to provide impetus for industrial development. These incentives are still continued in most of the countries even in changing context such as open, liberalized and market-based economies.

Tourism has become one of the important sectors of economy. When the significance of tourism in the economic growth and development is realized, it started to receive certain priority and attention in development planning. It started not only to receive the resources for the development of infrastructures but also to attract and encourage the private sector for the investment.

The mobilization of the tourism development strategy is dependent upon a partnership of public sector investment (especially in infrastructure) and private sector investment (especially in projects and enterprises). At every stage of implementation, there is a need for the governments to stimulate private investment by creating a favourable condition for investment with specific incentives including fiscal, financial and other (ESCAP, 2001).

Nepal provides the investment incentives exclusively for industries. Recently, they started to provide the incentives for tourism in general and hotel industry in particular, considering the huge initial capital investment. As such, all the incentives are general and consist of such measures as investment allowances, duty exemptions or concessions and tax holidays. It does not contain any grant finance to the private sector. The following are the major types of incentives offered to tourism (ESCAP: 2001: 210-211; HMG/N, 1992 and MOTCA, 1997):

Investment allowance: Investment allowance is the amount claimed in addition to the normal claim for depreciation. It is normally a percentage of total capital expenses excluding land cost. An additional depreciation is available as investment allowance presently at the rate of 25 percent of investment.

Duty concessions: Duty concessions are available for hotel and other industries (travels). The rate differs with the fiscal act.

Tax holiday: A five to seven year tax holiday is available in Nepal. Though travel trade and hotels both are eligible for such facility, it is more focused to hotels and resorts.

Relief from sales tax and VAT: Sales tax and VAT exemption is also available in Nepal for the hotels.

In the past, hotel sector has been the main focus area for the incentives. Tax concessions were made available almost exclusively to star hotels. Likewise, the current level of incentives for tourism business is low and somehow meaningless to encourage the development of the industry. The issues related to providing the incentives only to the certain type businesses, the level (size) of incentives and the extent of outreach are emerging as a debatable issue. Even some prominent business entrepreneurs started to question about the validity of incentives. In fact, these incentives should be aimed only for those entrepreneurs who were previously neglected (Government of South Africa, 1996: 28).

Similarly, there is a common complaint about the incentives only focused on the hotels not in other travel sector. The most justifiable complaint was the penal taxation on tourist coaches in Nepal, originally 200 percent and later to 100 percent. This level of tax makes it difficult to justify the purchase of new vehicles, as it is difficult to charge more in operating customers (Bennett, 1991: 196).

Nowadays it has been challenging to design a competent and modern package of investment incentive. Despite of its vast scope, fiscal incentives may not be sufficient to attract the desirable and appropriate level of tourism development. Rather, it is necessary to design of general investment incentives, revenue and taxation legislations, or incorporation of project legislations. In the meantime, it is necessary to include some other incentives including training facilities, profit repatriation and work permits along with a range of companion incentives. Companion incentives basically are related to the problem of obtaining land for the development of hotels and resort facilities in suitable locations, the system of land ownership and land leasing, the level of national savings and private savings as well as the availability of local entrepreneurial and managerial expertise and experience.

The availability of fiscal and financial incentives may not be sufficient to attract the level of private investment in tourism at least in this changing context. Thus, it seems necessary to design a range of complementary incentives, including:

- Seed money as loan equity;
- Assistance with land negotiations, especially with indigenous landowners;
- Providing training facilities (i.e., courses, schools, colleges and teaching staff);
- Guarantees of promotion through the Visitor's Bureau;
- Ease of repatriation of profits;
- The provision of work permits for key workers and staffs;
- Write-off facility for the costs of critical appliances and plants (air conditioners and solar heaters)

In short, in order to a design a major incentive, it is necessary to declare the nation as a "tax haven", removing all restrictions on corporate tax, income tax, estate duties, capital gains tax and sales tax.

The investment incentive process must be conspicuous, transparent, regular (following a time scale), clear and defined, supported by legal enactment and composed of incentives package (fiscal, financial and companion incentives). In addition, political and economic stability is primary requirement for the creation of a favourable investment climate.

"The purposes of the incentive package are to relieve the national budget of undue burdens, provide initial development momentum, support programme acceleration of that momentum, and provide flexibility so that projects can be encouraged and facilitated. Such a package should not be considered immutable or permanent. Each aspect of investment incentives should be subject to regular review, with a frequency at least as regular as the national economic strategy." (ESCAP, 2001: 40-41)

3.8 CONTRIBUTION OF TOURISM

Tourism has definitely been one of the important sectors in the world economy, and it is now considered as an efficient tool for promoting economic growth. The foreign currencies receipts from tourism contribute to finance the expansion of manufacturing by financing imports of capital goods (Jimenez and Ortuno, 2005). That is how the tourist activity can benefit the overall economy of the country and helps for the economic development and growth. The contribution of tourism can be explored with various methods depending upon the motive of such analysis. The prominent contribution of the tourism is economic benefits followed by socio-cultural, environmental and direct, indirect and induced effects in other sectors of the economy.

The economic benefits of tourism can be derived directly or indirectly. The primary effect is direct benefit from tourist expenditures for goods and services whereas the secondary effect is indirect benefit generated by the circulation of tourism expenditures in the destination.

In addition, tourism spending can create induced benefits. As income levels rise due to the direct and indirect effects of change in the level of tourism expenditure, some portion of the additional personal income will be spent within the destination resulting in induced benefits. Hence, the spending by tourists at the destination can create direct benefits in tourism-related services such as accommodation, hospitality, attractions, events and transportation indirect benefits such as increased income and employment and induced benefits such as local income and jobs in the manufacturing and service sector (ESCAP, 2001).

The tourism expenditures have primary and secondary effects. The economic impact of tourism can be measured as the difference in economic well being between the income levels that would have existed without tourism activity and the income levels after tourism activity. There are a number of tangible and less tangible economic benefits and costs (ESCAP, 2001).

However, economic benefits of tourism are of various types some of them can be traced for the discussion. These benefits include increase in direct, indirect and induced income; improvement in standard of living; generation of new employment opportunities; the rise in tax base; improvement in infrastructure and facilities; and development of local handicrafts.

Tourism is not a panacea, it certainly includes some potential costs including seasonal employment; availability of low status/paying jobs; inflation; increased costs (land, housing, food and services); pollution; increased traffic/congestion, crime, taxes; leakage of revenues and over dependency on tourism as a prime economic activity (ESCAP, 2001).

In addition to the economic costs discussed above, other costs may have an indirect or long-term impact on the economic contributions of tourism. For example, land values may change as high-priced projects replace traditional and less profitable land uses. If agricultural landowners sold or developed their land for tourism, the tourism economy would rely on food imports. The loss of traditional land values can also have an impact on the local heritage and sense of place. Moreover, conflict may arise between those landowners who do not wish to see the loss of the historic character of their community and area, and pro-tourism proponents. Residents and speculators who suffer or benefit from rising land prices might join in the fray. Such conflict could escalate as tourism pressures increase, and the resulting scars on the community might take a long time to heal.

It is also important to view economic impacts from a long-term perspective. Environmental degradation and pollution will result in short-term. There could also be considerable long-term economic costs to the local, regional, and national economies if the destination is no longer desirable due to the effects of degradation and pollution (ESCAP, 2001: 3-5). The sixth chapter also contains the empirical analysis for the contribution of the tourism.

3.9 CONCLUSION

The dealing about the evolution of tourism, organization involved for the operation and development of tourism, policies and plans designed to broaden the tourism and the discussion about its contribution clearly show the where about of the tourism industry in Nepal.

Nepal certainly lacks integrated tourism planning. It is the result of improper and myopic planning over the years. "Yet the industry has over the years been unable to develop a common vision or a cohesive mission to guide itself to meet the emerging market challenges in a proactive manner. It has also lacked farsighted and focused leadership as a result of secular business interests of a few in powers, instability in political leadership and resultant lack of continuity of government and bureaucracy" (Maharjan, 2004: 9). However, it has been developed on its own. Not surprising, the tourism sector has produced some unique product concepts ultimately creating a model for world tourism.

It may not be necessary to stress the vital role of the organization in the tourism industry. A sound and updated organization is necessary to formulate the policy, to frame out the guidelines and to issue the direction, to implement the plans and instruct the employees to achieve the targets. They provide with the structure, role, cooperation and coordination, integration and differentiation, responsibility and authority and finally so much about the operation of the tourism industry. The major point here is to remember about the essence and importance of management in tourism.

Similarly, the attraction of foreign visitors as well as to sell the product is not an easy task. It certainly requires improvement of tourist facilities; preservation of existing tourism resources; regulation and supervision of tourism industry in desired manner; enhancement of education for the employees; and designation and development of new tourist sites. In addition, it would be desirable to promote both international and domestic tourism, aggressively publicize and finally to establish a joint fund for tourism promotion and development.

REFERENCES

Cooper, C. P. ed. (1993). **Progress in Tourism, Recreation and Hospitality Management**. U.K.: University of Survey, Vol. 1.

ESCAP (1991). **Investment and Economic Cooperation in the Tourism Sector in Developing Asian Countries**. Report of a Seminar Organized by ESCAP Bangkok, 5-21 October 1991 Tokyo and Sendai Japan

ESCAP (2001). **Opportunities and Challenges for Tourism Investment**, ESCAP Tourism Review No. 21. New York: United Nations

FNCCI (1996). **Directory of Tourism**. Kathmandu: tourism Committee, Federation of Nepalese Chambers of Commerce and Industries.

HMG/N (1972). **Nepal Tourism Master Plan, 1972**. Kathmandu: His Majesty's Government of Nepal

HMG/N (1992). **Industrial Enterprises Act, 1992**. Kathmandu: Ministry of Law and Justice His Majesty's Government of Nepal.

Maharjan, Narayan P. (2004). **Tourism Planning in Nepal**. A Ph. D. Thesis submitted to Faculty of Management, Tribhuvan University Kathmandu, Nepal.

MOTCA (1997). **Tourism Policy, 1995**. Kathmandu: His Majesty's Government of Nepal, Ministry of Tourism and Civil Aviation.

MOTCA (1998). **Annual Statistical Report**, 1997. Kathmandu: His Majesty's Government of Nepal Ministry of Tourism and Civil Aviation

MOTCA (1998). **Nepal Tourism Statistics, 1997**. Kathmandu: His Majesty's Government of Nepal, Ministry of Tourism and Civil Aviation.

MOTCA (2005). Accessed from worldwide web site. http://www.motca.gov.np.

NTB (2003). **Destination Nepal: Travel Manual**. Kathmandu: Nepal Tourism Board.

NTB (2004). **Annual Operational Plan 2004-05 (2061-62 B.S.)**. Kathmandu: Nepal Tourism Board.

Satyal, Yagna Raj (2004). **Tourism in Nepal: A Profile**. New Delhi: Adroit Publishers.

Travers, Robert (2004). **Tourism Marketing Strategy for Nepal 2005-2020**. Kathmandu: Tourism for Rural Poverty Alleviation Programme.

UN ESCAP (2001). **Promotion of Investment in Tourism Infrastructure**. New York: UN ESCAP

Upadhyay, Rudra Prasad (2001). **A Study of Tourism as Leading Sector in Economic Development in Nepal**. A Ph. D. Thesis submitted to Department of Economics, University of Lucknow India.

CHAPTER

TOURISM FINANCE: AN IMPACT ANALYSIS

4.1 INTRODUCTION
4.2 INVESTMENT POLICY ENVIRONMENT

PART – ONE
TOURISM FINANCING FROM VARIOUS SOURCES

4.3 SOURCES OF TOURISM FINANCING
4.4 THE GOVERNMENT (PUBLIC SECTOR)
4.5 ROLE OF NEPALESE FINANCIAL SYSTEM IN TOURISM FINANCING
4.6 FOREIGN DIRECT INVESTMENT IN TOURISM

PART – TWO
ECONOMIC IMPACT OF TOURISM AND TOURISM FINANCING: AN EMPIRICAL ANALYSIS

4.7 ECONOMIC IMPACT ANALYSIS
4.8 ECONOMIC IMPACT OF TOURISM: AN EMPIRICAL ANALYSIS
4.9 ECONOMIC IMPACT OF TOURISM FINANCING: AN EMPIRICAL ANALYSIS
4.10 CONCLUSION

CHAPTER IV

TOURISM FINANCING: AN IMPACT ANALYSIS

4.1 INTRODUCTION

Capital (money) is one of the basic factors of production. Every enterprise needs it to run and achieve the organizational objectives. The organization gets money from shareholders in the form of share capital. Similarly, it may use other sources of capital to fulfill the demand of funds. Thus, it can either mobilize the share capital in terms of long-term liability or borrow money from banks and financial institutions. In addition, it can opt for the trade credit in order to manage the cash flow. The choice and size of the funding as well as selection of the agency basically depends upon the requirement and opportunity cost.

The primary purpose of this chapter is to illustrate the status of tourism financing, role of various sources of financing as well as to examine the role of tourism and tourism financing in economic growth of the country.

Therefore, the study in the first part examines the existing status of tourism financing from various sources, such as budget allocation of the government, credit disbursement of bank and financial institutions, foreign aid and loan assistance as well as the magnitude of foreign direct investment. The role is lauded basically in providing funding resources for the tourism development and in improving the development infrastructure.

The study in the second part empirically inquires about role of the tourism and tourism financing in the economic growth and development. As such, it attempts to assess the role on the basis of analysis inquiring the role of tourism earning on various development indices. Thus, the basic thrust of this discussion is to assess the impact of tourism and tourism financing in the economy. This chapter basically employs the secondary data for the period from Fiscal Year 1974/75 to 2004/05 along with some primary data collected from the field survey.

4.2 INVESTMENT POLICY ENVIRONMENT

In order to present the role and status of existing tourism investment, it is tried first to illustrate the role of various policies related to the tourism investment. In fact, it is designed in such a way to provide the premises in terms of policy environment over the period. The following discussion essentially deals about the various policies such as fiscal, monetary, industrial, tourism, and foreign investment.

The rationale for the investment goes back to the beginning of the periodical development plans. The under development status of the country, agro based subsistence economy, low level of saving, limited monetization and low level of investment provide only the hindrances. In addition, underdeveloped capital and money market, lack of private entrepreneurship and capital also provided the obstacles. The advent of the democracy inside the country, gradual exposure towards the outside world and growing awareness about the economic well being all provided for the initiation of development. It was coupled with the tremendous growth in other friendly countries and their generous assistance in the form of grants and loans also provided the impetus for the investment. Thus, Nepal started to crawl for the initiation of economic activities, to design the sound policies and to create the conducive environment for the investment.

In Nepal, national saving and investment has not been encouraging over the years thus providing limited resources for economic sectors. Deficit budget and expansionary monetary policy as well as supply leading approach, though conflicting with each other in some cases, have provided the policy environment for the investment financing. As such, the lack of long-term investment due to small and underdeveloped capital market and ever mounting regular expenditure of the government during past couple of years have hindered development efforts in general and provided very limited resources for most of economic sectors, in particular. Tourism sector is not an exception thus received meager budget allocation and investment.

Recently, "several policy measures have been adopted in line with open market and liberal economic policy. The monetary policy is being fine tuned to increase domestic resources mobilization, enhance efficiency of capital and provide credit to the priority and productive sectors" (Maharjan, 2005: 145). In fact, the government policy is aimed at assigning a dominant role to the private sector. Private enterprises are expected to increase the efficiency and productivity in industrial and commercial operations through private entrepreneurship. The role of the government is confined as a facilitator in providing the infrastructures for the development. In addition, the role is expected to be a catalyst in creating the conducive environment in which the private sector could perform its task effectively (Planning Commission, 1992; Maharjan, 2005: 145)

The industrialization though has been a slogan in most of the national plans could not be an ingredient for the economic development of the country. Lack of sound and investment friendly policies posed development obstacles. So, the government implanted a new industrial policy, 1992 including foreign investment and one window policies through the adoption of open and liberal industrial environment and enhancement in the participation of the private sector (Shrestha, 2003: 63).

The Industrial Enterprise Act, 1993 has been a leap forward in the policy environment. It has shown even shifting in its premise from the planned (controlled) economy to the market economy. It has also been enriched with further amendments from time to time. In fact, it offers the de-licensing for the establishment, expansion and diversification of the enterprise (institution). The policy has reserved cottage and small industries to Nepalese citizens and security and basic services for the government owned establishments. Thus, medium and large industries are left open to foreign entrepreneurs. Further large and medium scale industries have been opened even for the 100 percent foreign investment whereas small and cottage scale industries can also mobilize the foreign resources in terms of the transfer of technology. Industries are classified into four categories according to the size of capital investment, such as cottage, small, medium and large scale (MOL, 1993).

The Industrial Enterprises Act is formulated and implemented in line with the overall economic policy and along with some supplementary policies including Foreign Investment Policy and Technology Transfer Act, which are discussed in appropriate place of the current chapter.

Tourism policy, 1995 specifically spells about the private investment and thus reads as "The private sector participation shall be highly encouraged in the development and expansion of tourist activities and His Majesty's Government's involvement in this field shall mainly be focused to the development of the tourism infrastructures and in addition to that His Majesty's Government shall also play a role as a coordinator as well as a catalyst" (MOTCA, 1997: 4)

Further, it also includes the provision for the other investment as "Local investment will be encouraged in service-oriented, travel and trekking agency businesses in which local investors have proven capability. Foreign investment including joint ventures will be promoted in areas, which transfers skills and technology or in capital-intensive industries like hotels and resorts" (MOTCA, 1997: 5). Thus, it is to create an environment necessary to enable the private sector to play a principle role in the development endeavor of the country.

PART – ONE
TOURISM FINANCING FROM VARIOUS SOURCES

4.3 SOURCES OF TOURISM FINANCING

As mentioned earlier, national saving and investment has not been encouraging over the years thus tourism sector has been receiving a meager budget allocation from the government. Similarly, underdeveloped capital market, limited credit outreach to the rural mass and prevalence of the informal or unorganized financial market have provided very limited resources for the tourism investment. Nevertheless, Nepalese tourism has continuously been enjoying the investment financing basically from banks and financial institutions. Commercial banks and financial institutions are found to be extending credit in tourism. The increase in loans and advances to the private sector also hints about the rise in tourism investment. Similarly, the emerging private sector inside the country and foreign direct investment also provided the endurable source for the supply of funding.

The surge in import credit and introduction of new debt products (such as housing loan, educational loan, consumer financing etc) and increased competition between commercial banks and other financial institutions have definitely provided the economic sectors with a broad based financing (Bhetuwal, 2005: 8).

To finance the tourism infrastructure needs, several strategies and sources may be tapped. Among these, domestic private investment, foreign private investment and foreign aid (international or government), and government financing are vital for the development of tourism (ESCAP 2001: 27-30 and UN ESCAP, 2001: 177). In addition to these sources, loans from international and multilateral institutions/agencies as well as loans from domestic banks and financial institutions have played a significant role in the development of tourism industry. In this context, Oliver Bennett (1991: 204) has enlisted following funding sources available for tourism development.

- Government budget
- Multilateral and bilateral grant, loans and aid
- Development banks
- State enterprises
- Commercial banks
- Private sector
- Overseas investors

The funding sources comprise a mix of the above financial resources and appear very much similar with the financing of other sectors. The selection of the source and its mixture highly depends upon the demand of the beneficiaries of the investment.

Present chapter essentially deals with the investment sources available for the financing of tourism, such as the government, foreign investment (both FDI and foreign aid) and lending of commercial banks and financial institutions whereas the next chapter follows the discussion about the financing of tourism business enterprises.

4.4 THE GOVERNMENT

Every government has a certain interest in developing all economic sectors such as agriculture, industry and others including tourism. Because it provides foreign exchange earning, contributes in government revenues, generates the employment and income and facilitates for the regional development (Bahuguna, 2005).

The role of the government is indispensable in every economic sector, because it plays a vital role in the development of natural resources, preparation of the qualified human resources and in building of a firm foundation for the promotion and development of the industry (ESCAP, 2001). Mill and Morrison (1992) and Hall (1994) suggested that the government plays various roles in planning, coordinating, controlling and implementing national tourism policies (UN ESCAP, 2001:3). As such, the government is involved in sectors such as tourism for public objectives to be achieved and for such sectors to survive and prosper. It is only the government that has legitimacy to establish national objectives and policies, resources to perform the functions as well as the power to direct and control many diverse bodies involved in tourism (Elliott, 1997: 54). It equally functions to develop a wide range of tourism products, to implement development plans, to maximize positive impacts from tourism such as the creation of jobs to generate income and employment and finally to foster the balanced regional development.

The role of the government may not always be obvious particularly in some specific sectors such as tourism. In such cases, it appears to be better to assess the role in totality considering the various socio-cultural aspects and basic features of the economy.

Government in Nepal has a very limited involvement in hotels and leaves travel agency operation to the private sector (Bennett, 1991: 197). The Tourism Policy, 1995 also defines the government's role as a catalyst for the private sector investment (MOTCA, 1997: 4-5). Nevertheless, tourism as a distinct and productive economic sector has been successfully attracting the attention of the government particularly to develop the infrastructure needed for tourism development (UN ESCAP, 2001: 176).

Obviously, the government has realized the crucial role of tourism in strengthening economy and fostering the economic development. Otherwise, the economic benefits of tourism industry would be at risk. Consequently, the government has been continuously engaged in policy issues and regulation of the investment. It has enacted various investment legislations, designed regulatory frameworks, introduced investment incentives, and published trade and business directories. In addition, it has mobilized the foreign aid and loan assistance for infrastructure development.

A. DIRECT GOVERNMENT INVESTMENT

The government allocates the budget for the development of tourism as well as for the investment (expenses) in civil aviation. However, the development expenditure in tourism in terms of annual development budget appears to be meager over the period, accounting less than one percent of total annual budget.

Table: 4.1

Direct Government Investment

Rs. in '000

Fiscal Year	TEXP	Annual Change Percent	Total Dev. Budget	Share of Tourism Exp in Total Budget %	GICA	AnnualChange Percent	Share of civil exp to Total %
1980/81	4		2731.1	0.15	74.2		2.72
1984/85	6.1	-10.3	5488.7	0.11	347.1	287.0	6.32
1989/90	18.4	7.0	12997.5	0.14	410.3	29.7	3.16
1994/95	147.4	116.4	19794.9	0.74	316.8	7.8	1.60
1999/00	221.5	43.7	31749.2	0.70	417.8	-3.0	1.32
2000/01	383.7	73.2	37065.9	1.04	508.9	21.8	1.37
2001/02	253.9	-33.8	31482.2	0.81	194.9	-61.7	0.62
2002/03	189.7	-25.3	29033.0	0.65	242.5	24.4	0.84

Source: Economic Survey (various issues). Ministry of Finance HMG/N

The percentage of annual changes in development expenditure for tourism and investment in civil aviation show great fluctuation over the years as presented in Table: 4.1. The share of development expenditure for tourism in total annual development expenditure remained to be minor usually not more than one percent over the period. The share of development expenditure for civil aviation remained relatively at a higher level.

B. FOREIGN AID AND LOAN ASSISTANCE

Foreign aid continues to play a vital role in meeting government budgetary and development needs as well as the provision of foreign exchange (ESCAP, 2001: 31). Table: 4.2 presents the details of foreign aid over the period and share of tourism in overall loan disbursement.

Over the review period, the foreign aid and foreign loan has been gradually increasing. However, in recent years particularly after the F.Y. 2001/02, there has been a sharp decrease in foreign loan. Such decrease has a great impact in the total foreign assistance.

The share of tourism sector in total foreign aid and loan has increased from 2.5 percent in F.Y. 1979/80 to 16.6 percent in F.Y. 2004/05. This necessarily indicates the sector is gaining importance in the portfolio of foreigners. The fluctuation in foreign aid and loan disbursement can be attributed to domestic and international reasons.

Table: 4.2

Foreign Aid and Loan Disbursement

Year	Foreign Aid	Foreign Loan	Total	Foreign aid and loan in tourism sector #	
				Amount	Share Percent
1979/80	805.6	534.9	1,340.5	33.7	2.5
1984/85	923.5	1,752.9	2,676.4	135.8	5.1
1989/90	1,975.4	5,959.6	7,935.0	1,021.0	12.9
1994/95	3,937.1	7,312.3	11,249.4	570.8	5.1
1999/00	5,711.7	11,812.2	17,523.9	1,411.5	8.1
2000/01	6,753.4	12,044.0	18,797.4	1,888.1	10.0
2001/02	6,686.1	7,698.7	14,384.8	1,453.1	10.1
2002/03	11,339.1	4,546.4	15,885.5	1,470.3	9.3
2003/04	11,283.4	7,629.0	18,912.40	4,116.5	21.8
2004/05	14,391.2	9,266.1	23,657.30	3,935.1	16.6

\# Figures are in Rs. Million and also includes local development, supply and other social services and labour etc.

Source: Economic Survey (Various Issues) Ministry of Finance, HMG/N.

Figure 4.1

Foreign Aid and Loan Disbursement

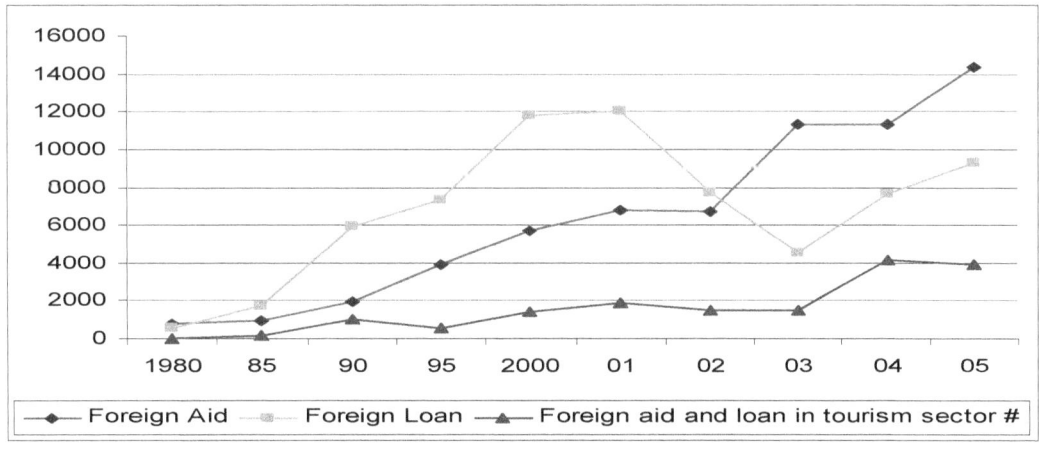

\# Figure also includes local development, supply and other social services and labour etc.

It is worthwhile to note that the principal bilateral aid arrangements are conducted at the government-to-government level, and results in aid transfer as budgetary assistance. Likewise, special aid arrangements may be negotiated on a government-to-government or government-to-agency basis for particular prestige projects, environmental rehabilitation schemes or some other projects related to regional cooperation.

4.5 ROLE OF NEPALESE FINANCIAL SYSTEM IN TOURISM FINANCING

In short, Nepalese financial system is composed of commercial banks, financial institutions and contractual saving organizations. The financial institutions include development banks, micro-credit development banks, finance companies, financial cooperatives, non-government organizations (financial) performing limited banking activities (NRB, 2005).

Figure: 4.2

Nepalese Financial System

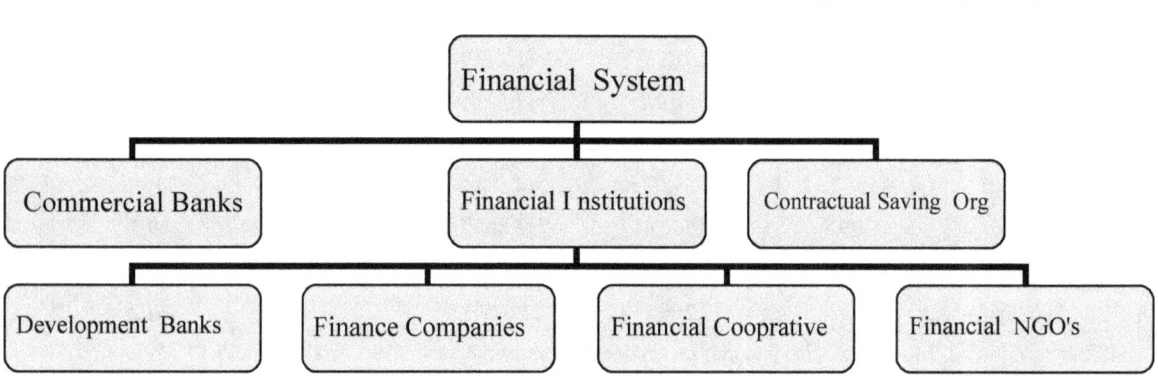

Likewise other contractual saving organizations (popularly known as other financial institutions) comprise insurance companies, employee's provident fund, citizen investment trust, postal saving offices and Nepal stock exchange. However, this study concentrates for those banks and financial institutions which are licensed and report to Nepal Rastra Bank and are engaged in the financing of tourism business. Figure: 4.2 presents brief structure of Nepalese financial system.

In July 2005, there were 17 commercial banks, 26 development banks, 59 finance companies, 20 financial cooperatives, and 47 financial non government organizations.

A. COMMERCIAL BANKS AND PURPOSE-WISE LOAN DISBURSEMENT

The trend of loan disbursement for the particular sector of the economy provides the imprints to assess the role of bank lending. Such lending provides the resources for the promotion and development of the sector, albeit based on banking regulation for the portfolio diversification. Table: 4.3 and Figure: 4.3 depict loan disbursement of commercial banks by purpose summarizing in terms of percentage for the review period.

Table: 4.3

Purpose-wise Loan Disbursement of Commercial Banks

In Percentage

Year	Agriculture	Industrial	Commercial	General/ other	Service
1975	0.06	5.08	45.47	48.04	1.35
1980	0.92	11.96	62.16	20.98	3.98
1985	3.21	18.78	44.08	30.03	3.89
1990	12.98	32.36	28.58	23.61	2.48
2000	8.91	45.13	32.93	7.28	5.74
2001	8.86	45.20	32.08	7.13	6.74
2002	8.60	45.41	31.29	6.98	7.72
2003	8.60	45.41	31.29	6.98	7.72
2004	3.58	37.88	26.78	21.38	10.37
2005	2.77	37.17	27.07	23.58	9.41
Average	**5.8**	**32.4**	**36.2**	**19.6**	**5.9**

Source: Banking and Financial Statistics and Economic Survey (various issues)

Over the review period, the share of industrial credit in total loans has gradually increased from 5.1 percent in 1975 to 45.1 percent in 2000 and remained at 37.2 percent in 2005.

Over the review period, the industrial sector has gradually assumed the major share accounting on an average 32.4 percent in total credit lending whereas the commercial sector maintained its level with 36.2 percent share on an average. More recently the situation has changed a lot. The service sector is emerging and registered gradual growth in its share from meager 1.4 percent in 1975 to 9.4 percent in 2004 in contrast with the share of agriculture and general purpose. The tourism sector is included in the service sector.

Figure: 4.3

Loan Disbursement of Commercial Banks by Purpose

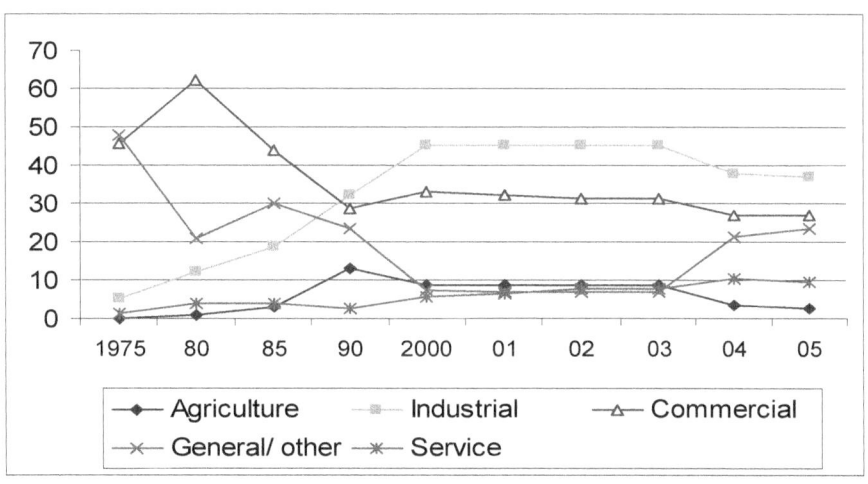

B. LENDING OF COMMERCIAL BANKS IN TOURISM SECTOR

The total credit disbursement as well the disbursement to the tourism sector by the Commercial Banks for the period from Fiscal Year 1991/92 to Fiscal Year 2004/05 (as covered in primary survey) is summarized in Table: 4.4. The table is especially designed to provide the details such as the ratio of credit outstanding in tourism to total credit outstanding and that of credit disbursement in tourism to total credit disbursement. In addition, the table also provides the annual rate of change (growth or decline) in percentage for credit disbursement in tourism over the period.

The annual credit disbursement by commercial banks to tourism sector has been fluctuating over the review period. It was Rs. 142.0 million during F.Y. 1991/92 and it reached to Rs. 4,298.89 millions in 2003/04. The annual rate of change for the credit disbursement to the tourism sector is highest at 323.3 percent (positive) during F.Y. 2001/02 and the lowest 31.7 percent (negative) during F.Y. 2004/05.

Table: 4.4

Loan Disbursements and Outstanding of Commercial Banks in Tourism

(Rs. In '000)

Year ending Mid July	O/S on Tourism	O/S Total	O/S Ratio	Disbursement on Tourism	Total Credit Disbursement	Disb. Ratio	Change % in Disbu. on Tourism
1992	165,597	31,794,800	0.5	142,000	18,797,600	0.8	
1993	277,708	36,221,600	0.8	154,400	21,477,000	0.7	8.7
1994	537,605	43,650,900	1.2	174,040	29,339,100	0.6	12.7
1995	932,347	55,112,500	1.7	236,730	40,590,300	0.6	36.0
1996	1,321,293	69,014,400	1.9	261,550	52,619,800	0.5	10.5
1997	1,817,431	78,511,900	2.3	383,280	60,476,600	0.6	46.5
1998	1,934,244	93,797,700	2.1	288,310	71,244,200	0.4	- 24.8
1999	2,249,497	111,968,800	2.0	353,079	84,082,500	0.4	22.5
2000	3,465,075	136,184,800	2.5	295,972	99,453,800	0.3	- 16.2
2001	4,929,914	160,919,300	3.1	574,388	112,860,600	0.5	94.1
2002	5,651,284	173,319,200	3.3	2,431,462	118,028,400	2.1	323.3
2003	6,987,871	201,822,520	3.5	3,270,123	120,754,600	2.7	34.5
2004	7,458,789	228,235,000	3.3	4,298,888	137,080,900	3.1	31.5
2005	6,881,850	260,867,000	2.6	2,935,254	164,005,900	1.8	- 31.7

Source: Field Survey, 2006 and Economic Survey (various issues)

The ratio of credit disbursement to tourism sector to total credit disbursement is fluctuating over the review period. The ratio registered the highest (3.1 percent) in F.Y. 2003/04 against the lowest (0.3 percent) in F.Y 1999/2000. The average ratio over the review period stood at 1.1 percent.

In contrast, the ratio of credit outstanding in tourism to total credit outstanding produced slightly different picture. Figure 4.4 summarizes the result. The ratio was 0.5 percent in Fiscal Year 1991/92 and increased gradually to 3.5 percent in F.Y. 2002/03 except minor fluctuations in between. However, the average ratio over the review period stood in a tune of 2.2 percent.

Figure 4.4 also depicts the variation of growth (decline as well) in both the ratios. During the early years of review period the disbursement ratio was high and later outstanding ratio was high.

Figure: 4.4

The Ratio of Tourism in Total Credit Disbursement and Credit Outstanding

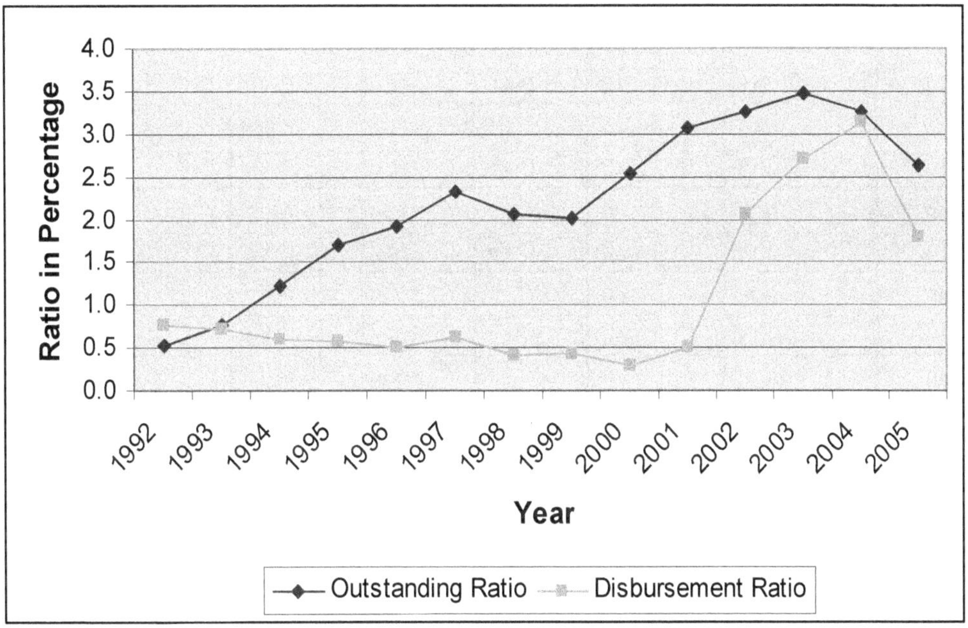

C. ROLE OF NEPAL INDUSTRIAL DEVELOPMENT BANK

Nepal Industrial Development Corporation (NIDC) was established in June, 1959 under a special charter to fulfill the growing demand of providing promotional and financial assistance.

Table: 4.5 summarizes the outstanding financial assistance of NIDC for the review period based on the classification of industry. The manufacturing sector grabbed the major share in total loan outstanding (financial assistance). On an average the manufacturing sector has registered 51.4 percent share followed by hotel sector with 27.2 percent average share.

Table: 4.5

Outstanding Financial Assistance of NIDC (Classified by Industry)

(Rs. in million)

Year	Manufacturing	Transport	Electricity	Hotel	Services	Miscellaneous	Total
1975	66.3	14.4	2.6	38.8	3.7	19.5	145.3
	45.6	*9.9*	*1.8*	*26.7*	*2.5*	*13.4*	*100.0*
1980	80.9	7.1	0.3	130.2	5	87.1	310.6
	26.0	*2.3*	*0.1*	*41.9*	*1.6*	*28.0*	*100.0*
1985	199	5.5	5	185.2	23	130.8	543.5
	36.6	*1.0*	*0.9*	*34.1*	*4.2*	*24.1*	*100.0*
1990	414.3	4.9	7.6	239.9	33.3	138.2	1,023.60
	40.5	*0.5*	*0.7*	*23.4*	*3.3*	*13.5*	*100.0*
1995	739.8	0	0.5	359	122.7	179.4	1,401.40
	52.8	*0.0*	*0.0*	*25.6*	*8.8*	*12.8*	*100.0*
2000	1,465.20	0	0	571.5	197.7	147.7	2,382.10
	61.5	*0.0*	*0.0*	*24.0*	*8.3*	*6.2*	*100.0*
2001	1,384.90	0	0	532.2	172.1	134.5	2,223.70
	62.3	*0.0*	*0.0*	*23.9*	*7.7*	*6.0*	*100.0*
2002	1,382.10	0	0	463.1	158	132.5	2,135.70
	64.7	*0.0*	*0.0*	*21.7*	*7.4*	*6.2*	*100.0*
2003	1,337.70	0	0	462.6	154.7	127.4	2,082.40
	64.2	*0.0*	*0.0*	*22.2*	*7.4*	*6.1*	*100.0*
2004	1,182.90	0	0	561.3	120.5	125.4	1,990.10
	59.4	*0.0*	*0.0*	*28.2*	*6.1*	*6.3*	*100.0*
Average %	*51.4*	*1.4*	*0.4*	*27.2*	*5.7*	*12.3*	*100.0*

Note: Figures in bold and italic indicate the percentage in total amount.
Source: Quarterly Economic Bulletin (2005) Vol. XXXIX No. 3, Nepal Rastra Bank

Other sectors held minor share over the review period. Interestingly, in F.Y. 1979/80, the hotel sector has enjoyed the major share of 41.9 percent in total credit outstanding surpassing the manufacturing sector. During the rest of the review period, the share of hotel sector (tourism) remained in the second position after manufacturing sector.

The total credit disbursement as well the disbursement to the tourism sector by the Nepal Industrial Development Bank for the period from F.Y. 1974/75 to F.Y. 2004/05 (in interval of five year) is summarized in Table: 4.6. The table is especially designed to provide the details such as the ratio of credit outstanding in tourism to total credit outstanding and that of credit disbursement in tourism to total credit disbursement. In addition, the Table also provides the annual rate of change (growth or decline) in percentage for credit disbursement in tourism (hotel) over the period.

The total credit disbursement during the F.Y. 1974/75 was Rs. 53.8 million. It gradually grew till F.Y. 1994/95 to Rs. 361.8 million except in 1979/80. The annual credit disbursement appeared to be decreasing in recent years reaching to Rs. 21.4 million during F.Y. 2003/04.

Table: 4.6

Loan Disbursement and Outstanding in Tourism (NIDC)

(Rs. in million)

Fiscal Year	Total Loan O/S	Loan O/S on Tourism	Ratio	Annual Loan Disbursement	Tourism Loan disbursement	Ratio
1974/75	149.3	38.8	**26.0**	53.8	18.1	**33.6**
1979/80	310.6	130.2	**41.9**	21.1	10.1	**47.9**
1984/85	556.3	185.2	**33.3**	80.1	13.2	**16.5**
1989/90	1023.6	239.9	**23.4**	206.5	62.7	**30.4**
1994/95	1244.5	359.0	**28.8**	361.8	71.5	**19.8**
1999/00	2139.1	571.5	**26.7**	107.7	17.3	**16.1**
2000/01	1589.8	532.2	**33.5**	81.6	10.6	**13.0**
2001/02	1582.3	463.1	**29.3**	77.2	7.8	**10.1**
2002/03	2233.0	462.6	**20.7**	36.7	4.1	**11.2**
2003/04	1861.1	561.3	**30.2**	21.4	1.1	**5.1**
Average			**29.4**			**20.4**

Source: Quarterly Economic Bulletin (2005), Economic Survey (various issues) and field survey, 2006

The annual credit disbursement through NIDC in tourism (hotel projects) seemed to be the most important (Sharma, 2001: 224-225). It was Rs. 18.1 million during F.Y. 1974/75 and seemed to be fluctuating over the review period. The disbursement reached to Rs. 71.5 million in F.Y. 1994/95 and to the lowest of Rs. 1.1 million during F.Y. 2003/04.

The ratio of credit disbursement in tourism sector to total credit disbursement also seemed to be fluctuating over the review period. The ratio is the highest at 47.9 percent in F.Y. 1979/80 against the lowest of 5.1 percent in F.Y. 2003/04.

In contrast, the ratio of credit outstanding in tourism to total credit outstanding produced slightly different picture. Figure: 4.5 summarizes the result. The ratio was 26.0 percent in F.Y. 1974/75 and increased to 41.9 percent in F.Y. 1979/80. The average ratio over the review period stood in a tune of 29.3 percent

Figure: 4.5
The Share of Tourism in Total Credit Disbursement and Outstanding

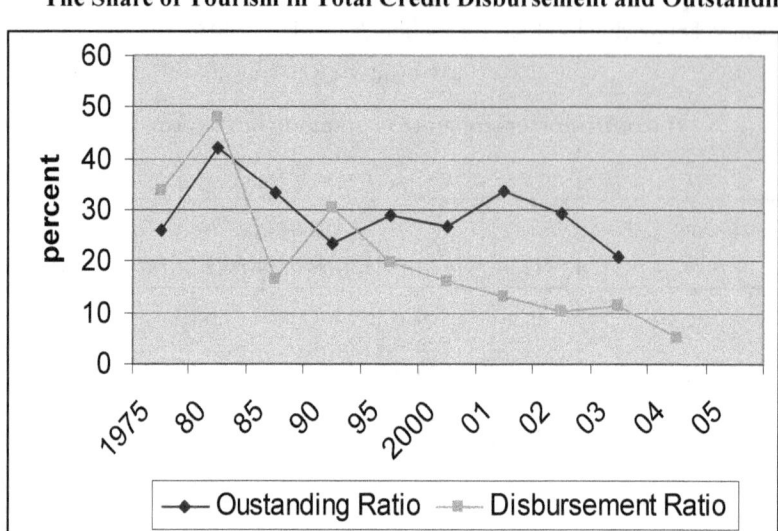

Figure: 4.5 also depicts the variation of growth (decline as well) in both the ratios. During the early years of review period the disbursement ratio was high and later outstanding ratio was high. It also indicates that tourism sector loans are usually long-term and repayment of such loan also has been poor.

D. TOURISM FINANCING FROM FINANCIAL INSTITUTIONS

Despite of the growing size of financial institutions they appeared shy to be lending to tourism sector. The status of loan disbursement to tourism sector during the period from F.Y. 1998/99 to F.Y. 2004/05 is summarized in following Table: 4.7.

The loan disbursement to tourism sector from the financial institutions over the review period seems to be nominal. It was Rs. 40.6 million in F.Y. 1998/99 and increased by more than four fold to reach Rs. 206.5 million in F.Y. 1999/00. Further, in F.Y. 2000/01 and F.Y. 2001/02 it increased by 84 percent (Rs. 166 million) and Rs. 547 million and reached to Rs. 379.6 million and Rs. 926.1 million respectively. Afterwards, there has been gradual decline in loan disbursement to tourism sector.

Table: 4.7

Loan Disbursement to Tourism by Financial Institutions [1]

Figures are in Rs. thousand

	ADB/N	NDB	DCBL	FC*	TOTAL
1998/99	-	-	-	40,640	**40,640**
1999/00	-	192,867	-	13,680	**206,547**
2000/01	-	367,552	5,372	6,650	**379,574**
2001/02	18,655	755,064	110,940	41,468	**926,127**
2002/03	20,772	855,162	16,399	32,317	**924,650**
2003/04	43,479	653,696	9,656	30,276	**737,107**
2004/05	77,089	693,957	-	33101	**804,147**
Total	**159,995**	**3,518,298**	**142,367**	**198,132**	-

* The figure comprises the amount from the sample survey of 13 Finance Companies.

Source: Compiled and self calculated from the Field survey (2006)

The development banks such as Nepal Development Bank, Development Credit Bank and Agriculture Development Bank (with some exceptions), have more exposure than that of 13 finance companies. It is not feasible to find out the tourism investment through other non bank financial institutions over the period. It is particularly because of the lack of regulatory framework to classify the lending and reporting to the designated institution. The primary survey also could not produce the remarkable response for such figures and trend of financing for the review period.

4.6 ROLE OF FOREIGN DIRECT INVESTMENT

The history of foreign investment in Nepal goes back to 1951-52 when Nepal Commercial Corporation was set up as a joint venture with 67 percent equity of Indian investors.

"Foreign investment and technology transfer is imperative as it plays a catalytic role to move towards independence, provide robustness, dynamism, and competitiveness in the economy through mobilization of human and natural resources in the industrialization process. Foreign investment together with capital and modern technology brings in qualities of business culture, management and technical skills, access to international market and development of competitive business for the industrial development of the country. It also contributes for the independent and self reliant national economic development with the increase in revenue base" (Ministry of Finance, 2004: 133).

---

[1] Financial institution essentially includes all development banks, finance companies, financial cooperatives financial NGOs as well as other contractual saving institutions such as Employees Provident Fund, insurance companies and Citizen Investment Trust. The table neither includes the figures of Nepal Industrial Development Bank, a prominent development bank in Nepalese Financial System nor the figures of other contractual saving institutions.

The importance of attracting the foreign investment in general and tourism sector in particular does not need any exaggeration. As the role of tourism has been recognized as a benign agent for the economic development and growth in the country, the special focus and attention has been provided.

A. FDI INVESTMENT POLICY AND CLIMATE

The ability of a tourism destination to attract foreign investment (as in domestic as well) is basically influenced by several characteristics (ESCAP, 2001: 4) such as: political constraints and incentives (attractiveness of the taxation, policies regarding local and foreign investment and imports); the resources and conveniences offered (attractions, transportation, access, hospitality, medical and other services, pricing etc.); market characteristics (visitor tastes and preferences, disposable income, propensity to travel, proximity to destination etc.); political stability; and the ability of the destination to market and promote itself effectively.

The investment policy has given a special place for the tourism sector. Priority in initiating tourism related industry and business is given to the nationals. Fear of nationalization of industry no more exists. Private ownership of the industries at various levels and sizes is permitted by the policy. The procedure of obtaining import license is gradually simplified (Maharjan 2004, 148). The investment climate of Nepal nowadays seems quite liberal and congenial for the foreign investment.

B. FOREIGN DIRECT INVESTMENT IN TOURISM

The size of foreign direct investment in Nepal is still in its infant stage. As a result of continuous efforts to attract the foreign investment by adopting the time-suitable, practical, liberal and open policy; a total of 1,063 industries received the permission to operate under the foreign investment by March 2006. The fixed capital of these industries amounted to 76,863 million rupees and the total project cost amounted to 92,809.7 million rupees. About 104,848 people are expected to be additionally benefited from the operation of these industries (Ministry of Finance, 2006: 103).

Table: 4.8 presents the details about the magnitude of the foreign direct investment as well as the share of tourism industry in the total (foreign direct investment) during the period from F.Y. 2001/02 to 2004/05.

The share of tourism sector (FDI) both in terms of project numbers and absolute amount in total foreign direct investment is fluctuating over the period. In Fiscal Year 2001/02, it has assumed 31.0 percent share in total projects and 5.1 percent share in total amount of foreign direct investment. The share increased to 34.6 percent and 5.4 percent respectively in the following year. However, the share declined afterwards and stood at 18.8 percent and 2.3 percent respectively in F.Y. 2004/05.

The tourism sector held 26.8 percent projects, on an average during the review period. During the review period, the share of tourism in total project cost, fixed capital and number of employment stood as 3.1 percent, 3.6 percent and 8.5 percent, on an average respectively. It is necessary to mention that the figure for F.Y. 2003/04 covers only first eight months of the Fiscal Year.

Table: 4.8

Foreign Direct Investment and Share of Tourism Industry

(Rs. in Million)

Year	2001/02		2002/03		2003/04*		2004/05	
Details	Tourism	Total	Tourism	Total	Tourism	Total	Tourism	Total
No. of Projects	22	71	27	78	8	35	12	64
Percent in Total	*31.0*	*100.0*	*34.6*	*100.0*	*22.9*	*100.0*	*18.8*	*100.0*
Foreign Investment	89.9	1767.3	148.0	2764.0	16.0	543.0	37.0	1639.0
Percent in Total	*5.1*	*100.0*	*5.4*	*100.0*	*2.9*	*100.0*	*2.3*	*100.0*
The Project Cost	147.7	4877.6	150.0	4323.7	29.0	1080.0	57.0	1801.1
Percent in Total	*3.0*	*100.0*	*3.5*	*100.0*	*2.7*	*100.0*	*3.2*	*100.0*
Total Fixed Capital	123.5	3577.3	138.0	3776.0	22.0	690.0	46.0	1151.0
Percent in Total	*3.5*	*100.0*	*3.7*	*100.0*	*3.2*	*100.0*	*4.0*	*100.0*
Number of Employment	512	3543	274	2144	86	3787	254	5576
Percent in Total	*14.5*	*100.0*	*12.8*	*100.0*	*2.3*	*100.0*	*4.6*	*100.0*

* igures are only for first eight months of the Fiscal Year. Source: Economic Survey (various issues) Ministry of Finance, HMG/N

Tourism industry stands as one of the important sectors in which Nepal has its unique advantages. Despite of this, it is observed that it could not create the momentum and even could not maintain its previous increasing trend. The main reasons behind this can be various, ranging from deteriorating law and order situation, insufficient infrastructural facilities, lengthy administrative system to the competition for FDI itself and other factors related to the investors.

In fact, the attraction of FDI has become very competitive. It has to offer more generous and attractive incentives to potential investors compete with other countries in attracting FDI. It also needs an integrated approach and congenial environment with specific targets to attract the foreign direct investment (Pant and Sigdel: 2004).

In addition, apart from attractive incentives, the investors consider other factors such as political stability, sound economic policies and good legal environment good labor practices, skilled labor force, and continuity in policies as well as access to the market (ESCAP, 2001 and UNCTAD, 2003). Therefore, these factors need proper attention in order to overcome the challenge of attracting more foreign direct investment in the country.

It is also observed that the government has initiated several policy reforms to promote foreign investment. In order to design a congenial environment for the FDI, it has amended the respective laws, provided with a guarantee of equal treatments for foreign investors and has offered various investment incentives for the investment.

PART - TWO
ECONOMIC IMPACT OF TOURISM AND TOURISM FINANCING: AN EMPIRICAL ANALYSIS

4.7 ECONOMIC IMPACT ANALYSIS

Tourism is one of the productive business activities directed for the production of the goods and services. It provides the goods and services for the customers (visitors, generally foreigners) while providing employment and income for the locals. With this not only the tourism business enterprises generate the earning from the operation of the business activities but also the people related directly or indirectly with such business generate their earning. Moreover, tourism as an economic activity produces various direct, indirect and induced impacts in the economy. It ultimately increases the foreign exchange earning, generates the employment opportunity and increases the income. Again, the resultant income again flows and circulates in economy, other economic activities and people inducing many rounds of income. Therefore, the role of tourism has been distinct and significant in the economic growth and development of the country. Here, it is imperative to test the hypothesis that tourism leads for the overall economic growth in the economy.

Gross domestic product can be considered as the main economic indicator of the development since it is composed of all the final goods and services produced in the economy over a year period (Sharma, 2001: 71). In addition, various development indices such as internal revenue, tax revenue, trade volume and contribution of hotel, trade and restaurant on GDP are considered to be significantly affected by the foreign exchange earning from tourism. Similarly, foreign exchange earning from tourism can be considered as an indicator of tourism development. Subsequent sections intend to examine these aspects.

A. METHODS OF ANALYSIS AND MODEL

The present study examines effects of tourism on various development indices through regression analysis using Ordinary Least Square Method. Initially, we use both simple linear and log linear model and on the basis of the test (Gujarati, 1995: 209-210) as mentioned below we selected the final model.

$$Y = \alpha + \beta X + \omega \qquad \text{Simple linear}$$

Where, Y takes the value of development variable, α = constant, β = slope, X = independent variable and ω = unexplained variable.

$$\ln Y = \ln \alpha + \beta \ln X + \omega \qquad \text{Log linear}$$

Where, lnY takes the log value of development variable, α = constant, β = slope, lnX = log value of independent variable and ω = unexplained variable.

Moreover, the model is also corrected to deal with the problem of autocorrelation through Chochrane-Orcutt (C-O) two-step method as explained below.

B. FORM OF ANALYSIS (SIMPLE OR LOG LINEAR)

In order to determine a correct functional form either simple or log linear, both the equations are estimated and the final model is selected on the basis of the following method based on Gujarati (1995: 209-210). On the basis of the log model estimated value of Y in the log form is derived. These values are converted into antilog. The value of R² is then derived. Now this R² value is compared with R² of the simple equation and whichever is higher, that functional form is accepted for further analysis.

C. AUTOCORRELATION AND REMEDIAL MEASURES

The Durbin-Watson 'd' statistics is used to find out the presence or absence of autocorrelation. To solve the problem of autocorrelation, Chochrane-Orcutt (C-O) Two-step Method (Gujarati, 1995: 431-32) is used. Such analysis is expected to provide for the improvement in the estimation of the models. The regression model is as follows.

$$(Y_t - \hat{p}Y_{t-1}) = \beta_1(1-\hat{p}) + \beta_2(X_t - \hat{p}X_{t-1}) + (u_t - \hat{p}u_{t-1})$$

In fact, this is a shortened version of the iterative process. First of all, row value 'p' is estimated and it is used in step two in the generalized differences equation. So to estimate the row value 'p', standard OLS routine is undertaken for two-variable model and obtained the residuals $\hat{u}_t$. Then in the second step values of estimated residuals are used to run the following regression to get the $\hat{p}$:

$$\hat{u}_t = \hat{p}u_{t-1} + v_t$$

4.8 ECONOMIC IMPACT OF TOURISM: AN EMPIRICAL ANALYSIS

A. EFFECTS OF TOURISM ON DEVELOPMENT INDICES

In the beginning of the impact analysis, it is desirable to examine the direct relationship between the development indices and foreign exchange earning from tourism (FXET). Table: 4.9 is designed to summarize the result of the simple linear regression analysis with foreign exchange earning from tourism as the explanatory variable and development indices such as government internal revenue (GIR), tax revenue (TXR), trade volume (TRAV) and gross domestic product (GDPN) as the dependent variable. In addition, the analysis is continued further to examine the relationship between foreign exchange earning from tourism (FXET) and other development indices such as contribution of hotel, trade and restaurant on domestic product (GDPT) and ratio of GDPT to GDPN (RGDPT).

Table: 4.9

The Regression Results on Development Indices (Simple Linear)

Equation	Dependent Variable	Coefficients		Statistics		
		Constant	FXET	R²	F	DW
4.1	GIR	-452.633 (-0.212)	3.827* (12.846)	0.850	165.00	1.100
4.2	TAXR	-273.254 (-0.167)	2.965* (12.958)	0.850	167.92	1.120
4.3	TRAV	-3299.8 (-0.545)	12.689* (15.038)	0.890	226.14	1.440
4.4	GDPN	13021.94 (0.941)	29.859 (15.48)	0.890	239.63	1.450
4.5	GDPT	364.65 (0.297)	3.366* (19.633)	0.93	385.4	**1.77**
4.6	RGDPT	0.062 * (8.584)	4.72E-06 *(4.715)	0.434	22.23	0.28

Figures given in the parentheses indicate t values.
Asterisks (*) signifies that the coefficient is significant at 1% level.

The result showed a positive impact of tourism earning on development indices. All the slope coefficients are statistically significant at 1 percent level implying positive impact of foreign exchange earning from tourism on various development indices. Moreover, in all the regressions except 4.6, the intercept is not statistically significant; which shows the direct and proportionate relationship between two variables.

The regression analysis is carried out in log form and following results are obtained.

Table: 4.10

The Regression Results on Development Indices (Log Linear)

Equation	Dependent Variable	Coefficients		Statistics		
		Constant	Ln. FXET	R^2	F	DW
4.1	Ln. GIR	1.841 * (6.706)	0.933 * (26.987)	0.962	728.280	0.689
4.2	Ln. TAXR	1.727 * (6.287)	0.918 * (26.529)	0.960	703.793	0.677
4.3	Ln. TRAV	2.191 * (7.581)	1.024 * (28.113)	0.965	790.335	0.755
4.4	Ln. GDPN	5.193 * (21.968)	0.803 * (26.956)	0.962	726.617	0.684
4.5	Ln. GDPT	0.133 0.335)	1.121* (22.53)	0.95	507.6	0.59
4.6	Ln.RGDPT	-5.061* (-16.70)	0.3185* (8.345)	0.71	69.6	0.40

Figures in parentheses indicate t values. Asterisk (*) signifies that the coefficient is significant at 1% level. The analysis is based on log linear model.

Table: 4.11

A comparison of R^2 and comparable R^2

Equation	Regression equation for FXET (as Dependent)	R^2 from Simple Linear	Comparable R^2 from log model
4.1	GIR	0.8527	0.8495
4.2	TAXR	0.8527	0.8515
4.3	TRAV	0.8863	0.8859
4.4	GDPN	0.8920	0.8936
4.5	GDPT	0.9300	0.9201
4.6	RGDPT	0.4339	0.6307

As stated earlier, comparative R^2 from log equation is derived which are presented in Table: 4.11 (as above) in order to select the better model of analysis.

Both R^2s are approximately same in all the equations except the last one. Therefore, we interpret both the types of equations.

Looking at the DW statistics in both the types of equations except of GDPT, it shows the presence of first order autocorrelation and therefore Chochrane-Orcutt method is followed to deal with the problem.

Table: 4.12

Regression Analysis on Development Indices (Simple Linear C-O two step)

Equation	Dependent Variable	Coefficients		Statistics		
		Constant	FXET	R^2	F	DW
4.1	GIR	2248.43 (1.126)	3.161* (6.912)	0.63	47.77	1.17
4.2	TAXR	60.367 (0.67)	0.773* (136.09)	0.99	18521	2.28
4.3	TRAV	1595.55 (0.256)	11.838* (10.334)	0.79	106.8	1.55
4.4	GDPN	16530.98 (1.15)	28.818* (12.274)	0.84	150.66	1.52
4.6	RGDPT	0.013* (5.324)	1.15E-06 (1.094)	0.041	1.197	1.72

Table: 4.13

Regression Analysis on Development Indices (Log linear C-O Two Step)

Equation	Dependent Variable	Coefficients		Statistics		
		Constant	Ln.FXET Independent	R^2	F	DW
4.1	Ln. GIR	0.864* (3.628)	0.853* (10.197)	0.788	103.9	**1.50**
4.2	Ln. TAXR	-0.530* (-6.833)	0.002 (0.090)	0.003	0.008	**2.03**
4.3	Ln. TRAV	0.962* (3.760)	0.949* (11.894)	0.835	141.5	**1.63**
4.4	Ln. GDPN	1.919* (9.573)	0.751* (10.599)	0.80	112.3	**1.54**
4.6	Ln.RGDPT	-0.827* (4.426)	0.206*** (1.891)	0.11	3.58	**1.59**

Both types of the equations (simple and log form) estimated through the Chochrane-Orcutt method show that slope coefficient is statistically significant at one percent level. Moreover, the value of R^2 is high indicating the corresponding variations in the dependent variable due to the change in foreign exchange earning from tourism.

To sum up foreign exchange earning from tourism has significant positive impact on GIR, TAXR, TRAV, GDPN, GDPT and RGDPT. Therefore, the foreign exchange earning form tourism plays a significant role in the economy. Thus, the tourism sector in Nepal has a significant impact on economic growth.

In the next section, the study analyzes the role of tourism development in the economic growth and development of Nepal.

B. ROLE OF TOURISM DEVELOPMENT IN ECONOMIC GROWTH

This section attempts to examine the effects of tourism development on gross domestic product of the country. FXET, TTAR, TNTB, and TNHR are the variables included in the model as explanatory variables indicating tourism development in the country. Analysis, therefore, includes above variables in different combinations to determine the explanatory power of different independent variables.

Hence, the estimation is undertaken employing the variables such as FXET, TTAR, TNTB, TNHR and TNHB with respect to gross domestic product (GDPN) in the first equation. The coefficient of TNHB is statistically significant at 1 percent level with theoretically expected sign. Similarly, TNTB and TNHR are significant at 10 percent level with expected sign. Here, the FXET is not found to be statistically significant though in Table: 4.10, it is statistically significant. This can be due to the problem of multicollinearity.

The partial elasticity coefficients of FXET, TNTB, TNHR and TNHB with respect to GDPN are found to be 0.12, 0.18, 0.11 and 0.67 percent respectively. It implies that one percent increase in these variables have the impact on GDPN by respective percentage values. For example, one percent increase in FXET has an impact of 0.12 percent on GDPN.

Moreover, the effect of TTAR on GDPN is expected to be positive, i.e. with the increase in the number of tourist arrival, we expect increase in GDPN. In this equation, the coefficient is negative but not statistically significant. When ln. GDPN is regressed only on ln.TTAR, the coefficient turns out to be positive and statistically significant (refer third equation in Table: 4.14). However, the model as a whole is very good as the value of R^2 is very high.

Further, in the second equation (Table: 4.14), FXET and TNTB variables are included as explanatory variables. The variable FXET is found statistically significant at 5 percent while that for TNTB at 1 percent significance level. Both the variables possess theoretically expected signs. Again, the model has a good explanatory power as well as good fit in terms of adjusted R^2 and F statistics respectively.

Table: 4.14

Regression Results of Ln. GDPN as Dependent Variable

Constant	Independent variable (ln. value)					Adj.R^2	F stat	DW
	(FXET)	(TTAR)	(TNTB)	(TNHR)	(TNHB)			
5.46*	0.12	-0.22	0.18***	0.11***	0.67*	0.99	266.6	0.81
(2.87)	(0.94)	(-1.26)	(1.99)	(1.81)	(6.12)			
6.43*	0.34**		0.42*			0.97	454.1	0.57
(12.09)	(2.19)		(3.43)					
-17.55*		2.339*				0.88	209.56	0.52
(-8.751)		(14.48)				(R^2)		

Note: GDPN = Gross domestic product at nominal price, FXET = Foreign exchange earning from tourism, TTAR = Tourist arrival in the country, TNTB = Total number of tourism business, TNHR = Total number of trained human resources and TNHB = Total number of hotel beds.

Figures given below the coefficient of variable in parentheses indicate t values. Asterisks (*) signifies that the coefficient is significant at 1% level, asterisks (**) at 5% level and asterisks (***) at 10% level. The analysis is based on log linear model.

In summing up the first model presented in Table: 4.14 is considered to be better model to show the impact of tourism development on economic growth of the country. It is because, this model has a good coverage of the variables, better fit, significance of the elasticity coefficients and theoretical expected signs of the variables. Therefore, the economic growth of the country is explained by the indicators of tourism development such as FXET, TTAR, TNTB, TNHR and TNHB. It shows that the tourism development has a significant impact on the economic growth.

4.8 ROLE OF TOURISM FINANCING IN ECONOMIC GROWTH

A. ROLE OF TOURISM FINANCING

Shrestha's (1995: 64) study had compared all the lending programmes of the commercial banks along with their contributions to respective GDP values. It had analyzed role of bank lending on the respective share of GDP and concluded that without the bank lending, the sectoral GDP as well as the national income is largely affected. The study thus, argued for the credit (support) on the various sectors of the economy and concluded that the bank lending in such sectors have been the key determining variables ultimately leading to economic growth.

The transmission mechanism of bank lending in the economy does not appear much complex because in case of increase in loan, the borrower may quickly spend the money on real goods and services that increase the economic activities and ultimately affect the national income. In case of increase in bank investment on securities, the seller may not invest it immediately on real goods rather they invest in purchasing another financial asset (Shrestha, 1995: 74). Hence, the role of tourism financing in the sectoral GDP as well as overall economic growth and development of the country becomes clear.

However, an attempt has been made to determine the role of tourism financing in the economy through an empirical analysis. The effects of tourism financing on GDPT, GDPN and RGDPT is examined through log model and results are presented in Table: 4.15. The calculations are carried out in log linear form based on the respective analysis of R^2 as mentioned earlier and upon selection of the better explaining model.

The theoretical expected sign of the coefficient (β_1) is positive i.e. $\beta_1 > 0$. It implies that tourism financing as an independent variable has a positive impact on economic growth (dependent variable). Contribution of hotel, trade and restaurant (GDPT) to the overall nominal GDP can also be proxied as an important economic growth variable because an increase in this particular variable certainly has positive impact on overall GDP performance. Further, it does not need any explanation why GDPN is proxied as an important economic growth variable. In addition, the ratio of GDPT/GDPN (RGDPT) is also proxied as the growth variable. Similarly, it is imperative to see the impact of tourism financing which is proxied by supply of tourism financing which is derived by summing up of credit exposures of banks and financial institutions, development expenditure of the government as well as foreign aid assistance in tourism.

Table: 4.15

Regression Results on Tourism Financing

Dependent variable	Constant	Independent variable Ln. (TFSD)	R^2	F stat	DW
Ln. (GDPT)	1.861* (2.891)	0.970* (11.155)	0.81	124.4	0.75
Ln. (GDPN)	6.28* (16.82)	0.72* (14.17)	0.87	200.8	1.32
Ln. (RGDPT)	-4.421* (-13.08)	0.255* (5.589)	0.52	31.24	0.31

Note: TFSD = Tourism financing, GDPT = Contribution of hotel trade and restaurant on GDP, GDPN = Gross domestic product at nominal price and RGDPT = Ratio of GDPT to GDPN.

Figures given below the coefficient of variable in parentheses indicate t values. Asterisks (*) signifies that the coefficient is significant at 1% level.

The elasticity coefficient of the tourism financing is significant at 1 percent level for all the indices of economic growth. In addition to that, the coefficients are possessing theoretical expected sign. The coefficient of determination (R^2) value, which shows the goodness of fit, is 0.81, 0.87 and 0.52 respectively which is considered relatively high in the context of data being time series. It also signifies that the variation in the dependent variable is explained by the independent variable. The F statistic is also statistically significant.

All the equations seem statistically significant and possess theoretical expected signs. Durbin-Watson 'd' statistic shows problem of autocorrelation. Therefore, all equations are corrected for the problem of autocorrelation through Chochrane-Orcutt (C-O) two-step procedure as discussed on earlier pages. Table: 4.16 presents the result of the estimation.

The theoretical expected sign of the coefficient is positive i.e. > 0. It implies that tourism financing has a positive impact on various indices of economic growth (dependent variable). The calculated DW value came to be 0.96, 1.67 and 1.61 for the equations. The calculated DW value is again compared with the given table value and found that there is no autocorrelation except in the first equation. The equations possess theoretical expected signs.

Not only this, since GDPN is a major growth variable, possesses significant coefficients and it has good fit too, it confirms about the significant impact of the tourism financing on economic growth but TFSD is not affecting RGDPT in a significant way.

To sum up, it is clear that the indices of development are sensitive enough to the tourism financing. With this analysis and results, it permits to conclude that the tourism financing has a significant impact on the overall economic growth in the economy.

Table: 4.16

Further Regression Results on Tourism Financing (C-O two step method)

Dependent variable	Constant	Independent variable Ln. (TFSD)	R^2	F stat	DW
Ln. (GDPT)#	1.974* (5.624)	0.518* (4.373)	0.41	19.12	0.96
Ln. (GDPN)	4.539* (12.752)	0.632* (8.908)	0.74	79.35	1.67
Ln. (RGDPT)	-0.201* (-6.121)	0.771 (1.462)	0.07	2.14	1.61

Note: # Analysis was also undertaken following the C-O iterative process up to fifth step and 'd' value in the forth and fifth is found to be same (1.15).

B. ROLE OF VARIOUS SOURCES OF TOURISM FINANCING

Further, it is also desirable to find out the contribution of various sources of tourism financing separately on economic growth. It is clear that there are different sources for the tourism financing such as lending of banks and financial institutions, government budget (investment) as well as foreign loan and assistance in tourism. Hence, in order to assess the impact of such sources in the development indices, further regression analysis is carried out in simple linear model. It takes the growth variable, GDPT as dependent variable and the different sources of investment financing as independent variable in respective equations, both separately and in combination. Table: 4.17, however, presents the considerable results only.

The theoretical expected signs of the coefficient are positive i.e. > 0. It implies that tourism financing from each of sources has a positive impact on GDPT (dependent variable). As already mentioned earlier, the contribution of hotel, trade and restaurant to the nominal GDP (GDPT) can also be proxied as an important economic growth variable because it is one of the economic sectors and an increase in this particular variable certainly has positive impact on GDPN, the economic growth of the country.

This section attempts to examine the effects of tourism financing from various sources on the growth variable, GDPT. Here, LTDNIDC, LSDCB, TEXP, GICA and FADOT are the variables included in the model as explanatory variables indicating tourism financing in the country. Analysis, therefore, includes above variables in different combinations to determine the explanatory power of different independent variables.

Hence, the estimation is undertaken employing the variables such as LTDNIDC, LSDCB, TEXP, GICA and FADOT with respect to sectoral gross domestic product (GDPT) in the first equation. The coefficients of LDSCB and TEXP are statistically significant at 1 percent level with theoretically expected signs. Similarly, LTDNIDC and GICA are significant at 5 percent level with expected signs. The FADOT is not found to be statistically significant because of the inclusion of more variables.

The partial coefficients of LTDNIDC, LSDCB, TEXP and GICA with respect to GDPT are found to be 47.13, 1.81, 64.04 and 2.29 respectively. It implies that one rupee increase in these variables have the impact on GDPT by respective rupees increase. For example, one rupee increase in LTDNIDC has an increase of Rupees (Rs.) 47.13 on GDPT.

Moreover, the effect of FADOT on GDPT is expected to be positive, i.e. with the increase in the amount of foreign aid and loan disbursement, we expect increase in GDPT. In this equation, the coefficient is negative but not statistically significant. When GDPT is regressed only on FADOT, the coefficient turns out to be positive and statistically significant (refer the fifth equation in the Table: 4.17).

However, the model, in terms of F statistic is found to be a good fit. Further the adjusted R^2 is also found 0.92 which is quite high.

Further, in the second equation (Table: 4.17), the combination of independent variables comprising TEXP and GICA are included. The variables possess the theoretical expected signs. It is significant at 1 percent level. The value of coefficient of determination (Adj.R^2) which shows the goodness of fit is 0.87 which is considered quite satisfactory. Further, the DW value shows the absence of an autocorrelation. This equation shows the significant impact of government budget allocation in the tourism sector that induces the economic growth.

Table: 4.17

Regression Results for GDPT (Simple Linear)

Constant	Independent variable					Adj. R^2	F - stat	DW stat
C	LDTNIDC	LDSCB	TEXP	GICA	FADOT			
351.72	47.125**	1.806*	64.040*	21.45**	-0.288	0.92	57.16	1.51
(0.154)	(2.127)	(2.863)	(3.847)	(2.291)	(-0.123)			
-402.488			115.575*	31.94*		0.87	83.17	1.85
(-0.145)			(8.415)	(3.120)				
1131.69			95.989*	23.49**	3.578**	0.89	66.70	1.80
(0.425)			(6.193)	(2.303)	(2.197)			
2568.81	118.74*	3.73*				0.87	96.81	0.54
(1.436)	(4.961)	(13.633)						
8177.2*					12.99*	0.62	45.49	0.59
(3.244)					(6.744)	(R^2)		

Note: TFSD = Tourism financing, GDPT = Contribution of hotel trade and restaurant on GDP, LDTNIDC = Tourism sector loan disbursement of NIDC, LDSCB = Service sector loan disbursement of Commercial banks, TEXP = Development exp. of government in tourism sector, FADOT = Foreign aid disbursement in other sector including tourism and GICA = Government investment in civil aviation

Figures given below the coefficient of variable in parentheses indicate t values. Asterisks (*) signifies that the coefficient is significant at 1% level, asterisks (**) at 5% level and asterisks (***) at 10% level.

Similarly, in the third equation, TEXP, GICA and FADOT variables are included as explanatory variables. The variable TEXP is found statistically significant at 1 percent while that for GICA AND FADOT at 5 percent significance level. All the variables possess theoretical expected signs. Again, the model has a good explanatory power as well as good fit in terms of adjusted R^2 and F statistics respectively. The DW ('d') value also shows the absence of an autocorrelation. Therefore, this result also proves the significant role of these sources of tourism financing in the growth variable.

In addition, in order to map out the impact of lending in tourism industry from the banks and financial institutions, the fourth equation is undertaken. Here, the coefficient of loan disbursement of NIDC (LTDNIDC) is significant at 5 percent level and that of the service sector loan disbursement of commercial banks (LDSCB) 1 percent level with respect GDPT. The adj.R^2 signifies that around 87 percent of the variation in the dependent variable is explained by the independent variables.

To sum up the analysis the first model presented in Table: 4.17 is considered to be a better model to show the impact of tourism financing from various sources in the development index. It is because, this model has a good coverage of the variables, better fit, significance of the coefficients and theoretical expected signs of the variables. Therefore, the economic growth in the sector is explained by the indicators of tourism financing such as LTDNIDC, LSDCB, TEXP, GICA and FODOT. It shows that the tourism financing from various sources has a significant impact on the growth variable i.e. economic growth in the sector (hotel, trade and restaurant).

Hence, with all these analysis and corresponding results from different combinations of independent variables, it permits to conclude that different sources of financing have considerable impact on the economic growth.

4.10 CONCLUSION

The tourism financing over the years has reached to some heights though it has a long way to go. To finance the tourism sector, several strategies and sources may be tapped. Among these, domestic private investment, foreign direct investment, government budget and foreign aid (bilateral and multilateral) are vital. During the review period, the role of the government appeared to be very limited leaving tourism industry operation in the private sector. The budget allocation of the government also has been meager. The foreign aid and loan disbursement in tourism sector also has been in similar fashion without showing any great achievements. Despite of this, the government might have realized the value of tourism investment because if it does not, economic benefits will be at risk. Thus, the government have introduced investment promotion incentives, investment legislation, and published trade and business directories.

During the review period, there has been a tremendous growth in the number of banks and financial institutions. At the beginning of the 1980s when financial sector was not liberalized, there were only two commercial banks and two development banks performing banking activities in Nepal. There were no micro-credit development banks, finance companies, cooperatives and NGOs therefore most of the people had the only access of informal sector.

After the liberalization of the financial sector, financial sector has made a hall-mark progress both in terms of the number of financial institutions and beneficiaries of financial services. Similarly, the loan and advances as well as investment increased persistently signifying strong uplift in the financial business (BFIS, 2005: 45). It has certainly provided with enough resources for the development and advancement of every sector including tourism. Over the years tourism industry has enjoyed the financial resources for the infrastructure and superstructure though there has been some slackness during the last 5 years or so. The tremendous growth in the financial assets and loan-able funds of the banks and financial institution in these years could not result for the corresponding growth in loan and advances and so is the situation in tourism. Thus, there is still a certain space to improve the situation with some shifting in lending behavior of commercial banks and financial institutions diverting the resources in productive and promising sectors of the economy.

There has been very little private foreign investment in tourism. It is because "potential investors may be discouraged by the difficulty of dealing with some government agencies, inadequate infrastructure, the difficulties of tackling the complex land tenure system, and insufficient investment incentives (ESCAP 2001: 27-28). Foreign investment in tourism is expected to promote responsible tourism, diversify the products, and transfer the capital, skill and technology even in rural and less developed areas. But in general, it is difficult to attract private foreign investment and gain high priority for tourism. Hence, it is desirable to target specialist donor agencies (such as the World Tourism Organization or the United Nations Development Programme (UNDP) to solicit support for tourism financing and development exercises.

The discussion and analysis permits to conclude that the government expenditure for tourism promotion and investment on civil aviation, as well as the loan disbursed by the commercial banks, NIDC and other financial institutions has been significant for the development of tourism industry. Moreover, it has been a benign agent for hotels and other tourism business. It is the investment that has brought the significant changes in the infrastructure and superstructure necessary for tourism in order to ripe the benefits from such industry.

The first empirical analysis on the role of tourism found the significant impact of tourism earning (foreign exchange from tourism) on the development indices and particularly on gross domestic product. It has shown the significant impact of tourism in the economic growth of the country.

Further, the second empirical analysis about the effectiveness of tourism financing also found the significant impact of tourism financing on growth variables such as GDPT, GDPN and RGDPT. It clearly showed that tourism financing has significant impact on development indices (variables) related to the sectoral growth (including tourism development) and growth of the economy in general. Further, the analysis also showed the significant impact of various sources of tourism financing such as the government, banks and financial institutions as well as foreign aid and loan disbursement in both the forms, separately and combination of two or more than two sources.

REFERENCES

Acharya, Keshav R. et al (2003). **The Sequencing of Economic Liberalization in Nepal**. Kathmandu: Centre for Policy Studies.

Andriesz, Ewa; D. Asteriou and K. Pilbeam (2005). The Linkage between Financial Liberalization and Economic Development: Empirical Evidence from Poland. **Journal of Economic Integration**, 20 (2)

Bahuguna, Anjali (2005). Tourism in India: Development Perspective. **The Indian Economic Journal** Vol. No.39

Basyal, Tula Raj (1994). Developments in Domestic Saving Mobilization in Nepal: An Overview. **Economic Review** Vol. No. 7 p.

Bennet, Oliver (1991). "Tourism financing" in ESCAP (1991) **Investment and Economic Cooperation in the Tourism Sector in Developing Asian Countries**. Report of a Seminar Organized by ESCAP Bangkok, 5-21 October 1991 Tokyo and Sendai Japan

Bhetuwal, Khem Raj (2005). **Assessment of the Effectiveness of Financial Sector Reforms in Nepal**. A Ph.D. Thesis submitted to the Maharaja Sayajirao University of Baroda Gujarat India.

Chandra, Prasanna (2002). **Projects: Planning, Analysis, Financing, Implementation and Review**. New Delhi: Tata McGraw Hill Publishing Company Limited.

Elliott, James (1997). **Tourism: Politics and Public Sector Management**. London and New York: Routledge.

ESCAP (1991). **Investment and Economic Cooperation in the Tourism Sector in Developing Asian Countries**. Report of a Seminar Organized by ESCAP Bangkok, 5-21 October 1991 Tokyo and Sendai Japan

ESCAP (2001). **Opportunities and Challenges for Tourism Investment**, ESCAP Tourism Review No. 21. New York: United Nations

FNCCI (1996). **Directory of Tourism**. Kathmandu: tourism Committee, Federation of Nepalese Chambers of Commerce and Industries.

FNCCI (2004).**Nepal and the World 2005: A Statistical Profile**. Kathmandu: Federation of Nepalese Chamber of Commerce and Industry

Gujarati, Damodar (1995). **Basic Econometrics.** Third Edition. New York: McGraw-Hill Inc.

HMG/N (1972). **Nepal Tourism Master Plan, 1972**. Kathmandu: His Majesty's Government of Nepal

Maharjan, Narayan P. (2004). **Tourism Planning in Nepal**. A Ph. D. Thesis submitted to Faculty of Management, Tribhuvan University Kathmandu, Nepal.

Ministry of Finance (2004). **Economic Survey 2003/04**. Kathmandu: Ministry of Finance, His Majesty's Government of Nepal.

Ministry of Finance (2006). **Economic Survey 2005/06**. Kathmandu: Ministry of Finance, His Majesty's Government of Nepal.

MOCTCA (2005). http://www.motca.gov.np.

MOLJ (1974). **Commercial Banking Act, 1974**. Kathmandu His Majesty's Government of Nepal, Ministry of Law and Justice.

MOLJ (1992). **Industrial Enterprises Act, 1992**. Kathmandu: Ministry of Law and Justice His Majesty's Government of Nepal.

MOTCA (1997). **Tourism Policy, 1995**. Kathmandu: His Majesty's Government of Nepal, Ministry of Tourism and Civil Aviation.

MOTCA (1998). **Annual Statistical Report**, 1997. Kathmandu: His Majesty's Government of Nepal Ministry of Tourism and Civil Aviation

MOTCA (1998). **Nepal Tourism Statistics, 1997**. Kathmandu: His Majesty's Government of Nepal, Ministry of Tourism and Civil Aviation.

NATA (1995). **Investment in Tourism**. Kathmandu: Nepal Association of Travel Agents

Nepal Rastra Bank (1995). **Summary Report of Rural Credit Survey**. Kathmandu: Nepal Rastra Bank, Central Office.

Nepal Rastra Bank (1997). **Forty Years of Nepal Rastra Bank**. Kathmandu: Nepal Rastra Bank, Central Office.

Nepal Rastra Bank (2005). **Banking and Financial Statistics** Kathmandu: Nepal Rastra Bank, Bank and Financial Institution Regulation Department.

Pant, Bhubanesh and Bama D. Sigdel (2004). **Attracting Foreign Direct Investment: Experiences and Challenges**. Nepal Rastra Bank Working Paper Serial Number NRB/WP/1. Accessed from web site - http:// www.nrb.org.np/publications

Quarterly Economic Bulletin (2005)**.** Nepal Rastra Bank, Research Department. Kathmandu

Satyal, Yagna Raj (2004). **Tourism in Nepal: A Profile**. New Delhi: Adroit Publishers.

Sharma, Om Prakash (2001). **Tourism Development and Planning in Nepal**. A Ph. D. Thesis presented to Faculty of Social Sciences, Banaras Hindu University India.

Shrestha, Sunity (1995). **Portfolio Behaviour of Commercial Banks in Nepal**. Kathamandu: Mandala Book Point.

Siddiqui, S. A. and A. S. Siddiqui (2005). **Managerial Economics and Financial Analysis**. New Delhi: New Age International (P) Limited, Publishers.

UN ESCAP (2001). **Promotion of Investment in Tourism Infrastructure**. New York: UN ESCAP

UNCTAD (2001). **Foreign Investment Guide to Nepal**. New York and Geneva: United Nations

UNCTAD (2003). **Investment Policy Review Nepal**. New York and Geneva: United Nations

Upadhyay, Rudra Prasad (2001). **A Study of Tourism as Leading Sector in Economic Development in Nepal**. A Ph. D. Thesis presented to Department of Economics, University of Lucknow India.

World Bank (1989). **World Development Report, 1989**. Washington D.C.: Oxford University Press.

V

CHAPTER

TOURISM INVESTMENT FINANCING IN NEPAL: AN ANALYSIS OF RESPONDENTS OF TOURISM BUSINESS ENTERPRISES

5.1 INTRODUCTION

5.2 REPRESENTATIVENESS OF THE SAMPLE

5.3 PROFILE OF TOURISM BUSINESS (RESPONDENTS)

5.4 COMPOSITION OR MAGNITUDE OF TOURISM FINANCING

5.5 BALANCE SHEET AND STRUCTURE OF FINANCING

- Structure of Balance Sheet
- Fixed Assets
- Working Capital

5.6 FINANCING PATTERN OF TOURISM BUSINESS ENTERPRISES

- Aggregate Sources and Uses of Funds of TBE
- Sources and Uses of Funds by Types of Business
- Sources and Uses of Funds by Ownership Pattern

5.7 ESSENTIAL ASPECTS OF FINANCING

- Financial Planning
- Cost of Financing
- Selection of Financing Sources

5.8 OPERATING PERFORMANCE AND FINANCIAL POSITION

5.9 EFFECTIVENESS OF THE INVESTMENT

5.10 BORROWING NEED AND PROSPECTS OF FINANCING

5.11 CONCLUSION

CHAPTER V

TOURISM INVESTMENT FINANCING IN NEPAL: AN ANALYSIS OF THE RESPONDENTS OF TOURISM BUSINESS ENTERPRISES

5.1 INTRODUCTION

The primary purpose of this chapter is to assess the existing status and system of tourism financing from the demand side. Other purposes are to examine the relative role and position of various sources of finance in the total financing of tourism business enterprises. The chapter basically, employs the data collected from the field survey using the structured questionnaire (Appendix: A.1). It certainly analyses the data based on their financial statements (balance sheet, profit and loss a/c) and questionnaire response of the surveyed tourism business enterprises (business). In addition, it also employs some relevant secondary data for the analysis.

This chapter, therefore after examining the representativeness of sample carries out thorough analysis of data related to the pattern, magnitude and structure of financing. It also contains assessment of financing, its essential aspects, performance of the tourism business enterprises and the assessment of business prospects and borrowing need.

The importance of financial management in tourism industry can be hardly overemphasized (Singh, 2001: 124). Financing decisions are more crucial because they have an impact on profitability (Witt and et al, 1997: 103). Financing policy, practice and system thus includes all activities pertaining with planning, acquisition and management and evaluation of the funding in the organization.

The study intends to assess the existing status of financing, funding sources, patterns and effectiveness of tourism financing. It requires an analysis from both demand and supply side. The previous chapter discussed about the tourism financing from various sources (the supply side). Here, it attempts to study from demand side. Naturally, the demand side of the tourism finance will include within its scope, various enterprises engaged in tourism industry. As on July 2005, there were 2,780 Tourism Business Enterprises in Nepal (MOCTCA, 2005: 78; please refer Chapter – I for details).

According to Anil Sharma (2006: 106), "In most industries, manufacturers have predominant control over product design, distribution, promotion and pricing. On the other hand, in tourism sales intermediaries like tour operators, travel agents, reservation services and hotel brokers play a very dominant role and enjoy superior marketing strength from the stand point of tourism marketing, the strong position of the travel trade has significant implications."

Tourism business enterprises largely comprise the intermediation in one way or the other dealing mostly either as wholesalers and retailers or as independent service providers. In recent years, particularly after the restoration of democracy and adoption of market friendly economic policies in Nepal most of the economic activities are left for the private ventures. The government has limited itself only for some essential activities only and started to play a catalyst role.

"The modern corporate sector in Nepal is still at a nascent stage, although considerable developments have taken place over the last decade. Though most businesses are still family-owned, there are a number of companies with a broad shareholder base, run by professional management, and the number of such companies is on the increase. Banks, other financial services, airlines, spinning mills, textile factories and hotels are some of the areas in which companies tend to be publicly held and listed on the stock exchange" (UNCTAD and ICC, 2003: 34).

Considering the importance of the business intermediaries, the primary survey has attempted to include various tourism business enterprises. The study basically requires financial information of the enterprises. Such type of the information is not accessible for the small, family owned business and some other located in the far remote places. Basic thrust of the selection thus was to cover most of them considering the availability of financial information. Some business enterprises did not supply the complete information despite of vigorous efforts.

5.2 REPRESENTATIVENESS OF THE SAMPLE

As discussed earlier, the present study attempts to analyze the financing pattern and structure of the surveyed tourism business enterprises. In addition, it attempts to assess about the effectiveness of the tourism financing as well as about role of tourism and tourism financing in economic growth and development of country.

In order to find out whether the sample selected for the study represents the population or not, two methods are undertaken viz. statistical test and simple comparison of the proportion in total distribution. Statistical test comprises the standard error test, which is given by 1.96 SE $\overline{X}$ whereas simple average test is concerned with the comparison of the proportion of the sample with population i.e. Tourist Service Provider (licensed) based on the type of business. In fact, the standard error test examines the difference between population mean and sample mean and enables to confirm whether it is significant or not (refer Gupta, 2002).

Table: 5.1
A comparison of the Population with Survey Response
(Representativeness of the Sample)

FXET in US$	Population	Sample	Difference
Mean	91,709.27	57,423.42	34,285.85
Standard Deviation	302,946.21	302,946.21	
Standard Error of Mean		27,655.078	
1.96 Standard Error of Mean			54,203.95

The sample is said to represent the population when the difference between population mean and sample mean is less than 1.96 SE $\overline{X}$ (Gupta, 2002: 902; also Kantawala, 1996: 59). For the purpose of applying this test, the data were collected about the foreign exchange earning from tourism, from secondary sources, as this was the common aspect for population and sample. The population data are taken for the year 2003/04, because it was only after that the data collection was to start. As is evident from the table, the difference between the population mean and sample mean is less than 1.96 Standard error of the mean. Hence, it confirms that the sample represents the population.

In addition, the comparison on Table: 5.2 also confirms the proportional representation of population by the proportional distribution of the sample.

Table: 5.2

A Proportional Distribution of Tourism Business Enterprises (Population and Sample)

Type of Business \ Year	Population				Sample
	2003	2004	2005	Average	
Travel Agency	31.7	32.9	34.0	32.8	25.7
Adventure					
Trekking	25.9	26.4	26.6	26.3	24.8
Rafting	3.6	3.4	3.3	3.4	7.3
Accommodation	38.8	37.3	36.1	37.4	42.2
Grand Total	100.0	100.0	100.0	100.0	100.0

Source: Nepal Tourism Statistics, 2005

5.3 PROFILE OF TOURISM BUSINESS (RESPONDENTS)

In the primary survey, it was intended to cover 130 tourism business enterprises currently operating in the market. The sample thus comprised 28 travel agencies, 38 adventure agencies (trekking, mountaineering and rafting), 48 accommodation businesses (hotel, resort and lodging) and 16 other businesses. Here, other business enterprises include curio shops, restaurants, cyber café, retail craft and retail garment sellers exclusively dealing with foreign tourists. Out of 130 enterprises contacted, 120 tourism business enterprises comprising 28 travel, 35 adventure, 46 accommodation and 11 other business enterprises supplied the information. Table: 5.3 summarizes the distribution of the respondents.

The composition of the respondents (tourism business enterprises) depicts an important picture. The Figure 5.1 and Figure 5.2 are particularly, designed to present the distribution of the samples and respondents of tourism business enterprises in terms of percent respectively.

Table: 5.3

Distribution of Sample and Response of Tourism Business Enterprises

Tourism Business	Sample		Response		Response Rate
	Number	Percent	Number	Percent	
Travel Agency	28	21.5	28	23.3	12.6
Adventure Agency	38	29.2	35	29.2	7.3
Accommodations	48	36.9	46	38.3	20.7
Other business	16	12.3	11	9.2	4.3
Total	130	100.0	120	100.0	10.2

Source: Primary Survey, 2006

Thus, the response of the survey comprised accommodation business with 38.3 percent share followed by adventure agencies with 29.2 percent share. Likewise, the travel agency business has 23.3 percent share and that of other business (miscellaneous sector) with 9.2 percent share in total distribution. However, the distribution indicates the majority share of hotel and adventure business. It is in line with the importance of such business too.

Figure 5.1   Figure 5.2

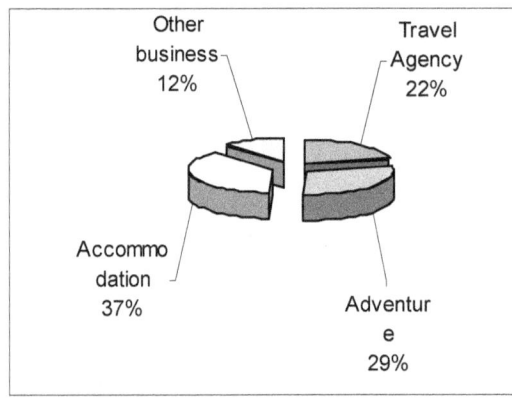
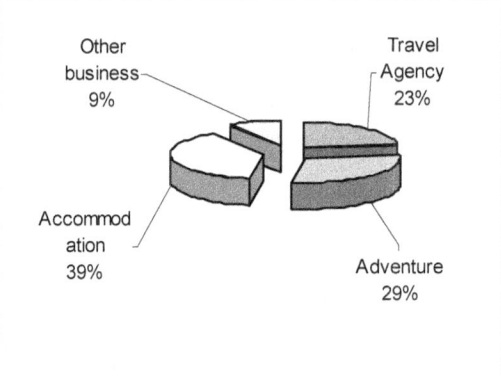

A. OWNERSHIP PATTERN OF THE RESPONDENT

The ownership pattern of the respondent shows very dominant share of private limited companies in the distribution. It has occupied staggering 77.5 percent share in the distribution. Proprietorship and partnership firms have 10.8 percent and 9.2 percent share respectively.

Table: 5.4

Type of Business vs. Ownership Pattern

Particulars Ownership Pattern	Type of Business				Total
	Travel Agency	Adventure	Accommodation	Other	
Proprietorship Firm	1 (3.6)	6 (17.1)	3 (6.5)	3 (27.3)	**13 (10.8)**
Partnership Firm	3 (10.7)	4 (11.4)	3 (6.5)	1 (9.1)	**11 (9.2)**
Private Limited	24 (85.7)	25 (71.4)	37 (80.4)	7 (63.6)	**93 (77.5)**
Public Limited	-	-	3 (6.5)	-	**3 (2.5)**
Total	**28 (100)**	**35 (100)**	**46 (100)**	**11 (100)**	**120 (100)**

Note: Figures in the parentheses indicate the percent in total.

Source: Primary Survey, 2006

The primary survey largely tried to cover most of the public limited companies currently functioning in the tourism market though the share in total distribution has been only 2.5 percent. As such, the survey has incorporated 13 proprietorship firms, 11 partnership firms, 93 private limited companies and 3 public limited companies as the respondents. The table also depicted the information about both the types and ownership pattern of the surveyed tourism business enterprises.

B. NATIONALITY OF PRINCIPAL PROMOTER OR CEO

During the survey, it was primarily tried to find out the nationality of the Business Executives comprising various titles such as Principal Promoter or Managing Director or Executive Chairman or Chief Executive Officer of the business enterprises. It was felt necessary to find out the entrepreneurship quality of the Nepalese business executives as well as the supply of foreign business executives. Table: 5.5 is designed to provide distribution of the business executives in terms of both absolute number and percentage.

Table: 5.5

Nationality of Business Executives

Nationality	Frequency	Percent	Share in Foreigners
Nepalese	107	89.2	
Foreigners	13	10.8	
Total	**120**	**100**	
Indian	6	5.2	46.2
Japanese	2	1.9	15.4
Thai	1	0.9	7.7
Chinese	2	1.9	15.4
Canadian	1	0.9	7.7

Source: Primary Survey, 2006

130 *Opportunities and Challenges of Tourism Financing*

The response from the survey was in line with the assumption and finding of Investment Policy Review Nepal (UNCTAD and ICC, 2003: 8), thus showed the majority share of Nepalese business executives with 89.2 percent. The share of foreigners stood at 10.8 percent. As such, the composition of the foreign executives has also been examined. The share of Indian executives in the total distribution stood at 5.2 percent, even though, it has topped among the foreign executives with an overwhelming majority share of 46.2 percent. The Japanese and Chinese executives stood at the second position in foreigners with 15.4 percent share followed by both Thai and Canadian in the third place with 7.7 percent share.

C. DURATION OF BUSINESS OPERATION

The survey has covered various business enterprises with diverse business duration. As such, it has covered some old business enterprises with more than 35 years of operation and some new business enterprises with just more than 3 years of business operation. Figure 5.3 is designed to provide the details about the duration of the business operation of the respondents.

Figure 5.3

Duration of Business Operation

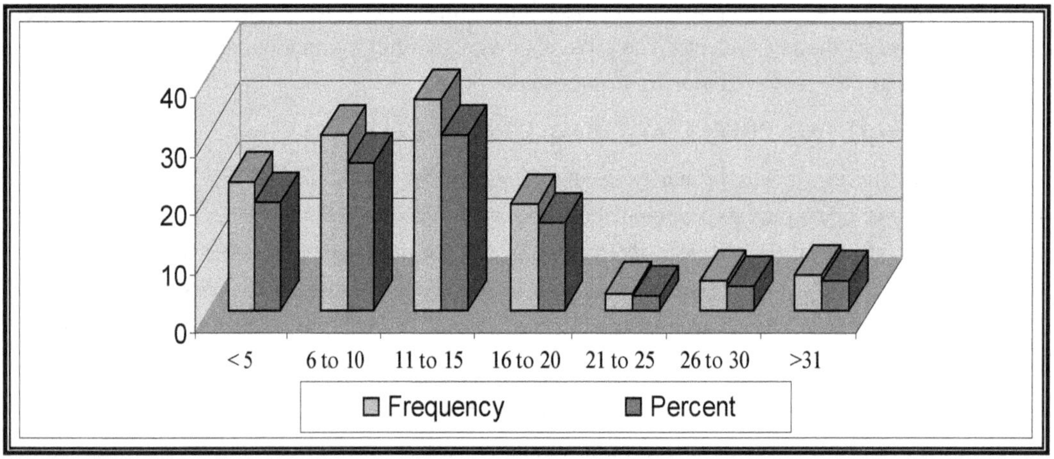

The Figure: 5.3 and Table: 5.6 summarize the distribution of the duration of business operation of the respondents both in terms of number of business enterprises and percentage. The majority of the business enterprises were found to be operating for 11 to 15 years accounting for 30.0 percent followed by that of 6 to 10 years with 25.0 percent and below 5 years with 18.3 percent. The business operating for 21 to 25 years found to be at minimum with just 2.5 percent. Other business operating for 16 to 20 years, 26 to 30 years and more than 31 years accounted for 15.0 percent, 4.2 percent and 5.0 percent respectively. In fact, the survey did not include any tourism business enterprise with less than 3 years of business operation.

Table: 5.6

Duration of Business Operation

Duration of Business Operation (Years)	Frequency	Percent
3 to 5 years	22	18.3
6 to 10	30	25
11 to 15	36	30
16 to 20	18	15
21 to 25	3	2.5
26 to 30	5	4.2
More than 31 years	6	5
Total	120	100.0

5.4 COMPOSITION OR MAGNITUDE OF FINANCING

In fact, the assessment of the composition and structure of financing is the fundamental aspect of the financing. It clearly describes pattern and magnitude of the financing as well as about the growth pattern over the period.

"The analysis of financial structure is concerned with the types of capital funds used to finance the enterprise ranging from patient and permanent equity capital to short term funds that are temporary and more risky source" (Bernstein, 1993: 597).

The mix of debt and equity is called capital structure of the organization. As such, the financing policy of an organization has an important bearing upon the survival of the organization because it influences the flexibility in the operations of the business. Too much of debt in the organization means high fixed cost or interest obligations, which may even endanger the survival of the organization (Singh, 2001: 126). Flexibility means the organization's ability to adapt its capital structure to the needs of the changing circumstances. "The organization should be able to raise funds, without undue delay and cost, whenever needed to finance the profitable investments. It should also be in a position to redeem the debt whenever warranted by the future conditions" (Pandey, 2004: 730).

Here the central issue is to determine the appropriate proportion of equity and debt. In fact, neither too much of debt nor too much of equity is desired in the overall capitalization of the organization. Optimal financing policy means a balance between debt and equity (Singh, 2001: 126). Therefore, it is really important to strive for the best financing mix or the optimum capital structure of the firm.

The importance of financial management in tourism industry can be hardly overemphasized (Singh, 2001: 124). Financing decisions are more crucial because they have an impact on profitability (Witt and et al, 1997: 103). Financing policy and system thus includes all activities pertaining with planning, acquisition and management and evaluation of the funding in the organization.

Therefore, the following sections deal about the sources of funding including equity and borrowing as well as to present the composition and status of financing for the tourism business enterprises over the review period.

It is already mentioned that the tourism business enterprises can mobilize the various internal and external sources to achieve an appropriate mix and size of the financing. The primary survey was intended to examine the magnitude of the financing for the review period. In this section, the attempt is made primarily to assess the financing in two categories viz. Share capital financing and loan financing through banks financial institution and that of current assets financing. It also summarizes the financing from foreign direct investment as well as from the funding from the share market in terms of public share issue.

A. SHARE CAPITAL FINANCING

I. M. Pandey (2004: 442) viewed ordinary shares, preference shares and debentures as important types of securities that the firms generally use to raise funds to finance their activities whereas Whitehouse and Tille (1993: 122) viewed the equity and borrowings as the main types of business finance in addition to the raising finance from internal sources. Similarly, Lawrence Gitman (2004: 522) viewed the total capital as composed of debt capital and equity capital.

Equity (simply share capital) is the owners' interest in the business and consists of the resources put in by them (shareholders) and the retained earning i.e. accumulation of the after tax profit over the years (reserves) within the business. In fact, the equity is a risk capital (Whitehouse and Tilley, 1993: 122). Ordinary shares essentially, provide the ownership rights for shareholders of the company (Pandey, 2004: 438).

There are two basic sources of equity capital viz. preferred stock and common stock. Common stock is typically the most expensive form of equity, followed by retained earning and then preferred stock. Equity capital is expected to remain in the firm for an indefinite time-period (Gitman: 2004: 522).

To examine the proportion of equity share capital financing by respondents, the segregation is also made between promoters' share, foreign equity and equity share capital financed through public issue. Table: 5.7 provides the details of the share capital financing of the surveyed tourism business enterprises during the review period.

In fiscal year ending mid-July 2000, the aggregate share capital (paid up equity capital) of the tourism business enterprises was Rs. 813.34 million. It increased by 43 percent and 24 percent to reach Rs. 1,162.17 million and Rs. 1,439.64 million in F.Y. 2000/01 and 2001/02 respectively. There has been a remarkable growth in share capital with 47 percent during F.Y. 2002/03. However, in the fiscal years of 2003/04 and 2004/05 there has been slight increase of 4 percent and 0.1 percent respectively. Thus, the share capital in the last year of the review period reached to Rs. 2,205.60 from Rs. 2,204.33 million of preceding year.

Table: 5.7

Share Capital Financing of Tourism Business Enterprises

(Amount in Rs. '000)

Fiscal Year ending mid-July	Total Paid up Capital		Promoters Share		Foreign equity		Public Issue	
	Amount	Share	Amount	Share	Amount	Share	Amount	Share
2000	813,342	100	717,233	88	26,109	3	70,000	9
2001	1,162,170	100	1,061,921	91	30,249	3	70,000	6
Growth %	43	-	48	3	16	-	-	-
2002	1,439,640	100	1,263,183	88	106,457	7	70,000	5
Growth %	24		19		252		-	
2003	2,113,982	100	1,655,322	78	338,660	16	120,000	6
Growth %	47		31		218		71	
2004	2,204,333	100	1,742,690	79	341,643	16	120,000	5
Growth %	4		5		1		-	
2005	2,205,595	100	1,743,951	79	341,644	16	120,000	5
Growth %	0.1		0.1		0		-	
Average Amount	1,656,510	100	1,364,050	82	197,460	12	95,000	6
Growth over the period %	171	-	143	-	1,209	-	71	-

Note: Share refers the percentage in total
Source: Primary Survey, 2006

The composition of the equity financing during the review period showed a dominant position in the domestic equity finance from the Nepalese promoters. It has on an average 82 percent share during the review period. The average share of the foreign equity investment (foreign direct investment) during the period stood in a tune of 12 percent followed by public issue with just 6 percent share on an average.

During the review period, there has been a gradual increase in private sector equity investment. Thus, it reached to Rs. 1,743.95 million in F.Y. 2004/05 from Rs. 717.23 million of F.Y. 1999/00. However, its share in total equity financing seemed to be decreasing from 88 percent in mid-July 2000 to 79 percent at the end of fiscal year 2004/05.

Similarly, there has been a remarkable increase of foreign equity investment during the review period. It was just Rs. 26.11 million in fiscal year 1999/00 and it increased to Rs. 341.64 million in fiscal year 2004/05. The increase in terms of percentage was remarkable particularly in fiscal year 2001/02 and 2002/03 with more than two folds. However, there has been a slow down in this source of financing particularly after fiscal year 2002/03. However, the pattern of foreign equity financing in terms of types and ownership pattern of business appeared to be distinct. Accommodation and other business in terms of type of business and private and public limited business in terms of ownership pattern have mobilized the foreign equity finance. It is to be noted that the foreign equity is not allowed in adventure and travel agency business (except TSA) as well as in proprietorship and partnership firms.

Moreover, there has been a satisfactory rise of public share investment in tourism business during the period. It was just Rs. 70.0 million in fiscal year 1999/00. It remained constant until Fiscal Year 2001/02 against the significant increase of 71.0 percent to reach Rs. 120 million at the end of F.Y. 2002/03. However, it remained at the par afterwards without showing any progress.

The initiation and practice of public share offering by some tourism business enterprises (hotels) during the period under review has produced the enthusiasm and opened up the new vistas for future resource mobilization.

B. DEBT FINANCING

This is the most popular and most widely used source of finance. It is a flexible form of finance because the interest is charged only for the amount utilized for the business activities. Lenders have no voting rights or direct control over management, but invariably require security over the business assets and occasionally, personal guarantees, which means that the owners' personal assets may be at risk in the event of the business failures (Whitehouse and Tilley, 1993: 123).

Term loans are directly obtained from the banks and financial institutions. They are the sources of short, medium and long-term debt. They are generally obtained to finance large expansion, modernization and diversification of the business (Pandey, 2004: 440).

Therefore, the borrowing (debt capital) can take various forms ranging from debenture, overdraft, mortgage, hypothecation, term loan to leasing and hire purchase. It must be paid and repaid at some future date based on the term and conditions of the credit. It is less risky rather more costly source of finance but the selection and utilization basically depends up on the situation and requirement. A debenture is a long-term promissory note for raising loan capital. The firm promises to pay interest and principal as stipulated. It is also called bond (Pandey, 2004: 438). There are various types of debentures.

The debt financing has a significant role for the growth and promotion of the tourism business. The impact of debt financing is presented in the previous (fourth) chapter. The discussion in this section concentrates mainly on the magnitude of debt financing of the tourism business during the review period. In addition, it will incorporate the shares of bank and financial institutions (BFIs) as well as that of the informal sector.

The loan from banks and financial institutions basically, comprises the loan and advances received from commercial banks, development banks and finance companies (as discussed in Chapter - IV). Similarly, the other loan composed the advance received mainly from the director or promoters themselves without any interest charges and the borrowing from the relatives, moneylenders or other informal sources. Table: 5.8 provides the details of the debt financing of the surveyed tourism business during the review period.

The share of the loans from BFIs in total debt financing of the tourism business enterprises remained at 96 percent on an average whereas that of the other loan (informal sector) remained at 4 percent only. The average amount of loan over the period from both the sources remained at Rs. 2,651.82 million and Rs. 119.03 million respectively. Similarly, there has been a net increase of Rs. 2,393.30 and Rs. 89.04

millions during the review period thus making a total net increase of Rs. 2482.34 million in debt financing.

Table: 5.8

Debt Financing of Tourism Business Enterprises

Fiscal Year ending mid-July	Loan from BFIs		Other Loan		Total Loan	
	Amount	Growth Rate %	Amount	Growth Rate %	Amount	Growth Rate %
2000	1,493,368		74,940		1,568,308	
Percentage	*95*		*5*		*100*	
2001	1,479,575	(0.9)	156,488	108.8	1,635,613	4.3
Percentage	*90*		*10*		*100*	
2002	1,698,680	14.8	68,026	(56.5)	1,766,706	8.0
Percentage	*96*		*4*		*100*	
2003	3,408,629	100.7	102,729	51.0	3,511,358	98.8
Percentage	*97*		*3*		*100*	
2004	3,944,005	15.7	148,005	44.1	4,092,010	16.5
Percentage	*96*		*4*		*100*	
2005	3,886,665	(1.5)	163,982	10.8	4,050,647	(1.0)
Percentage	*96*		*4*		*100*	
Average Amount	**2,651,820**		**119,028**		**2,770,849**	
Percentage	*96*		*4*		*100*	
Growth over the period %	160		119		158	

Source: Primary Survey, 2006

In the fiscal year 1999/00, tourism business enterprises have borrowed Rs. 1,493.37 million from the banks and financial institutions. However, it slightly decreased by 0.9 percent and declined to Rs. 1,479.58 million in F.Y. 2000/01. In contrast, it started to increase and thus in F.Y. 2001/02 there has been a rise of 14.8 percent to reach Rs. 1,698.68 million. Afterwards, it gradually increased until the fiscal year 2003/04 and slightly decreased in F.Y 2004/05. Interestingly, there has been a significant rise with more than cent percent in F.Y 2002/03 to reach a height of Rs. 3,408.63 million followed by a rise of 15.7 percent to reach Rs. 3,944.01 million in F.Y 2003/04. As in other cases, there has been a decline of 1.5 percent in F.Y 2004/05 accounting to Rs. 3,886.67 million.

The movement of the debt from other sources during the review period had a different trend. It increased remarkably by 108.8 percent to 156.49 million in F.Y. 2000/01 from Rs. 74.94 million of F.Y. 1999/00. However, it decreased by 56.5 percent to Rs. 68.03 million in F.Y. 2001/02. The declining trend did not continue for long time, thus in F.Y. 2002/03 it regained its rising trend with 51.0 percent growth rate. Such rising trend continued until the end of review period with significant growth of 44.1 percent and 10.8 percent in F.Y. 2003/04 and F.Y. 2004/05 respectively. Thus, the debt from informal source finally reached to Rs. 163.98 million by the end of fiscal year 2004/05.

The total loan and advances from BFIs and other source in the review period registered a significant growth during the review period. There had been a gradual growth of about 32 percent in average during the first four years under review. In Fiscal Year 2000/01 and 2001/02, it increased by 4.3 percent and 8.0 percent to Rs.1,635.61 million and Rs. 1,766.71 million from Rs. 1,568.31 million of the year 1999/00. Similarly, in F.Y. 2002/03 it increased remarkably by more than 98 percent to reach Rs. 3,511.36 million followed by an increase of 16.5 percent in F.Y. 2003/04. However, there has been a decline of 1.0 percent in fiscal year 2004/05 thus the total loan and advances of the surveyed companies remained at Rs. 4,050.65 million.

On the whole, it can be inferred that for the debt financing banks and financial institutions are the major suppliers. The year 2002/03 marked a considerable growth in the level of debt financing.

C. FINANCING OF CURRENT ASSETS

The debt financing in the preceding paragraphs discusses the fund supplied from banks and financial institutions for business purpose. The financing of current assets is mainly by the outstanding expenses, or advance received/ booking received from probable future customers. Table: 5.9 presents the result of such financing during the review period.

The current asset financing of tourism business enterprises in the review period registered a significant growth during the review period. There had been a growth of more than three folds during the period although the annual growth rate varied significantly. In the first year of the review period, the current asset financing amounted to Rs. 569.13 million. It decreased by 0.04 percent (Rs. 0.22 million) to remain at Rs. 568.91 million in Fiscal Year 2000/01. However, it increased persistently by 10.7 percent (Rs. 60.86 million) in F.Y. 2001/02 and more than 2.6 folds (Rs. 1,644.60 million) in F.Y. 2002/03 thus reached to Rs. 2,274.37 million. In contrast, it declined slightly by 3.2 percent to Rs. 2,204.54 million in F.Y. 2003/04. It regained growth by 8.3 percent in fiscal year 2004/05 thus the total current asset financing of the surveyed enterprises reached at Rs. 2,385.10 million.

Table: 5.9

Current Assets Financing of Tourism Business Enterprises

(Amount in Rs. '000)

Fiscal Year ending mid-July	Current Assets Financing	Increase (decrease) Amount	Growth Rate Percentage
2000	569,131	-	-
2001	568,913	-218	-0.04
2002	629,769	60,856	10.7
2003	2,274,369	1,644,600	261
2004	2,201,539	-72,830	-3.2
2005	2,385,104	183,565	8.3
Average Amount	1,438,138	-	-
Growth over the period %	318	-	-

Source: Primary Survey, 2006

The average amount of current asset financing remained at Rs. 1,438.14 million. Similarly, there has been a net increase of Rs. 1,815.97 million during the review period thus registering a tremendous growth of more than three folds within six years.

D. TOTAL FINANCING OF TOURISM BUSINESS

The firm mobilizes any one or combination of different sources considering the cost, requirement and availability of the sources. However, the real choice of financing depends upon the type of assets to acquire or finance. In fact, the business enterprise needs to analyze the types and methods of financing along-with their corresponding effects on its return and risk (Pandey, 2004: 579).

The financing of the tourism business enterprises witnessed continuous growth over the last six years signifying strong uplift in the tourism business. It increased persistently at an average rate of 28.6 percent per annum over the review period.

Table: 5.10

Composition of Total Financing

(Amount in Rs. '000)

Fiscal Year ending mid-July	Total Financing		Percentage Share in Total Financing		
	Amount in Rs. million	Increase %	Capital Financing	Debt Financing	Financing of C.A.
2000	2,950,781	-	27.6	53.1	19.3
2001	3,367,146	14.1	34.5	48.6	16.9
2002	3,836,115	13.9	37.5	46.1	16.4
2003	7,899,709	105.9	26.8	44.4	28.8
2004	8,497,882	7.6	25.9	48.2	25.9
2005	8,641,346	1.7	25.5	46.9	27.6
Average	5,865,497	28.6	30.1	46.8	23.1
Growth over the period %	182.6	-	-	-	-

Source: Primary Survey, 2006

In fiscal year ending mid-July 2000, the aggregate financing of the tourism business enterprises was Rs. 2,950.78 million. It increased by 14.1 percent and 13.9 percent to reach Rs. 3,367.15 million and Rs. 3,836.12 million in Fiscal Year 2000/01 and 2001/02 respectively. There has been a remarkable growth in total financing with 105.9 percent during F.Y. 2002/03. The basic reason behind such increase among others is the incorporation of financing data from most of the enterprises. In fact, some of the enterprises did not provide data for the earlier years of the survey period. Moreover, in the fiscal years of 2003/04 and 2004/05 there has been satisfactory growth of 7.6 percent and 1.7 percent respectively. Thus, the total financing during the last two years of the review period reached to Rs. 8,497.88 and Rs. 8,641.35 million respectively.

138 *Opportunities and Challenges of Tourism Financing*

Figure: 5.4

Composition of the Total Financing

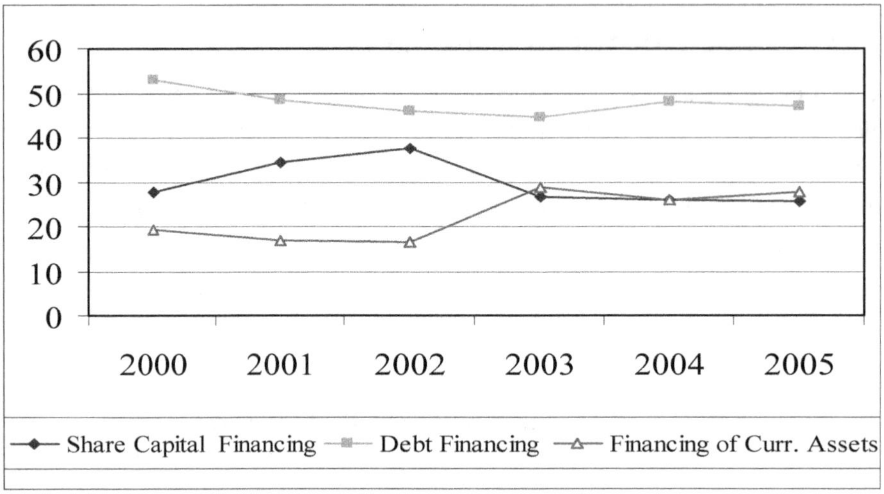

```
         Share Capital Financing    Debt Financing    Financing of Curr. Assets
2000              ~28                    ~53                    ~19
2001              ~34                    ~49                    ~17
2002              ~37                    ~46                    ~17
2003              ~27                    ~45                    ~29
2004              ~26                    ~48                    ~26
2005              ~26                    ~47                    ~28
```

The total financing of the tourism enterprises during the review period did not register any fundamental change in its composition though there had been a slight change in the shares of financing of equity and current assets during the second half of the review period. Debt financing continued to acquire more than 46.8 percent share in total financing over the last 6 years.

Similarly, the share of equity and current asset financing remained at the average of 30.1 percent and 23.1 percent during the review period. Figure 5.4 is designed to provide share of respective components in total financing of the surveyed tourism business enterprise over the review period.

5.5 BALANCE SHEET AND STRUCTURE OF FINANCING

A. STRUCTURE OF BALANCE SHEET

A Balance Sheet provides the structure of assets and liabilities of the firm or company. It is a summary statement of the firm's financial position at a given point of time. The statement balances the firm's assets – 'what it owns' against its financing, which can be either debt – 'what it owes' or equity – 'what it was provided by the owners' (Gitman: 2004: 44). Balance sheet provides the information related to the state of affairs of the company at a point of time.

Share Capital, Reserve and Surplus, Borrowing, Current Liabilities and other liabilities are the major constituents of liability side of the balance sheet whereas Current assets, Fixed Assets and other Assets are the major constituent of the asset side of the balance sheet. The distribution of these items forms the structure of liabilities and assets respectively. Table: 5.11 is designed to provide the structure of assets and liabilities (aggregate sources and uses of funds, in other words) of the surveyed tourism business enterprises through common size statements.

The aggregate sources or uses of funds of the surveyed tourism business enterprises have recorded a significant increase during the review period despite of an adverse impact posed by the negative balance of reserve and surplus.

Share capital, the major constituent of total liabilities, had on an average 33.4 percent share during the review period. The ratio was at minimum of 29.4 percent in F.Y. 1999/00 and at maximum of 43.1 percent in F.Y. 2001/02. Similarly, the ratio of borrowing in the total liabilities during the review years was found to be overwhelmingly high with 53.9 percent, on an average. The ratio appeared to be less fluctuating with a minor band of 6.5 percent over the period.

The average share of creditors during the review period was found to be 25.5 percent. Comparatively, its ratio has been in a wide range with a minimum of 18.4 percent in F.Y. 2000/01 to the maximum of 32.9 percent of F.Y. 2004/05. The average share of other item and that of reserve and surplus during the period found to be 1.0 percent and 13.8 percent (negative).

Current assets, the major constituent of the total assets had on an average 15.9 percent share during the review period. The ratio was at minimum with 11.9 percent in F.Y. 2002/03 and at maximum with 19.0 percent in F.Y. 1999/00. The ratio maintained a modest band of 7.1 percent in total assets.

Table: 5.11

Aggregate Balance Sheet of Tourism Business Enterprises

(In percentage of total)

Liabilities	2000	2001	2002	2003	2004	2005	Average
Share Capital	29.4	37.7	43.1	29.8	29.9	30.5	**33.4**
Reserve/Surplus	-8.1	-10.6	-16.7	-11.7	-15.8	-19.9	**-13.8**
Borrowing	56.7	53.0	52.9	49.4	55.6	55.9	**53.9**
Creditors/current liabilities	20.6	18.4	18.9	32.0	29.9	32.9	**25.5**
Other Liabilities	1.5	1.5	1.9	0.5	0.4	0.5	**1.0**
Total Assets or Total Liabilities	**100**	**100**	**100**	**100**	**100**	**100**	**100**
Assets							
Current assets	19.0	18.7	17.3	11.9	14.0	14.3	**15.9**
Fixed assets	76.6	79.2	80.6	86.0	82.7	83.6	**81.5**
Other assets	4.3	2.1	2.1	2.1	3.3	2.1	**2.7**

Source: Primary Survey, 2006

However, fixed asset stands not only a major constituent but also a determinant of the total assets with a hallmark share of 81.5 percent, on an average during review period. It was found to be at minimum with 76.6 percent in 1999/00 and at maximum with 86.0 percent in F.Y. 2002/03. The ratio in remaining years seemed to be less fluctuating. Further, the average share of other assets in the total found to be at 2.7 percent during the review period. The picture had been different if the accumulated loss (negative reserve and surplus) is transferred in asset side of the balance sheet. The balance sheet in absolute figures is available in Appendix: E.1.

B. FIXED ASSETS

In this section, the discussion continues for the fixed capital first and working capital in next section. In fact, a balance sheet provides information about the structure of investment on the one hand and the structure of its financing sources on the other (Gitman, 2004: 598).

Fixed assets remained major component in total assets of the tourism business enterprises during the period 2000-2005. Table: 5.12 presents the details of fixed asset of tourism business enterprises during the review period.

The fixed assets of tourism business enterprises showed a mixed trend during the review period. The size of the fixed assets increased in the fiscal year ending mid-July 2000, 2001, 2002 and 2003 but decreased in 2004 and 2005. It was Rs. 2,120.80 million in fiscal year 1999/00 and expanded to Rs. 2,445.19 million and Rs. 2,692.57 million in mid-July 2001 and 2002 respectively. It again, rose tremendously to Rs. 6,108.66 million in mid-July 2003. However, it declined to Rs. 6,091.66 million and Rs. 6,055.46 million in the recent years of review period (2004 and 2005) respectively. During the period, it expanded on an average 26.9 percent per annum and increased by 1.6 folds over the period. There has been a growth of Rs. 3,934.66 million during the same period. However, the basic reason behind such increase among others is the increase in the number of respondents for the latter years.

Table: 5.12

Fixed Assets of Tourism Business Enterprises

(Amount in Rs. '000)

Fiscal Year ending mid-July	Accommo-dation	Travel agency	Adventure	Others	Grand total
2000	1,720,961	19,728	100,929	279,178	2,120,796
2001	2,053,395	11,489	103,933	276,374	2,445,191
2002	2,332,841	10,572	106,354	242,805	2,692,572
2003	5,762,012	10,874	111,806	223,966	6,108,658
2004	5,824,603	14,235	109,877	142,944	6,091,659
2005	5,689,535	15,477	109,425	241,020	6,055,457
Growth Rate %	230.6	-21.5	8.4	-13.7	185.5

Source: Primary Survey, 2006

The Table: 5.12 also provides the variation of fixed assets based on the type of tourism business enterprises. Throughout the review period, the accommodation business has registered an increasingly large proportion of fixed asset among the tourism businesses. It has witnessed a significant growth rate of 230.6 percent over the period. Such type of growth rate for travel agencies was 8.4 percent. However, the growth rate for the adventure and other agencies has been negative with 21.5 percent and 13.7 percent respectively. It indicates the slackness and slow down in their business.

In addition to the fixed assets, it seems desirable to examine the total assets of the tourism business enterprises. Table: 5.13 is designed to provide the summary of total asset and its distribution based on type of business.

Table: 5.13

Total Assets of Tourism Business Enterprises

(Amount in Rs. '000)

Fiscal Year ending mid-July	Accommodation	Travel	Adventure	Others	Grand total
2000	2,222,765	143,412	114,850	287,138	2,768,165
2001	2,475,671	156,898	124,750	328,509	3,085,828
2002	2,721,162	187,812	136,246	294,777	3,339,997
2003	6,491,058	191,308	148,165	274,074	7,104,605
2004	6,614,815	242,147	200,323	305,732	7,363,017
2005	6,430,641	278,516	172,932	357,863	7,239,952
Growth over the period %	189.3	94.2	50.6	24.6	161.5

Source: Primary Survey, 2006

The size of total assets of tourism business enterprises increased continuously during the review period (except in 2004/05). The total asset, which was Rs. 2,768.17 million in mid-July 2000, expanded to Rs. 3,085.83 million and Rs. 3,340.00 million in the fiscal year ending mid-July 2001 and 2002 respectively. It rose tremendously to Rs. 7,104.61 million and Rs. 7,363.02 million in mid-July 2003 and 2004 respectively. However, it declined to Rs. 7,239.95 million in mid-July 2005. During the review period, it expanded 26.9 percent per annum, on an average. There has been an expansion of Rs. 4,471.79 million thus registering a significant growth of 161.5 percent during the review period. However, the basic reason behind such increase among others is the incorporation of the financial data from most of the surveyed tourism business enterprises.

The growth rate of total asset during the review period for accommodation, travel, adventure and other agencies stood at 189.3 percent, 94.2 percent, 50.6 percent, and 24.6 percent respectively. The growth rate of asset has been different for different types of tourism business. The hotel industry displayed highest growth among the other business.

The annual fluctuation in the quantum of total assets during recent years and particularly in fiscal year 2004/05 is attributable mainly to the macro business environment inside the country and international economic recession during the period.

C. WORKING CAPITAL

The financial planning of the organization also contains working capital financing. For some business/organizations, it becomes more important that deal with seasonal productions and operations. Similarly, the status of working capital during the review period also indicates the structure of financing for the tourism business enterprises.

Important components of the firm's financial structure include the level of investment in current assets and the extent of current liability financing. In US manufacturing firms current assets account for about 40 percent of total assets; current liabilities represent about 26 percent of total financing (Gitman, 2004: 598). Though such types of data are not available in Nepal, tourism business enterprises have been found to be extensively using current assets as well as current liabilities over the years.

Working capital represents the portion of investment that circulates from one form to another in the ordinary conduct of business. This idea embraces the recurring transition from cash to inventories to receivables and back to cash. As cash substitutes, marketable securities are considered to be a part of working capital (Gitman, 2004: 598).

Current liabilities represent the firm's short-term financing, because they include all debts of the firm that come due (must be paid). These debts usually include amounts owed to suppliers as account payable, employees and government as outstanding and banks as notes payable, among other payables (Gitman, 2004: 598).

The difference between the firm's current assets and its current liabilities is popularly known as **net working capital** (Gitman, 2004: 598) or simply as working capital. The conversion of current assets from inventory to receivables to cash provides the source of cash used to pay the current liabilities.

The change in working capital incorporates the changes in the current liabilities and current assets. Thus, an attempt has been made to incorporate the changes in working capital of the tourism business during the review period. The result is summarized in Table: 5.14. Working capital of the tourism business enterprises during the review period produced a picture with contrast figures along-with some variations.

Table: 5.14

Working Capital of Tourism Business Enterprises

(Amount in Rs. '000)

Fiscal Year ending mid-July	Accommodation	Travel	Adventure	Others	Grand total
2000	31,113	60,705	(51,314)	(82,496)	(41,992)
2001	(45,465)	75,345	(30,040)	8,303	8,143
2002	(104,722)	62,995	(17,391)	8,336	(50,782)
2003	(1,516,154)	83,387	(31,108)	34,455	(1,429,420)
2004	(1,334,825)	110,233	(26,373)	81,738	(1,169,227)
2005	(1,537,184)	115,403	(29,404)	101,833	(1,349,352)
Growth over the period %	-5040.6	90.1	42.7	223.4	-3113.4

Source: Primary Survey, 2006

Working capital of tourism business enterprises extensively remained at negative balance during the review period (except in 2000/01). It was Rs. 41.99 million (negative) in mid-July 2000, remarkably expanded (decreased either) to Rs. 1,429.42 million and Rs. 1,307.36 million (negative) in the fiscal year ending mid-July 2003 and 2005 respectively. Over the review period, the rate of the decline appeared to be 31.13 folds.

The rate of the growth or decline in the net working capital has been different during the review period for accommodation, travel, adventure and other agencies. Over the period, the accommodation business recorded further acceleration in negative working capital showing a net decline of 50.41 folds. In contrast, travel and other business recorded an increase in working capital with a growth rate of 90.1 percent and 2.23 folds respectively. Adventure business also recorded considerable increase in working capital with 42.7 percent growth; however, it could not offset the negative balance during the review period. In fact, the decline in the working capital of accommodation business can be attributed for the persistent decline on the aggregate working capital of the surveyed tourism business.

5.6 FINANCING PATTERN OF BUSINESS ENTERPRISES

The statement of sources and uses of funds generally incorporate the financial information of the institutions irrespective of its nature and size. It is the main reason why most of the corporate publication and regulatory statistics contain the funds flow analysis of various institution and business enterprises. This section attempts to inquire about the structure of financing, such as the composition of owner's investment in the form of equity and outsider's liabilities in the form of long-term and short-term debt. It also inquires about the sources of funds that were used to finance investment in assets. In other words, it examines financing pattern of enterprises and compares the share through common size statements (schedules) to reflect the changes and shifting, if any during the review period.

The share capital comprise of the paid up share capital (equity finance) and advance received for the share capital. It is the most conventional source of financing usually holding the major portion in financial structure of the enterprise. It is the most expensive source of financing. The reserve and surplus item comprise of retained earning, capital reserve, and the accumulated loss, if any.

The borrowing item in the source of financing comprise of outsiders' liabilities in the form of long-term and short-term debt that is used to finance the acquisition of the assets. In fact, the mix of equity and debt is called capital structure, which is generally used to evaluate the financing policy and practice of the enterprises. The current liabilities of the enterprises mainly comprise of sundry creditors, outstanding expenses and advances received from clients as well as from other parties. The structure also highlights the share of current liabilities in total capitalization of the business. The reminder liabilities are classified under the heading of other liabilities.

Similarly, the asset front comprise of current assets, fixed assets and other assets. The current assets of the enterprise comprise of cash and bank balance, sundry debtors, inventory (stock) and other receivables. Current assets indicate the liquidity position of the enterprise and structure of its total assets. Further, the fixed assets comprise of machineries and equipments, land and building, immovable properties whereas other assets comprise of fictious assets and other remainder. The survey of sources and uses of funds for all respondents of tourism business is presented in the Appendix: E (from Appendix: E_1 to Appendix: E_9).

A. AGGREGATE SOURCES AND USES OF FUNDS OF TOURISM BUSINESS ENTERPRISES

The aggregate sources or uses of funds of the surveyed tourism business enterprises have recorded a significant increase during the review period despite of an adverse impact posed by the negative balance of reserve and surplus (please refer Appendix: E. 1). To carry out the detailed analysis of the sources and uses of funds of tourism business enterprises, it was considered necessary to convert the absolute numbers in the common size. Table: 5.11 presents the balance sheet details in common size. One can simply refer the items of capital/liabilities as sources of funds and that of assets as uses of the funds.

It is not necessary to repeat the discussion but the constituents of sources and uses of funds rather, it is sufficient to state that it slightly produced a different picture. Amongst the items, share capital, slightly increased to 30.5 percent in F.Y. 2004/05 from 29.4 percent of F.Y. 1999/00. Current assets and borrowing as well as fixed assets and current liabilities showed similar variations during the review period. Other items of sources and uses such as other liabilities and other assets remained insignificant (less than 3 percent, on an average). However, the negative balance of reserve and surplus recorded a significant growth offsetting the real growth in other constituents of the sources and uses of funds of tourism business enterprises.

During the review period, accommodation business had an overwhelmingly majority share in aggregate sources and uses of funds[1]. These business enterprises appeared to be holding a majority share, on an average 85.7 percent during the review period. The variation in composition of aggregate sources and uses of funds as well as the respective increase or the decrease of funds of tourism business enterprises is attributable for the corresponding variation in the sources and uses of funds of the accommodation business.

In the foregoing sections of the chapter, an attempt has been made to examine the sources and uses of funds of the surveyed companies based on the type of the business and ownership pattern. As the study is based on the response pattern of the surveyed tourism business enterprises, it asks for the consideration of the actual number of respondents per annum (inserted in the last row in respective tables) and equally cautions all for the extensive interpretations, otherwise. The response could not incorporate the financial data of all surveyed business enterprises during the initial years of review period (particularly F.Y. 1999/00 and 2000/01 and in some cases F.Y. 2001/02 too).

B. SOURCES AND USES OF FUNDS BY TYPE OF BUSINESS

As mentioned earlier, it was considered necessary to convert the absolute numbers in the common size in order to have better idea about the proportion of each source in total source and proportion of each use in total use of funds. Moreover, if the number of various businesses are segregated and converted to common size analysis, it would indicate clearly the structure of sources and uses of funds according to the types of business.

---

[1] One can construct a table enumerating the figures from Appendix: E. 1 to Appendix: E. 5 to show the respective shares of the constituents in aggregate sources and uses of funds, considering various types of business.

The business enterprises under sample study though operate their business exclusively for tourism, the nature of business and dealing, mode of transaction and pattern of financing are quite different. Because most of accommodation businesses are capital-intensive with massive doses of finance in fixed assets whereas travel agents and other business are comparatively small and invest more on current assets. Travel agencies invest more on current assets because they deal in air ticketing business and need to maintain enough stock (ticketing). However, the adventure businesses have seasonal features and need to invest more on equipments, camping materials (tent and tarpaulins), kitchen utensils and mountaineering gears. Other business enterprises essentially comprised many small business units. Despite of this, the response also comprised one and only one big enterprise (i.e. airlines) among the respondents. Hence, the inclusion of financial figures of this particular business in the response has certain repercussions in the size of the fixed assets. Therefore, the size of fixed assets appeared to be high.

The following paragraph presents year wise common size analysis according to the types of businesses.

Accommodation Business

Table: 5.15 summarizes sources and uses of funds of respondents of accommodation business in terms of common size statements. Borrowing and share capital held majority share in liability side whereas fixed assets and current assets held such position in the asset side. Borrowing held 61.6 percent, 53.9 percent 56.7 percent, 50.4 percent, 58.0 percent and 58.1 percent share during the review period (from Fiscal Year 1999/00 to F.Y. 2004/05) respectively.

The share capital had 31.9 percent share at the end of Fiscal Year 1999/00. There had been a consistent increase in the share capital during the review period consequently, its portion in total sources increased to 46.0 percent (at maximum) in F.Y. 2001/02 and finally remained at 30.6 percent in F.Y. 2004/05.

The reserve and surplus item showed very much discouraging picture during the review period. It incorporated the accumulated loss because most of the accommodation enterprises have been suffering with loss in their business operation (please refer to operating performance). The share of reserve and surplus recorded a growing accumulated loss. This necessarily indicates the non-availability of the internal source of financing.

However, creditors/current liabilities showed a shift during the review period from 16.1 percent in F.Y. 1999/00 to 34.2 percent in F.Y. 2004/05. Similarly, the fixed assets registered the similar trend during the review period. Its share in total uses was 77.4 percent in Fiscal Year 1999/00 went up to 88.5 percent in F.Y. 2004/05. The growing debt capital of the accommodation agencies has financed investments in their business.

Table: 5.15

Sources and Uses of Funds of Accommodation Business

(In percentage of total)

Sources and Uses of funds	2000	2001	2002	2003	2004	2005	Average
Share Capital	31.9	40.3	46.0	29.6	29.7	30.6	34.7
Reserve/Surplus	-10.9	-13.5	-20.9	-13.1	-18.4	-23.3	-16.7
Borrowing	61.6	53.9	56.7	50.4	58.0	58.1	56.4
Creditors/current liabilities	16.1	17.7	16.7	32.5	30.3	34.2	24.6
Other Liabilities	1.3	1.6	1.6	0.5	0.4	0.5	1.0
Sources = Uses	**100.0**	**100.0**	**100.0**	**100.0**	**100.0**	**100.0**	**100.0**
Current assets	17.5	15.8	12.8	9.2	10.1	10.3	12.6
Fixed assets	77.4	82.9	85.7	88.8	88.1	88.5	85.2
Other assets	5.0	1.2	1.4	2.0	1.8	1.2	2.1
No. of Respondent	19	31	41	46	46	46	38

Source: Primary Survey, 2006

From the change in composition of current assets and current liabilities it can also be inferred that the rise in current liability has gone in financing the operating costs, which are higher than the revenue generated (i.e. negative rise in reserve/surplus).

Travel Agencies

The Table: 5.16 presents the common size statement of sources and uses of funds of travel agency business for six years beginning from Fiscal Year 1999/2000 to 2004/2005. The share capital had 13.7 percent share in F.Y. 1999/00. There had been a marginal increase in the share capital during the review period consequently, its portion in total sources increased to 15.4 percent (at maximum) in F.Y. 2000/01. It remained at 13.4 percent, 13.6 percent, 11.1 percent and 9.6 percent in F.Y. 2001/02, 2002/03, 2003/04 and 2004/05 respectively.

The reserve and surplus item though showed discouraging picture during three years from F. Y. 2000/01 to 2002/03 regained good position with 11.5 percent and 13.8 percent share in total sources of funds in F.Y. 2003/04 and 2004/05 respectively. It simply indicates about the emerging source of internal financing.

As is evident from the common size liability structure, these enterprises have been mobilizing the funds through debt. The percentage share of debt (borrowing) is quite high and varied within a narrow range of 40 percent to 43.3 percent in total capitalization.

Table: 5.16
Sources and Uses of Funds of Travel Agencies

(in percentage of total)

Sources and uses of funds	2000	2001	2002	2003	2004	2005	Average
Share Capital	13.7	15.4	13.4	13.6	11.1	9.6	12.8
Reserve/Surplus	1.8	-3.0	-4.3	-2.0	11.5	13.8	3.0
Borrowing	42.8	42.7	40.0	41.9	43.3	42.6	42.2
Creditors/current liabilities	41.5	41.7	49.3	45.7	32.8	33.2	40.7
Other Liabilities	0.1	3.1	1.5	0.8	1.4	0.8	1.3
Sources = Uses	100.0	100.0	100.0	100.0	100.0	100.0	100.0
Current assets	83.9	89.8	82.9	89.3	78.3	74.6	83.1
Fixed assets	13.8	7.3	5.6	5.7	5.9	5.6	7.3
Other assets	2.4	2.9	11.5	5.0	15.8	19.8	9.6
No. of Respondent	20	23	26	27	27	27	25

Source: Primary Survey, 2006

However, creditors/current liabilities remained important just next to debt capital with substantial variations during the review period. It was only 41.5 percent at the beginning of the review period. Its share increased to 49.3 percent (maximum) in F.Y. 2001/02 and finally remained at 33.2 percent in total sources by the end of F.Y. 2004/05.

The current assets, a major determinant of total uses of funds registered the persistent growth during the review period. Its share in total uses went up to 89.8 percent in F.Y. 2000/01 from 83.9 percent of F.Y. 1999/00 and finally it remained at 74.6 percent in F.Y. 2004/05. In contrast, the share of fixed assets varied within the range of 5.6 percent to 13.8 percent in total uses of funds during the review period whereas that of other assets within 2.4 percent to 19.8 percent.

Adventure Business

Table: 5.17 presents the sources and uses of funds of adventure business in common size form. These enterprises had recorded the gradual growth in their sources or uses of funds during the review period except in F.Y. 2004/05. In Fiscal Year 1999/00, the equity capital had 16.5 percent share in total financing of the adventure business. There had been a considerable rise in the share capital during the review period. Consequently, its portion in total sources increased to 25.0 percent (at maximum) in F.Y. 2001/02 and finally remained at 21.5 percent in F.Y. 2004/05.

The reserve and surplus showed an encouraging picture during the review period. It incorporated the consistent increase in profit and its corresponding role in internal financing. The share of reserve and surplus rose to 12.3 percent in F.Y. 2004/05 from 6.3 percent of F.Y. 1999/00.

The percentage share of debt (borrowing) has recorded a variation during the review period. The share gradually decreased to 15.1 percent in F.Y. 2004/05 (except F.Y. 2000/01) from 23.9 percent of F.Y. 1999/00. However, creditors/current liabilities showed a variation in its share during the review period. The share decreased to minimum of 30.8 percent in F.Y. 2001/02 from 52.9 percent of F.Y. 1999/00. Finally, by the end of review period, the share remained at 50.2 percent of total funding sources.

Table: 5.17

Sources and Uses of Funds of Adventure Agencies

(in percentage of total)

Sources and uses	2000	2001	2002	2003	2004	2005	Average
Share Capital	16.5	18.1	25.0	23.5	18.4	21.5	20.5
Reserve/Surplus	6.3	10.0	12.5	13.0	10.3	12.3	10.8
Borrowing	23.9	33.9	31.0	22.2	15.4	15.1	23.6
Creditors/current liabilities	52.9	36.8	30.8	40.7	55.2	50.2	44.4
Other Liabilities	0.4	1.2	0.7	0.5	0.7	0.9	0.7
Sources = Uses	100.0	100.0	100.0	100.0	100.0	100.0	100.0
Current assets	8.3	12.6	17.6	19.3	41.7	32.8	22.1
Fixed assets	87.9	83.3	78.1	75.5	54.8	63.3	73.8
Other assets	3.8	4.1	4.3	5.2	3.5	3.9	4.1
No. of Respondent	17	21	28	30	30	30	26

Source: Primary Survey, 2006

The current assets registered the persistent growth during the review period (except in F.Y 2004/05). Its share in total uses of funds went up to maximum of 41.7 percent in F.Y. 2003/04 from 8.3 percent of F.Y. 1999/00. Again, it finally remained at 32.8 percent. In contrast, the share of fixed assets varied and remained at 63.3 percent in F.Y. 2004/05 from 87.9 percent of Fiscal Year 1999/00. In fact, the share of fixed assets is consistently high in the total uses of funds during the review period whereas that of other assets remained below 5.0 percent, on an average.

Other Tourism Business

Table: 5.18 presents the common size statement of sources and uses of funds of other tourism business enterprises during the review period. These companies had recorded the great variation with several ups and downs during the review period.

The share capital had 23.1 percent share at the beginning of the review period. There had been a gradual increase in the share capital during the review period consequently, its portion in total sources increased to 35.5 percent, 43.7 percent, 47.1 percent and 57.0 percent in F.Y. 2000/01, 2001/02, 2002/03 and 2003/04 respectively. The share finally remained at 48.7 percent in F.Y. 2004/05. The share of reserve and surplus item in total sources of funds remained less significant. The share was 3.0 (at its maximum) in F.Y. 1999/00 decreased to insignificant figure in the following year. However, it revived and went up to 1.0 percent by the end of review period. It could not be an endurable source of internal financing.

The share of debt (borrowing) though has recorded a variation it remained as a determining factor in the total financing during the review period. The share varied considerably during the period and finally went up to 48.2 percent in F.Y. 2004/05 from 38.6 percent of F.Y. 1999/00. However, current liabilities showed a sharp decrease in its share during the review period. The share decreased to just 1.9 percent in F.Y. 2004/05 from 31.4 percent of F.Y. 1999/00.

Table: 5.18

Sources and Uses of Funds of Other Agencies

(in percentage of total)

Sources and uses	2000	2001	2002	2003	2004	2005	Average
Share Capital	23.1	35.5	43.7	47.1	57.0	48.7	42.5
Reserve/Surplus	3.0	0.0	0.5	0.7	0.8	1.0	1.0
Borrowing	38.6	58.2	36.4	46.6	40.0	48.2	44.7
Creditors/current liabilities	31.4	6.2	14.0	5.1	1.9	1.9	10.1
Other Liabilities	3.9	0.0	5.5	0.6	0.4	0.2	1.8
Sources = Uses	100.0	100.0	100.0	100.0	100.0	100.0	100.0
Current assets	2.7	8.8	16.8	17.7	28.6	30.3	17.5
Fixed assets	97.2	84.1	82.4	81.7	46.8	67.3	76.6
Other assets	0.1	7.1	0.8	0.6	24.6	2.3	5.9
No. of Respondent	5	6	9	10	10	10	8

Source: Primary Survey, 2006

The share of fixed assets of other agencies though varied considerably during the review period remained to be important in total uses of funds. It was 97.2 percent, 84.1 percent, 82.4 percent, 81.7 percent, 46.8 percent and 67.3 percent during review period from F.Y. 1999/00 to F.Y. 2004/05.

The share of current assets registered the persistent growth during the review period. Its share in total uses of funds remarkably went up to 30.3 percent in F.Y. 2004/05 from just 8.3 percent of F.Y. 1999/00. Further, the share of other assets remained variable during the review period.

In fact, there has been a considerable increase in current assets and decrease in current liabilities during the review period. It is a healthy sign from financing angle. However, the major reason behind such variation seems typical. As mentioned earlier, the response of 'other business' comprises one big enterprise (i.e. airlines) among others. Further, the response of that business clearly shows a considerable decline in its current liability and increment in its current assets. Therefore, the variation in these items of this particular business has a direct impact in the financial structure of 'other business.'

Comparative Analysis Based on the Type of Business

Table: 5.19 presents the comparative structure of financing in terms of common size (for the average percent) based on the types of business during the review period.

Table 5.19
Sources and Uses of Funds Tourism Business Enterprises
(Based on type of Business)

Sources and uses	Accommodation	Travels	Adventure	Others
Share Capital	34.7	12.8	20.5	42.5
Reserve/Surplus	-16.7	3.0	10.8	1.0
Borrowing	56.4	42.2	23.6	44.7
Creditors/current liabilities	24.6	40.7	44.4	10.1
Other Liabilities	1.0	1.3	0.7	1.8
Sources = Uses	**100.0**	**100.0**	**100.0**	**100.0**
Current assets	12.6	83.1	22.1	17.5
Fixed assets	85.2	7.3	73.8	76.6
Other assets	2.1	9.6	4.1	5.9

Note: Average percentage for the period.
Source: Primary Survey, 2006

From the table 5.19, it is apparent that the structure of the sources and uses of funds for various tourism businesses is different. In order to examine whether the variations in proportion of each of the item of the balance sheet is significantly different amongst as well as in between various types of business, ANOVA (one way) and t-Test is applied (refer Chapter – I for details of the methodology).

The analysis is based on the average percent in the data series (i.e. for six years) for each variable. For example, in order to run ANOVA for a particular item, say share capital among the various types of business, accommodation vs. travel agency vs. adventure vs. other business, first of all it takes the average percent of share capital (as shown in respective common size statements) for six years. Then, in order to determine whether the variance is significant or not, calculated F-value is compared with the table F-value i.e. 3.098 (d.f$_1$.= 3 and d.f$_2$ = 20) at 5 percent level of significance (Hildebrand and Ott, 1998: 810). Table 5.20 presents the summary of the ANOVA.

Table: 5. 20
Analysis of the Variance According to the Type of Business
(Accommodation vs. Travel vs. Adventure vs. Other business)

Variables	Calculated F - Value
Share Capital	21.44
Reserve/Surplus	34.85
Borrowing	31.21
Creditors/ current liabilities	17.46
Current assets	80.79
Fixed assets	63.37

Since the calculated F-value is more than the tabulated value, the variation is considered significant, which means that there is a significance difference in all the reviewed variables among the various types of tourism businesses.

Similarly, t-Test analysis is also based on the average percent in the data series (i.e. for six years) for each variable. For example, in order to run t-Test for a particular item, say share capital between accommodation and travel agency business, first of all it takes the average percent of share capital (as calculated in common size statements) for six years of accommodation business and compares with that of the travel agencies for the similar series. Then, calculated t-value is compared with the table value of 't' i.e. 2.571 at 5 percent level of significance (Hildebrand and Ott, 1998: 801) to find out the level of significance.

Table: 5.21 summarizes the result of various t-Tests for two sample means and verifies whether the variation is significant or not by comparing the computed value with table value.

As evident from the table, there is a significant difference for 24 cells out of 36 cells. Further, the result shows the significant difference in every variable during the comparison of accommodation business with travel agencies whereas it remained significant for some of the variables in other combinations such as accommodation vs. Adventure, Travel vs. adventure and travel vs. other and so on.

Table: 5.21

Results of t-Test for Two Sample Means (Average Percentage)

Based on Type of the Business

Variable	Accommodation vs. Travel	Accommodation vs. Adventure	Accommodation vs. Other	Travel vs. Adventure	Travel vs. Other	Adventure vs. Other
Share Capital	**8.85**	**5.34**	1.28	**4.52**	**5.50**	**5.03**
Reserve/ Surplus	**4.31**	**9.99**	**9.35**	2.31	0.63	**7.20**
Borrowing	**9.29**	**2.72**	**8.42**	0.77	**5.43**	**5.35**
Current Liabilities	**2.93**	**4.88**	1.92	0.58	**7.04**	**5.82**
Current Assets	**30.06**	1.50	0.86	**8.54**	**10.28**	**2.50**
Fixed Assets	**25.38**	**1.74**	1.02	**15.14**	**10.86**	1.13

Note: The figures in bold indicate significant at 5 percent level of significance.

It permits to conclude that there is a significant difference in the proportion of various components of sources and uses of the funds between the various types of tourism business.

C. **SOURCES AND USES OF FUNDS BY OWNERSHIP OF BUSINESS**

This section attempts to discuss the sources and uses of funds of the tourism business enterprises based on their ownership pattern. Hence, Table: 5.22 to Table: 5.25 are designed to present the distribution in terms of percentage.

Proprietorship Firms

The owners' fund (capital) appeared to be a determining factor in the financing of proprietorship business. During the review period, it held minimum share of 54.0 percent and maximum of 75.1 percent in total sources of funds. However, the reserve and surplus item showed very much discouraging picture during the review period. It incorporated the accumulated loss thus the share (negative) of reserve and surplus persistently increased during the review period. It simply indicates the non-availability of the internal source of financing.

It is also observed that during the year 2001/02, borrowing went down substantially and current liability rose from 11.0 percent to 45.4 percent. The major reason behind this should be the response pattern. Because, the number of respondents remarkably increased to 13 in F.Y. 2001/02 from 7 of previous year.

Table: 5.22

Sources and Uses of Funds of Proprietorship Firms

Sources and uses	2000	2001	2002	2003	2004	2005	Average
Share Capital	75.1	64.4	54.0	54.1	57.5	57.1	60.4
Reserve/Surplus	-5.0	-0.7	-11.9	-24.8	-27.1	-29.8	-16.5
Borrowing	23.2	24.3	8.9	28.6	31.7	32.8	24.9
Creditors/current liabilities	5.5	11.0	45.4	39.0	36.8	37.0	29.1
Other Liabilities	1.2	0.9	3.6	3.1	1.1	2.8	2.1
Sources = Uses	**100.0**	**100.0**	**100.0**	**100.0**	**100.0**	**100.0**	**100.0**
Current assets	16.7	27.1	24.0	27.1	25.5	25.9	24.4
Fixed assets	78.4	70.5	73.1	70.3	73.2	72.4	73.0
Other assets	5.0	2.5	2.9	2.5	1.3	1.8	2.6
No. of Respondent	6	7	13	13	13	13	11

Note: Figures are in percentage of total.
Source: Primary Survey, 2006

However, borrowing held considerable share in the financing of business ranging in between 8.9 percent to 32.8 percent. During the field survey, the respondents (of these businesses) informed about the difficulties they faced during the loan processing particularly for collateral of the loan and treatment. Creditors (current liabilities) also held similar position ranging its share in between 5.5 percent to 45.4 percent. Thus, to sum up they have been successfully mobilizing trade credit financing during the review period.

Partnership Firms

Table: 5.23 presents the sources and uses of funds of the partnership firms in common size statements. The share capital had been a major source of financing for the partnership business except year 1999/2000. Its share went up to 87.2 in F.Y. 2000/01 and finally stayed at 66.7 percent by the end of the review period. In fact, there had been a consistent increase in the share capital to provide with an eminent source of financing. In contrast, the reserve and surplus item registered negative growth incorporating the accumulated loss in their business operation.

Table: 5.23

Sources and Uses of Funds of Partnership Firms

Sources and Uses	2000	2001	2002	2003	2004	2005	Average
Share Capital	38.9	87.2	69.9	72.6	68.6	66.7	67.3
Reserve/ Surplus	-6.2	-13.6	-6.9	-8.1	-10.0	-10.4	-9.2
Borrowing	0.0	5.6	20.3	23.2	22.9	23.0	15.8
Creditors/current liabilities	61.9	19.7	16.4	12.0	18.3	20.6	24.8
Other Liabilities	5.4	1.0	0.3	0.3	0.2	0.2	1.2
Sources = Uses	100.0	100.0	100.0	100.0	100.0	100.0	100.0
Current assets	75.6	29.5	41.9	40.8	45.8	49.4	47.2
Fixed assets	15.7	66.9	42.7	42.7	38.4	36.3	40.4
Other assets	8.7	3.6	15.4	16.5	15.8	14.3	12.4
No. of Respondent	4	8	10	11	11	11	9

Note: Figures are in percentage of total.
Source: Primary Survey, 2006

As is evident from the common size liability structure, the enterprises have been adopting conservative financing policy relying less on debt capital. Though there was no borrowing in the first year, it took up a momentum in subsequent years to reach finally at 23.0 percent in F.Y. 2004/05 from 5.6 percent of F.Y. 2000/01. However, creditors/current liabilities showed a little bit shifting during the review period because it decreased sharply to 19.7 percent in F.Y. 2000/01 from 61.9 percent of previous year. Further, it remained at 20.6 percent by the end of F.Y. 2004/05. Again, the major reason behind this should be response pattern because the respondents did not report any borrowing during first year of the review period.

On the side of funds uses, share of fixed assets remained more than that of current assets. The share of current assets remained in between 29.5 percent (minimum) and 75.6 percent (maximum) compared to the share of fixed assets that remained in between 15.7 percent (minimum) and 66.9 percent (maximum). There has been a considerable variation in fixed assets and current assets during F.Y. 1999/00 and 2000/01. The reason for such variation can be attributed to the response pattern. Because in the year 2000, the respondents comprise only travel and adventure business whereas in 2001 it comprised accommodation business. Thus, travel business has more current asset and accommodation has more fixed assets. Other assets also registered a considerable share in total uses of funds, on an average 12.4 percent.

Private Limited Companies

Table: 5.24 presents the sources and uses of funds of private limited companies in common size statements. Borrowing and share capital are found to be holding the majority share in sources whereas fixed assets and current assets are found to be holding such position in the uses side. The borrowing registered the majority share in the sources of funds followed by equity capital and trade credit during the review period. Debt capital is found to be ranging in between 42.4 percent and 47.2 percent.

Likewise, the share of share capital and creditors are found to be ranging in between 30.3 percent to 38.2 percent and 27.8 percent to 37.6 percent respectively. In contrast, the negative share of reserve and surplus is found to be increasing. It not only incorporated the accumulated loss in the business operation but also the non-availability of the internal source of financing. However, the share of other liabilities remained at lower level less than 3.0 percent on an average.

Table: 5.24

Sources and Uses of Funds of Private Limited Companies

(in percentage of total)

Sources and uses	2000	2001	2002	2003	2004	2005	Average
Share Capital	30.3	36.2	38.2	37.2	37.8	36.7	36.1
Reserve / Surplus	-8.7	-9.7	-16.5	-20.9	-20.4	-21.3	-16.2
Borrowing	42.4	42.9	44.5	46.9	43.5	47.2	44.6
Creditors/current liabilities	32.9	27.8	30.1	34.7	37.6	35.8	33.1
Other Liabilities	3.1	2.8	3.7	2.1	1.5	1.7	2.5
Total	100.0	100.0	100.0	100.0	100.0	100.0	100.0
Current assets	26.7	28.0	26.8	28.7	32.4	31.5	29.0
Fixed assets	71.0	68.7	70.0	67.5	58.3	63.6	66.5
Other assets	2.3	3.3	3.2	3.9	9.3	4.9	4.5
No. of Respondent	46	61	77	83	83	83	72

Source: Primary Survey, 2006

The fixed asset stood at an average of 66.5 percent. The current assets stood at 29.0 percent, on an average. Thus, the majority of the investments of these companies are found to be financed through growing debt capital and sundry creditors and other payables.

Pubic Limited Companies

Table: 5.25 clearly depicts the considerable variation in the constituents of the sources and uses of funds during the review period. As is evident from the common size liability structure, the enterprises have been mobilizing considerable debt capital in their total financing. In fact, there had been a consistent increase in the debt capital during the review period, consequently, its portion in total sources remained at 59.9 percent by the end of the review period from 69.7 percent (at maximum) of beginning year. However, the share of equity capital is also found to be increasing because of public issue of the shares.

The share of equity capital went up to the maximum 47.3 percent in F.Y. 2001/02 from 28.4 percent of F.Y. 1999/00. The basic reason behind such increase was the response pattern of the share capital (data received from another company). Finally, it remained at 27.5 percent in F.Y. 2004/05.

The share of reserve and surplus in total financing has been negative during the review period. The share of reserve and surplus recorded a persistent increase during the review period indicating the ever-growing share of accumulated loss. It simply indicates the deficiency of the internal financing source.

Table: 5.25

Sources and Uses of Funds of Public Limited Companies

(in percentage of total)

Sources and uses	2000	2001	2002	2003	2004	2005	Average
Share Capital	28.4	38.3	47.3	26.8	26.5	27.5	32.5
Reserve/Surplus	-7.5	-11.5	-17.3	-8.6	-14.1	-19.3	-13.1
Borrowing	69.7	65.0	63.1	50.6	60.5	59.9	61.5
Creditors/current liabilities	9.5	8.2	6.9	31.2	27.1	31.9	19.1
Other Liabilities	0.0	0.0	0.0	0.0	0.0	0.0	0.0
Sources = Uses	**100.0**	**100.0**	**100.0**	**100.0**	**100.0**	**100.0**	**100.0**
Current assets	12.0	8.2	6.8	5.9	6.8	7.0	7.8
Fixed assets	81.9	91.1	92.7	92.7	92.3	92.2	90.5
Other assets	6.1	0.7	0.5	1.4	0.9	0.8	1.7
No. of Respondent	2	2	3	3	3	3	3

Source: Primary Survey, 2006

However, creditors/current liabilities showed a little bit shifting during the review period because it increased to 31.9 percent in F.Y. 2004/05 from 9.5 percent of F.Y. 1999/00. It also indicated the growing share of trade credit in total financing. The major reasons for such increase should be the slow down in the sales revenue and internal funds as well as the resultant dependency for alternative forms of financing such as the advance and trade credits.

Further, the distribution in uses of funds shows the investment into the fixed assets with more than 90.0 percent on an average. The share of the current assets decreased significantly to 7.0 percent in F.Y. 2004/05 from 12.0 percent of the beginning year.

As such, the role of capital market in tourism financing is negligible. Though capital market (particularly stock market) can be a benign agent for the investment in tourism, it is still far behind. It will take some more time to be at par compared to the development and diversity of money market. Nevertheless, three hotels viz. Soaltee Hotels 'Crownee Plaza', Oriental Hotels (Radditions) and Tara Gaon Regency Hotels (Hyatt Regency) have mobilized public issue of equity shares from the share market. These hotels are 5 – star category hotels. Not only this, they have franchise or TSA with renowned multinational hotel chains.

As they are suffering with operating losses, it is not feasible for them to issue the debentures or to issue the shares to the public or to increase the existing capital. Therefore, such type of financing source does not appear feasible, at least for some more time. Therefore, the capital market should come up with the appropriate financing schemes particularly for the endogenous tourism business.

Comparative Analysis Based on Ownership Pattern

The major portion of the respondents turned out to be private limited companies. In fact, they cover a major share in the samples, have detailed financial records and are ready even to furnish the information, in most of the cases. Thus, they appeared to be the dominant players to determine the structure and pattern of financing. The proprietorship firms are found to be holding a minor share in aggregate sources followed by the partnership firms. However, the public limited companies though are very small in number found to be holding considerable share in total financing.

Table: 5.26 presents the comparative structure of financing in terms of common size (incorporating the average percent) based on the ownership of business during the review period.

Table: 5.26

Sources and Uses of Funds Based on Ownership of Business

Sources and uses	Aggregate	Proprietor-ship	Partner-ship	Private Limited	Public Limited
Share Capital	33.4	60.4	67.3	36.1	32.5
Reserve/Surplus	-13.8	-16.5	-9.2	-16.2	-13.1
Borrowing	53.9	24.9	15.8	44.6	61.5
Creditors/current liabilities	25.5	29.1	24.8	33.1	19.1
Other Liabilities	1.0	2.1	1.2	2.5	0.0
Sources = Uses	100.0	100.0	100.0	100.0	100.0
Current assets	15.9	24.4	47.2	29.0	7.8
Fixed assets	81.5	73.0	40.4	66.5	90.5
Other assets	2.7	2.6	12.4	4.5	1.7

Note: Figures are in percentage of total.
Source: Primary Survey, 2006

From the table, it is apparent that the structure of the sources and uses of funds for various tourism business based on ownership pattern is different. In order to examine whether the variations in proportion of each of the item of the balance sheet is significantly different amongst as well as in between various types of business, ANOVA (one way) and t-Test (two sample means) is applied.

Table: 5.27

**Analysis of the Variance According to the Ownership of Business
(Proprietorship vs. Partnership vs. Private Ltd. vs. Public Ltd.)**

Variables	Calculated F – Value
Share Capital	18.34
Reserve/Surplus	1.31
Borrowing	43.94
Creditors/ current liabilties	1.12
Current assets	23.71
Fixed assets	32.48

The analysis is based on the average percent in the data series (i.e. for six years) for each variable. The results of ANOVA are presented in Table: 5. 27. Since the calculated F-value is more than the table value, it can be inferred that there is a significant difference in all the reviewed variables for various types of ownership forms of tourism businesses.

Based on the average percent in the data series T- value is computed. Table: 5.28 summarizes the result of various t-Test for two sample means and verifies its significance.

Table: 5.28

Results of t-Test Based on Ownership of the Business

Variable	Proprietorship vs. Partnership	Proprietorship vs. Private Ltd.	Proprietorship vs. Public Ltd.	Partnership vs. Private Ltd.	Partnership vs. Public Ltd.	Private vs. Public Ltd.
Share Capital	0.89	**5.43**	**5.35**	**5.64**	**5.68**	1.09
Reserve/ Surplus	1.41	0.10	0.76	**2.69**	1.91	1.48
Borrowing	1.85	**5.77**	**7.12**	**7.96**	**7.08**	**5.09**
Current Liabilities	0.32	0.64	1.66	1.07	0.54	**3.70**
Current Assets	**2.91**	**3.23**	**6.81**	**2.77**	**6.94**	**13.23**
Fixed Assets	**4.21**	**3.20**	**6.18**	**3.7**	**8.76**	**7.60**

As evident from the table, there is a significant difference between the most of the variables among the ownership of the businesses. If the calculated t-value is more than the table value it can be inferred that there is a significant difference between the variables. The result indicated that there is a significant difference between most of the variables of partnership vs. private limited business followed by other combinations except proprietorship vs. partnership business (only two variables are significantly different).

158 *Opportunities and Challenges of Tourism Financing*

D. FINANCING PATTERN BASED ON AVERAGE AMOUNT

Above analysis attempted to discuss the structure of financing. It focused on the common size statements and inquired that on the basis of types and ownership pattern of the tourism business enterprises. Further, it is desirable to undertake additional analysis on the structure of financing in terms of average amount of sources and uses of funds. To be more specific, it is not only the average amount but also the amount (certainly average) considering the actual respondents for the particular item for each and every items incorporating the sources and uses of funds.

Moreover, tables were constructed to present type-wise and ownership-wise details for the structure of financing (refer Appendix: E.10 to Appendix: E.17). Based on these appendices two tables viz. Table: 5.29 and Table: 5.30 are designed to present the details of the average amount during the review period considering both type and ownership pattern of the tourism business.

Table: 5.29

Sources and Uses of Funds of Respondents Based on Type of Business

(Average Amount for the period)

Sources and uses of funds	Accommodation	Travels	Adventure	Others
Share Capital	37,896.3	993.3	1,172.7	15,788.6
Reserve/Surplus	-21,530.9	345.9	638.4	1,028.9
Borrowing	86,789.9	8,083.7	3,250.4	27,672.0
Creditors/current liabilities	33,623.6	3,572.5	2,743.8	7,895.5
Other Liabilities	2,751.0	350.2	128.7	2,006.6
Current assets	13,932.3	6,569.3	1,299.7	6,781.8
Fixed assets	98,213.7	619.5	4,351.6	31,611.5
Other assets	3,343.0	1,474.8	318.1	3,755.5
Sources = Uses	114,654.1	7,930.8	5,823.8	39,783.2

Source: Primary Survey, 2006

From the tables it is clear that there are some variations in the structure of financing and pattern of sources and uses of funds. In order to examine the significance of variations ANOVA is applied.

Table: 5.30

Sources and Uses of Funds of Respondents Based on Ownership of Business

Sources and uses of funds	Proprietorship	Partnership	Private Ltd.	Public Ltd.
Share Capital	902.1	2,511.6	8,730.2	357,704.8
Reserve/Surplus	-414.7	-382.2	-4,277.8	-214,197.9
Borrowing	673.8	0.0	20,958.8	744,591.5
Creditors/current liabilities	682.8	952.5	8,862.9	311,681.8
Other Liabilities	128.5	143.1	2,036.4	0.0
Current assets	424.8	1,627.9	7,085.9	87,747.2
Fixed assets	1,129.6	1,600.1	16,381.5	1,097,750.2
Other assets	53.3	1,017.7	1,512.0	27,077.7
Sources = Uses	1,556.6	3,619.3	24,345.3	1,203,354.4

Note: Figures are in percentage of total.
Source: Primary Survey, 2006

Table: 5.31

ANOVA Summary (Type of Tourism Business)

Groups	Count	Sum	Average	Variance
Accommodation	9	369673	41075	2297856233
Travels	9	29940	3327	11043793
Adventure	9	19727	2192	3912064
Others	9	136323	15147	207453366
Source of Variation	*SS*	*df*	*MS*	*F*
Between Groups	8.82E+09	3	2938420545	**4.66***
Within Groups	2.02E+10	32	630066364	
			P-value	*F crit*
Total	2.90E+10	35	0.008175014	**2.90**

As evident from the calculations (see the results in ANOVA tables viz. Table: 5.31 and Table: 5.32), there is a significant variation between the distributions among the types and ownership pattern of tourism business enterprises. Since the calculated F-values (4.66 and 5.61 respectively) are greater than the table F-value (2.90), it can be concluded that there is significance difference in the distribution. It also supported a priori notion of the differences between the types and ownership of the tourism business.

Table: 5.32

ANOVA Summary (Ownership of Business)

Groups	Count	Sum	Average	Variance
Proprietorship Firms	9	5137	571	359121
Partnership Firms	9	11090	1232	1632765
Private Limited	9	85635	9515	89400714
Public Limited	9	3615710	401746	254293791319
Source of Variation	*SS*	*df*	*MS*	*F*
Between Groups	1.07E+12	3	3.56509E+11	5.61*
Within Groups	2.035E+12	32	63596295980	
			P-value	*F crit*
Total	3.105E+12	35	0.003	**2.90**

In addition to ANOVA, in order to find the variation between the variables of sources and uses of funds, t-Test is applied. The results of such analysis are summarized in Table: 5.33 and Table: 5.34.

Table: 5.33

Results of t-Test for Two Sample Means (Average Amount)

Based on Type of the Business

Variable	Accommodation vs. Travel	Accommodation vs. Adventure	Accommodation vs. Other	Travel vs. Adventure	Travel vs. Other	Adventure vs. Other
Share Capital	**16.49**	**16.53**	**8.71**	**4.97**	**13.68**	**13.36**
Reserve/ Surplus	**6.19**	**6.79**	**7.24**	0.98	0.94	0.56
Borrowing	**8.64**	**8.83**	**5.66**	**9.75**	**4.25**	**5.49**
Current Liabilities	**4.22**	**4.42**	**2.47**	1.70	0.93	1.15
Current Assets	**4.62**	**7.74**	**2.83**	**23.27**	0.17	**4.45**
Fixed Assets	**7.58**	**7.18**	**3.84**	**11.89**	**4.85**	**4.48**

The figure in bold letter shows significant at 5 percent level of significance

As evident in Table: 5.33, there is a significance difference between the most of the variables based on the type of businesses. Out of 36 results, 28 results are found to be significant. It is interesting to note that for share capital and fixed assets between all the types business, a significant difference is found.

Further, as depicted in the Table: 5.34, there is a significant difference between the most of the variables among the ownership of the businesses.

Table: 5.34
Results of t-Test for Two Sample Means (Average Amount)
Based on Ownership of the Business

Variable	Proprietor-ship vs Partnership	Proprietor-ship vs Private Ltd.	Proprietor-ship vs Public Ltd.	Partner-ship vs Private Ltd.	Partner-ship vs Public Ltd.	Private Ltd vs Public Ltd.
Share Capital	**5.37**	**27.89**	**7.08**	**15.44**	**7.06**	**6.91**
Reserve Surplus	0.26	**11.67**	**6.23**	**8.95**	**6.22**	**6.15**
Borrowing	1.73	**10.05**	**6.56**	**8.98**	**6.55**	**6.31**
Current Liabilities	0.94	**13.46**	**3.27**	**18.21**	**3.25**	**3.18**
Current Assets	**9.64**	**17.19**	**6.35**	**13.61**	**6.28**	**5.94**
Fixed Assets	1.50	**13.86**	**4.77**	**13.54**	**4.77**	**4.69**

The figure in bold letter shows significant at 5 percent level of significance.

However, it is important to note that no significant difference is observed in the financing pattern of proprietorship and partnership business, except the composition of share capital and current assets.

5.7 ESSENTIAL ASPECTS OF FINANCING

A. FINANCIAL PLANNING

The establishment, nursing and growth of the trade, industry and commerce owes to the finance. Finance is rightly said to be the lifeblood of the business. Funds are required to commence and carry on the business. It is also required for the expansion, growth and sustaining (Siddiqui and Siddiqui, 2005: 273). Therefore, every business enterprise whether large or small needs finance to run the operation. Business enterprises require capital in various forms comprising a number of assets and of various types both fixed (permanent) and current nature (Mahat, 1981:1).

A firm secures whatever capital it needs and employs it (finance activity) in activities such as production, marketing and finance. It requires real assets and financial assets to carry on its business. Real assets include tangible assets (plant, machinery, office, factory, furniture and building) and intangible assets (technical know-how, technological collaborations, patents and copyrights) whereas financial assets include securities or financial instruments (shares and debentures), lease obligations and borrowing from banks or financial institutions (Pandey, 2004: 3-4).

During the survey, it was tried to find out the practice of formulation of financial planning by the surveyed tourism business enterprises. Though the selection of person or consultant for the financial planning depends upon several factors, depends basically on the necessity and affording capacity. The basic objective to assess the financial planning of the tourism organizations is to determine the extent of financial planning practices and their exposure to the professional consultants.

The survey result about the financial planning is summarized in Table: 5.35. The table indicates that the majority (67.5 percent) of tourism business enterprises design financial planning within (inside) the organization. The business using the both the sources for the design of financial planning are found to be at 29.2 percent.

Table: 5.35

Financial Planning of the Company

Response on the Financial Planning	Respondents	Percentage in Total
Within Organization (only)	81	67.5
Outside the Organization (only)#	0	0.0
Both Within and Outside the Organization	35	29.2
No comment	4	3.3
Total	120	100

\# Outside the organization (total) were 19 respondents, which are included in next row.
Source: Primary Survey, 2006

However, the survey did not find any business formulating the financial planning, only outside the organization. The responsibility of the financial planning is found to be more relying on financial managers of the respective institutions.

Thus, the result supports the proposition that the design of the financial planning is a principal responsibility of the organization and its management. In certain cases, they can consult their auditors, advisors and consultants.

B. COST OF CAPITAL

Financing policy, in simple words means to design the capital structure with appropriate proportions of debt and equity. Every business firm aims at maximizing the firm value by minimizing the overall cost of capital. In fact, the cost of capital is useful in deciding about the methods of financing at a point of time (Pandey, 2004: 168).

In such broader view, the central issue of financial policy is the wise use of funds and the central process involved is a rational matching of advantages of potential uses against the cost of alternative sources so as to achieve the broad financial goals which an enterprise sets for itself (Soloman, 1969: 3).

During the survey, an attempt was made to find out the cost of the borrowing during the period. The respondents did not furnish the complete response for the cost of the borrowing. Nevertheless, Table: 5.36 is designed to summarize the response and disclose the average interest rate of the tourism business enterprises during the review period.

The average interest rate of the borrowing has been gradually decreasing during the review period. It decreased to 13.8 percent in F.Y. 2000/01 from 14.1 percent in fiscal year 1999/00. The interest has declined to 13.3 percent, 13.1 and 12.4 percent in F.Y. 2001/02, 2002/03 and 2003/04 respectively. The rate stood at the par of 12.4 percent in F.Y. 2004/05 with that of preceding year.

The interest rate had been slightly different among the various types of tourism business. The distribution showed that the rate stood in lower range for accommodation business followed by travel agency and adventure business. However, the rate had been in higher range for other agencies. The basic reason behind this should be exposure of the loans from formal and informal sector. In fact, hotel business can provide good collateral and get loans but other business do not possess much to offer as collateral. Small and indigenous business usually depend on informal source of finance which is more expensive.

Table: 5.36

Average Interest Rate on Borrowing (in percentage per annum)

Year	Accommodation	Travel agency	Adventure	Others	Average
2000	13.0	13.8	14.0	15.5	14.1
2001	13.0	12.5	14.0	15.7	13.8
2002	12.6	12.5	13.0	15.0	13.3
2003	12.2	12.1	13.5	14.5	13.1
2004	11.5	12.0	13.0	13.0	12.4
2005	11.5	13.0	12.0	13.0	12.4

Source: Primary Survey, 2006

The study undertakes a comparison for the interest rate structure between published (secondary) data with the results from the survey, during the review period. The interest rate structure for the industry of the banks was in a range of 10.5 percent to 15.5 percent in 2000 and 8.25 percent to 13. 5 percent in 2005 (NRB, 2005: 32). Hence, in 2000 it is found in higher range and in 2005 it is found even less than the higher range.

C. SELECTION OF FINANCING SOURCES

There can be varied modes of financing based on the purpose of financing, methods and time duration. It simply means that it can be classified as internal and external, formal and informal as well as domestic and foreign. However, the classification highly depends on the criteria used for such classification.

As organizations grow in size and expand their business, they will eventually face the problem of sufficient funding. In fact, they cannot finance the entire expansion from internal funds generated from their operations. A decision is required to fulfill the funding gap and to decide about the best type of finance (Whitehouse and Tille 1993: 122).

Further, Whitehouse and Tilley (1993: 122, 135) have discussed the sources and types of finance dividing them in two broad categories of commercial and non-commercial sources of finance. Again, they have divided commercial finance in short and mid-term finance as equity, borrowing, debt factoring, invoice discounting leasing, hire purchase and bills of exchange as well as medium and long-term finance such as venture capital, long-term borrowing (share issue, debenture).

Another classification of financing in internal and external source is based on the flow of funds. The internal source comprises the retained earning, reserves, surplus and depreciation whereas the external source comprises issuance of shares, debentures, borrowings from banks and financial institution as well as trade credits.

Practically, the enumeration of sources or types of financing can be different for the different types of business enterprises. As in other economic sectors, the tourism business can also mobilize various sources of financing such as internal and external; domestic and overseas; formal and informal. The selection of the financing sources and amount of financing, basically, rests on the business prospects, borrowing need (financing requirement), intensity of demand and availability of funding sources in the market. It largely depends upon the cost of financing too. In addition, some other macro economic variables determine the size and availability of the financing. Keeping all these factors in mind, the business enterprises can select the source, size and duration of the financing and adjust them considering their business peculiarities.

As in other economic sectors, tourism industry can also mobilize various sources of financing such as internal and external; domestic and overseas; formal and informal. The selection of the financing source and amount of financing basically, rests on the business prospects, borrowing need (financing requirement), intensity of demand and availability of funding sources in the market. It largely depends upon the cost of financing too.

Moreover, some other macro economic variables determine the size and availability of the financing. Keeping all these factors in mind, the business enterprise can select the source, size and duration of the financing and adjust that as per the situation and some other business peculiarities.

In this section of the chapter, an attempt has been made to find out the sources of financing based on the results of the primary survey. Tourism business enterprises in Nepal have been found to be using various sources of financing. The distribution of such financing is summarized in the Table: 5.37.

The Table: 5.37 clearly depicts that majority (58.3 percent) of tourism business enterprises use both the internal and external financing sources. However, 35.8 percent respondents are found to be using only internal financing sources while 5.8 percent did not provide the response in this matter.

Similarly, 86.7 percent and 2.5 percent respondents are found to be using only domestic and only foreign equity finance respectively. Five percent (5 %) of the respondents are utilizing both domestic and foreign source of financing. 5.8 percent did not provide the response about financing sources.

Further, the composition of financing in terms of formal and informal sources appeared to be different. There are 25.8 percent respondents using only the formal source of financing and 20.0 percent using only the informal source. Likewise, there are 12.5 percent respondents using both the formal and informal source of finance. However, the rest 41.7 percent respondents did not provide the response, because either they did not use the sources for further financing in the business or just avoid to furnish the information in the survey.

Table: 5.37

Distribution of the Financing Sources

S. N.	Sources	No. of business (Respondent)	Percentage in total Respondent
1.	**Internal vs. External Source**	120	100.0
	Internal Source (only)	43	35.8
	External Source (only) *	0	0.0
	Both the internal and external sources	70	58.3
	No comment	7	5.8
2.	**Domestic vs. Foreign Source**	120	100.0
	Domestic source (only)	104	86.7
	Foreign source (only)	3	2.5
	Both Domestic and Foreign sources	6	5.0
	No comment	7	5.8
3.	**Formal vs. Informal Source**	120	100.0
	Formal source (only)	31	25.8
	Informal source (only)	24	20.0
	Both the formal and informal source	15	12.5
	No Borrowing / No Response	50	41.7

* External Source (total) were 70 respondents.
Source: Primary Survey, 2006

5.8 OPERATING PERFORMANCE AND FINANCIAL POSITION OF RESPONDENTS

This section of the chapter contains the information about the financial position of the surveyed tourism business organizations. Such information is extracted from the survey questionnaire. In addition, the study contains further information based on their balance sheet, profit and loss account and statements. Similarly, the chapter contains ratio analysis (certainly basic or fundamental) to assess the financial position of the business enterprises.

The annual account and financial statements of a business can be used as a starting point to examine overall success and underlying financial strength of the enterprises. In fact, these statements can be used to assess efficiency and performance and to indicate areas that require further improvements (Whitehouse and Tilley, 1993: 33).

In order to understand the financing of the business enterprises it seems highly desirable to understand the financial position and operating performance during the period under consideration. In fact, the changes in the company's financial structure can be gauged by means of a number of measurements and comparisons. Some key ratios can be calculated and their longitudinal analysis can be undertaken through growth trend in various variables (Singh, 2003: 137).

This section of the chapter presents the information about the financial position of the surveyed tourism business organizations. In addition, it includes the brief discussion about the financial ratios and finally tries to summarize the analysis and implications.

Revenue Generation (Annual Turnover)

At the outset, the performance of the business organization can be assessed in terms of its sales, or revenue generation. It is generally known as the turnover. It simply means the revenue generated through the operation of the business or from the sale proceeds of the products and services of the enterprises. Table: 5.38 is designed to provide the details of the sales revenue during the review period.

The aggregate sales revenue of the tourism business enterprises did not register any significant growth during review period. Out of six years, it grew in fiscal year 2000/01, 2002/03 and 2003/04 with 2.9 percent, 34.4 percent and 24.9 percent respectively whereas it decreased in 2001/02 and 2004/05 with 23.1 percent and 20.1 percent respectively. The main reasons behind such decrease were decline in tourist arrival and deteriorating law and order situation inside the country as well as the economic recession and growing threat of terrorism outside the country. The sales revenue increased to Rs. 1,622.46 million in fiscal year 2004/05 from Rs. 1,529.48 million of 1999/00. The growth rate over the period stood at 6.1 percent. Therefore, the aggregate sales of the tourism business enterprises during the review period showed a mixed trend.

Table: 5.38

Sales Revenue of Tourism Business Enterprises

Fiscal Year ending mid-July	Accommo-dation	Travel agency	Adventure	Others	Grand total	Growth %
2000	1,096,870	103,785	90,771	238,050	1,529,476	
2001	1,146,018	93,709	91,422	242,701	1,573,850	2.9
2002	799,403	103,702	58,130	249,142	1,210,377	(23.1)
2003	1,107,332	144,211	88,339	286,609	1,626,491	34.4
2004	1,366,628	187,391	91,524	386,197	2,031,740	24.9
2005	669,347	160,418	109,849	682,843	1,622,457	(20.1)
Average	1,030,933	132,203	88,339	347,590	1,599,065	
Growth Rate %	-39.0	54.6	21.0	186.8	6.1	

Source: Primary Survey, 2006

Similarly, the sales revenue based on the types of business did not show much variation. Accommodation business has topped list followed by other business leaving the travel agency and adventure in third and forth position respectively. The sales revenue during the review years grew remarkably for other business with more than 1.86 fold while for travel and trekking agencies it rose moderately with 54.6 percent and 21.0 percent respectively. In contrast, the revenue of the accommodation agencies declined by 39.0 percent over the period. There can be many reasons behind this but the sharp decrease in the number of tourist for convention/conference purpose followed by the decrease in tourists with pleasure, business and official purposes have adverse impact for sales revenue of accommodation business (Please refer Table: 3.3 in Chapter - III).

There are a number of ratios which exist and which can be used to gain an insight into an organization's profitability, liquidity, solvency and general state of health (Whitehouse and Tilley, 1993: 52). However, some basic and fundamental ratios are calculated to indicate the financial position of the tourism business enterprises. It is to be mentioned especially here that the industry average for different types of tourism business could not be compiled. Nevertheless, the analysis indicates only some basic information.

Profit Margin

Generally, the performance of the business is gauzed in terms of its net profit. However, the surveyed tourism business enterprises could not show the profit during the review period. There can be various reasons behind this but it seems simply enough to state that these enterprises are in operating loss and eroding their share capital in recent years.

Therefore, the study does not discuss the net profit of the tourism business enterprises in absolute figures rather compares it with their sales revenue to find the net profit margin ratio. Such ratio is expected to indicate the profitability position of the business. The formula for the ratio is as follows (Chandra, 1998: 24.12):

Net Profit Margin Ratio = Net Profit / Net Sales

Table 5.39 is designed to provide the details based on the type of tourism business enterprises during the review period. The profitability position or simply the net profit margin ratio of surveyed tourism business enterprises during the review period stood at 0.2 (negative), on an average.

Table: 5.39

Net Profit to Sales Ratio of Tourism Business Enterprises

Fiscal Year ending mid-July	Accommodation	Travel agency	Adventure	Others	Aggregate
2000	(0.1)	0.0	0.1	0.02	(0.0)
2001	(0.1)	(0.0)	0.1	(0.05)	(0.1)
2002	(0.3)	0.3	0.1	(0.01)	(0.2)
2003	(0.4)	0.3	0.1	(0.01)	(0.3)
2004	(0.3)	0.1	0.1	0.03	(0.2)
2005	(0.6)	0.1	0.2	0.01	(0.2)
Average	**(0.3)**	**0.1**	**0.1**	**(0.001)**	**(0.2)**

Source: Primary Survey, 2006

The ratios for different types of tourism business showed slightly different picture and thus stood at 0.3 (negative), 0.1, 0.1 and 0.001 for accommodation, travel agencies, adventure and other business respectively. As accommodation business (Hotels) are suffering with continuous loss, the government came up with a package to treat such industries as sick industry and provide the financing.

It had been really difficult to get the figure particularly for net profit. After several commitments not to disclose the names of the business enterprises, they supplied data, which are incorporated in the study. The study has largely relied on the data supplied by the respondents. There was not even a single mean to verify such data and test the reliability. Thus, it cautions for the elaborative interpretations.

Interest Coverage Ratio

Interest coverage ratio is widely used for the financing decision. It simply measures the debt servicing capacity of a firm. The ratio depicts the strength of the firm as 'how many times the interest charges are recovered by profits.' The formula for the ratio is as follows (Kishore, 2004: 16):

Interest Coverage Ratio = PBIDT / Interest

The low ratio is a danger signal that a firm is using excessive debt and does not have the ability to offer assured payment of interest to creditors. However, too high ratio may imply unused debt capacity (Singh, 2003: 141). Table 5.40 summarizes the distribution based on the type of tourism business enterprises.

Table: 5.40

Interest Coverage Ratio of Tourism Business Enterprises

Fiscal Year ending mid-July	Accommodation	Travel agency	Adventure	Others	Aggregate
2000	1.1	1.9	21.3	1.8	1.7
2001	1.1	0.8	28.5	1.0	1.6
2002	(0.4)	6.3	20.9	3.1	0.9
2003	0.3	5.8	26.5	2.5	0.8
2004	0.6	2.8	22.6	2.7	0.9
2005	0.2	2.7	24.9	3.1	0.8
Average	**0.5**	**3.4**	**24.1**	**2.4**	**1.1**

Source: Primary Survey, 2006

The interest coverage ratio of tourism business enterprises for the entire reviewed period stood at 1.1 times, on an average. The low ratio of 0.5 times of accommodation business can be attributed to lower profitability/loss situation. However, too high ratio (24.1 times) for the adventure business indicates unused debt capacity.

Debt Equity Ratio

Debt equity ratio reflects the relative claims of the outsiders and the owners against the assets of the business enterprises (Chandra, 1998: 24.4). This ratio alternatively indicates the relative proportion of long-term debt and equity in financing the assets of a firm (Singh, 2003: 138).

A high debt equity ratio magnifies profitability and that of low reflects a conservative structure making creditors safer but lesser profitability to firm (Singh, 2003: 138). The formula for the ratio is as follows (Chandra, 1998: 24.12):

Debt-Equity Ratio = Debt / Equity Capital

Table: 5.41 summarizes the ratio for different tourism business enterprises during the review period. The debt equity ratio of tourism business enterprises for the review period stood at 1.7 on an average.

Table: 5.41

Debt Equity Ratio of Tourism Business Enterprises

Fiscal Year ending mid-July	Accommodation	Travel agency	Adventure	Others	Aggregate
2000	1.9	3.1	1.4	1.7	1.9
2001	1.3	2.8	1.9	1.6	1.4
2002	1.2	3.0	1.2	0.8	1.2
2003	1.7	3.1	0.9	1.0	1.7
2004	1.9	3.9	0.8	0.7	1.9
2005	1.9	4.4	0.7	1.0	1.8
Average	**1.7**	**3.4**	**1.2**	**1.1**	**1.7**

Source: Primary Survey, 2006

The distribution of the ratio for different types of tourism businesses has been slightly different. Thus, the ratio accounted for 1.7, 3.4, 1.2 and 1.1 for accommodation, travel agencies, adventure and other business respectively. Among these enterprises, the ratio for travel business stood at higher range followed by the accommodation business while that of adventure and other business stood at lower range.

The study attempts to link up and find out the relationship between the duration of business operation and capital structure of the surveyed tourism enterprises. It intends to find out whether the new tourism business enterprises (with few years of business operation) have different capital structure comparing with the old ones (with many years of business operation) or not employing the Karl Pearson's Correlation Coefficient method (refer Chapter – I for methodology). It simply tries to inquire about the debt equity ratio and duration of the business operation and their corresponding relation. From the calculation, the correlation coefficient is found to be 0.123. Therefore, it is to conclude that there is positive (but not strong) relationship between the duration of business operation and capital structure.

Debt to Total Assets

It measures the extent to which borrowed funds support the firm's assets (Chandra, 1998: 24.4). It also reflects the capacity of the enterprise to finance the total assets by the use of debt capital. The formula for the ratio is as follows (Chandra, 1998: 24.4):

Debt to Total Assets Ratio = Debt / Total Assets

Table 5.42 summarizes the distribution based on the type of tourism business enterprises. The debt to total assets ratio of tourism business enterprises for the review period stood at 0.5:1 on an average. The average ratio for the review period of accommodation and adventure business was 0.6 and 0.4 respectively while that for both of travel agencies and other business was 0.4 during the review period.

Table: 5.42

Debt to Total Assets Ratio of Tourism Business Enterprises

Fiscal Year ending mid-July	Accommodation	Travel agency	Adventure	Others	Aggregate
2000	**0.62**	0.43	**0.24**	0.39	**0.57**
2001	**0.54**	0.43	**0.34**	0.58	**0.53**
2002	**0.57**	0.40	**0.31**	0.36	**0.53**
2003	**0.50**	0.42	**0.22**	0.47	**0.49**
2004	**0.58**	0.43	**0.15**	0.40	**0.56**
2005	**0.58**	0.43	**0.15**	0.48	**0.56**
Average	0.6	0.4	0.2	0.4	0.5

Source: Primary Survey, 2006

Proprietorship Ratios

Proprietorship ratio expresses the relationship between net worth and total capital employed (Kishore, 2004: 16). It shows the proportion of the total funds that the shareholder of the business has provided as well as the proportion that the outside parties have provided.

Potential investors and lenders are interested in this ratio, because they may wish to see the owners of the business owning a large proportion of the assets. It can indicate about the owners' commitment to their business, on one hand and influence the decisions of potential investors for the investment on the other (Whitehouse and Tilley, 1993: 48-49). The formula for the ratio is as follows (Whitehouse and Tilley, 1993: 49):

Proprietorship Ratio = Shareholders Fund / Total Capital Employed.

Table 5.43 summarizes the result of the ratio analysis. The average proprietorship ratio for adventure and other business stood high (32.6 percent and 44.9 percent) compared to 18.4 percent of accommodation business during the review period. However, the ratio for travel business stood in a tune of 17.9 percent while that of tourism business enterprises, in aggregate stood at 20.1 percent during the review period.

Table: 5.43
Proprietorship Ratio of Tourism Business Enterprises (Percent)

Fiscal Year ending mid-July	Accommodation	Travel agency	Adventure	Others	Aggregate
2000	22.1	16.0	23.8	26.0	22.3
2001	27.2	12.8	29.3	38.3	27.7
2002	25.4	10.4	39.2	44.5	26.9
2003	16.9	12.2	38.5	48.1	18.4
2004	11.6	26.8	29.7	60.8	14.5
2005	7.4	29.2	35.2	51.7	10.8
Average	**18.4**	**17.9**	**32.6**	**44.9**	**20.1**

Source: Primary Survey, 2006

Current Ratio

The current ratio is also referred to as the working capital ratio and it gives an indication as to whether an organization has sufficient current assets. This means the assets, which can be converted into cash within a short period to cover those current liabilities that are due for payment either immediately or in the near future, usually over the next twelve months. This ratio is an indication of the organization's short-term financial strength (Whitehouse and Tilley, 1993: 43).

It generally measures the ability of the firm to meet its current liabilities (Chandra, 1998: 24.3). It also provides the liquidity status of the firm/enterprise and indicates the viability of the business. It can be calculated by dividing the current assets by the current liabilities thus the formula is as follows (Van Horne, 1995: 762):

Current Ratio = Current Assets / Current Liabilities.

Table: 5.44 is designed to provide the details of the current ratio during the review period. The analysis showed that travel agencies achieved the best current ratio of 2.1 on an average among the tourism business enterprises. Though the average current ratio of other tourism business stood at 6.2, it had a great variation during the review period.

Table: 5.44
Current Ratio of Tourism Business Enterprises

Fiscal Year ending mid-July	Accommodation	Travel agency	Adventure	Others	Aggregate
2000	1.1	2.0	0.2	0.1	0.9
2001	0.9	2.2	0.3	1.4	1.0
2002	0.8	1.7	0.6	1.2	0.9
2003	0.3	2.0	0.5	3.5	0.4
2004	0.3	2.4	0.8	15.1	0.5
2005	0.3	2.2	0.7	16.2	0.4
Average	**0.6**	**2.1**	**0.5**	**6.2**	**0.7**

Source: Primary Survey, 2006

The accommodation and adventure enterprises did not show an encouraging signs in terms of current ratio and so was the situation with surveyed tourism business enterprises, in aggregate. The response pattern of one big company is attributable for such high ratio for other business during the fiscal Year 2003/04 and 2004/05. Similarly, the basic reason behind the low ratio for the accommodation business is slow down in sales revenue and resultant decrease in current assets.

Current Assets Turnover

Turnover ratios generally measure the efficiency of the firm in the employment of the resources (Kishore, 2004: 21) whereas the current asset turnover measures the role of the current assets for the generation of the sales amount. The formula for the ratio is as follows (Pandey, 2005:528):

Current Assets Turnover = Sales / Current Assets

The analysis showed that travel agencies could not maintain the satisfactory current assets turnover ratio and thus stood at 0.8:1 on an average. In fact, other tourism business tamed the apex position with 10.1:1, on an average. Similarly, the average ratio during the review period for adventure and accommodation enterprises stood at 4.0 and 2.2 respectively. The aggregate ratio for the surveyed tourism business enterprises stood at 2.2:1, in aggregate.

Table: 5.45
Current Assets Turnover Ratio of Tourism Business Enterprises

Fiscal Year ending mid-July	Accommodation	Travel agency	Adventure	Others	Aggregate
2000	2.82	0.86	9.53	30.54	2.90
2001	2.93	0.67	5.81	8.43	2.73
2002	2.29	0.67	2.42	5.02	2.09
2003	1.86	0.84	3.08	5.92	1.93
2004	2.04	0.99	1.10	4.41	1.97
2005	1.01	0.77	1.94	6.29	1.57
Average	2.2	0.8	4.0	10.1	2.2

Source: Primary Survey, 2006

Fixed Assets Turnover

As the fixed asset turnover measures the role of the fixed assets for the generation of the sales amount. It measures the efficiency of the business enterprises too. The formula for the ratio is as follows (Pandey, 2005:527):

Fixed Assets Turnover = Sales / Net fixed assets

The highest fixed assets turnover ratio of the travel business during the review period indicated overtrading of total assets whereas the lowest ratio of 0.3 of accommodation business indicated the idle capacity of total assets during the review period. The ratio for the adventure and other business stood also in lower range with 0.8 and 1.6 times respectively.

However, the ratio for the surveyed tourism business enterprises in aggregate has been low with 0.4 times on an average for the review period.

Table: 5.46

Fixed Assets Turnover Ratio of Tourism Business Enterprises

Fiscal Year ending mid-July	Accommodation	Travel agency	Adventure	Others	Aggregate
2000	0.64	5.26	0.90	0.85	0.72
2001	0.56	8.16	0.88	0.88	0.64
2002	0.34	9.81	0.55	1.03	0.45
2003	0.19	13.26	0.79	1.28	0.27
2004	0.23	13.16	0.83	2.70	0.33
2005	0.12	10.36	1.00	2.83	0.27
Average	0.3	10.0	0.8	1.6	0.4

Source: Primary Survey, 2006

Working Capital Turnover

Working capital turnover ratio simply indicates the extent of working capital turned over in achieving sales of the firm (Kishore, 2004: 21). It also measures the efficiency of the business enterprises. The formula for the ratio is as follows (Pandey, 2005:528):

Net current assets turnover = Sales / Working capital

Working capital turnover ratio for the surveyed tourism business enterprises in aggregate has been high with 21.5 times on an average for the review period. The highest working capital turnover ratio (12.7 times) of other business during the review period indicated an extensive usage of working capital whereas the lowest ratio of 3.0 (negative) of adventure business indicated did not only indicate the inability in achieving sales but also the shortage of working capital during the review period. The ratio for the accommodation and travel business stood also in lower range with 0.04 and 1.6 times respectively.

Table: 5.47

Working Capital Turnover Ratio of Tourism Business Enterprises

Fiscal Year ending mid-July	Accommodation	Travel agency	Adventure	Others	Aggregate
2000	35.25	1.71	(1.77)	(2.89)	(36.42)
2001	(25.21)	1.24	(3.04)	29.23	193.28
2002	(7.63)	1.65	(3.34)	29.89	(23.83)
2003	(0.73)	1.73	(2.84)	8.32	(1.14)
2004	(1.02)	1.70	(3.47)	4.72	(1.74)
2005	(0.44)	1.39	(3.74)	6.71	(1.20)
Average	0.04	1.6	(3.0)	12.7	21.5

Source: Primary Survey, 2006

174 *Opportunities and Challenges of Tourism Financing*

5.9 RESPONSE ON INDICATORS OF TOURISM FINANCING

A. RAISING THE SHARE CAPITAL

During the survey, tourism business enterprises were asked to furnish the information related to the raising of further equity capital in their business during the review period. The result is summarized in Table: 5.48.

Table: 5.48

Response on Raising Equity Capital

Response	Frequency	Percent
Response Available	57	47.5
Response Not Available	63	52.5
Total Respondents	120	100

Source: Primary Survey, 2006

The table clearly indicated that 47.5 percent of respondents had provided the information related to the raising of further equity capital. The question was designed to find out the practice of equity financing particularly during the review period.

Table: 5.49

Easy to Raise Equity Capital

Response	Frequency	Percent
Yes	40	33.3
No	17	14.2
To Some Extent	6	5.0
No Comment	57	47.5
Total	120	100.0

Source: Primary Survey, 2006

Further, to find out the effectiveness of equity capital financing, the tourism business enterprises were asked to furnish the information related to the easiness in the raising of capital. The response is summarized in Table: 5.46. The majority of the tourism business enterprises i.e. 33.3 percent responded that it was easy to raise the share capital in contrast to 14.2 percent enterprises with opposite view. Further, 5.0 percent respondents felt that raising capital was easy to some extent only. However, 47.5 percent enterprises did not provide any comment in this connection.

B. GETTING THE LOAN

The survey is intended to find out the information related to the acquisition of the loan (borrowing). The effectiveness of financing should show that the acquisition of debt is feasible for the tourism business enterprises. Table: 5.50 is designed to provide the response related to the loan financing during the review period.

Table 5.50

Raising Debt Capital (Borrowing)

Response	Frequency	Percent
Available	70	58.3
Not Available	50	41.7
Total	120	100

Source: Primary Survey, 2006

The table clearly indicated that 58.3 percent respondents had provided the response related to the raising debt capital (borrowing or loan from the banks and financial institutions).

Further, to find out the effectiveness of debt (loan) financing, the tourism business enterprises were asked to furnish the information related to the easiness in the raising of loan in the business. Table: 5.51 summarizes the response. The majority of the tourism business enterprises i.e. 40.8 percent responded that it was easy to raise the loan. It was followed by 39.4 respondents viewing it, as it had been easy to some extent only. In contrast, 19.7 percent enterprises responded that it was not easy to raise the loans from the banks and financial institutions.

Table: 5.51

Easy to Get the Borrowing

Response	Frequency	Percent
Yes	29	40.8
No	14	19.7
To some extent	28	39.4
Total	71	100

Source: Primary Survey, 2006

Further another question was designed to find out whether these tourism business enterprises had received the loan as per their application i.e. demand for the loan financing. Table: 5.52 is designed to summarize the result.

Table: 5.52

Received the Loan as Proposed

Response	Frequency	Percent
Yes	25	35.2
No	46	64.8
Total	71	100

Source: Primary Survey, 2006

The majority of the tourism business enterprises i.e. 64.8 percent did not receive the loan as they had proposed. There could be many reasons behind such response; one of them could be overall performance of the tourism sector in recent years. The banks and financial institution became more conscious and conservative during the credit analysis and disbursement.

C. UTILIZATION AND IMPACT OF BORROWING

Further, another inquiry was undertaken to find out the response from the surveyed tourism business enterprises about the utilization of the loan (borrowing). The result is summarized in Table: 5.53.

Table: 5.53

Utilization of the Loan (Borrowing)

Response	Frequency	Percent
Yes	58	87.9
No	5	7.6
To some extent	3	4.5
Total	66	100

Source: Primary Survey, 2006

Thus, the response showed that an overwhelming majority (87.9 percent) of the enterprises had utilized the loan. Further, 4.5 percent of the respondents had utilized the loan to some extent only. However, very few (7.6 percent) replied that they could not utilize the loan.

The survey intended to find out the information related to the impact of the loan (borrowing). It may be the important financing indicator for the tourism business enterprises. Table: 5.54 presents the response related to the impact loan financing during the review period.

Table: 5.54

Impact of the Loan (Borrowing)

Response	Frequency	Percent
Excellent	7	12.3
Average	50	87.7
Total	57	100

Source: Primary Survey, 2006

The table depicts the overall impact of the loan (borrowing from the banks and financial institutions) had been average for an overwhelmingly majority of respondents (87.7 percent) while it has excellent for just 12.3 percent respondents. Only 57 tourism business enterprises provided the comment on the impact of loan.

D. PROJECT DROP OUT

During the survey of tourism business enterprises, an attempt was made to find out the project drop out in the past. They were asked to furnish the information related to the project drop out and the reasons for such drop out. Table: 5.55 and Table: 5.56 summarize the results related to the projects drop out.

Table: 5.55

Project Drop out

Response	Frequency	Percent
Yes	22	18.3
No	98	81.7
Total	120	100

Source: Primary Survey, 2006

Table: 5.55 showed that there were only 18.3 percent respondents that report about the project drop outs during the review period. As such, the majority of the tourism business enterprises had no project drop outs. It simply indicated that they were efficient in planning and implementing the projects and did not face any difficulties. However, it could not provide any assurance that there were no problems in project implementation.

Further, Table: 5.56 provides the year of project dropout. The response showed there had been many project drop out in the fiscal year 2000/01 with 22.7 percent in total distribution. It is followed by 18.2 percent in both F.Y. 2001/02 and 2003/04. Interestingly, there have been equal project drop outs (13.6 percent) in the fiscal year 1998/99, 1999/00 and 2002/03.

Table: 5.56

Number of Project Drop out during the Review Period

	Frequency	Percent
1999	3	13.6
2000	3	13.6
2001	5	22.7
2002	4	18.2
2003	3	13.6
2004	4	18.2
Total	22	100

Source: Primary Survey, 2006

There could be many reasons for such drop outs. Some reasons can be basic or primary and others can be secondary. Figure: 5.5 depicts the reasons for the project drop out during the period under study. The major reason for the drop out was related to the Strike and Bandha. It is a political problem and creates many hindrances for the growth and development of almost every sectors of economy. Other reasons for the project drop out are general ranging from the slow down in the business, deteriorating law and order situation to lack of government initiation.

During the survey, many respondents were complaining about the Maoist insurgency and deteriorating law and order situation inside the country and regional and international situation for the slow down of the tourism business outside the country. However, they did not provide detail information in the questionnaire (response).

Figure: 5.5

Reasons for Project Drop Outs

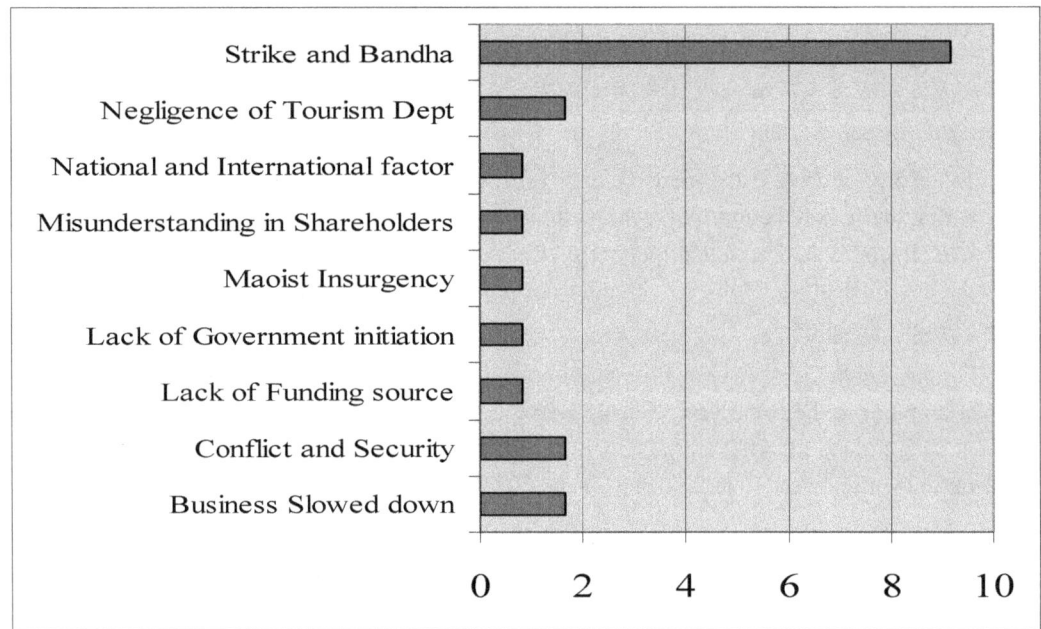

Source: Primary Survey, 2006

E. TIME AND COST OVER-RUNS

The survey also attempted to find out frequency of time and cost over-runs of the projects during the review period. The tourism business enterprises were asked to furnish the information with underlining reasons for such over-runs.

Table: 5.57

Time and Cost Over-Runs

	Time over-run		Cost Over-run		Both Time and cost Over-run	
	Frequency	Percent	Frequency	Percent	Frequency	Percent
Yes	15	12.5	10	8.3	11	9.2
No	91	75.8	95	79.2	94	78.3
No Comment	14	11.7	15	12.5	15	12.5
Total	120	100.0	120	100.0	120	100.0

Source: Primary Survey, 2006

Table: 5.57 summarizes the responses about the time over-run, cost over-run or both the time and cost over-runs during the review period. There were 12.5 percent respondents having the time over-run, 8.3 percent respondents having the cost over-run and 9.2 percent respondents having both time and cost over-runs. The distribution also showed that the majority of the tourism business enterprises did not have such time and cost over-runs during the period under study.

Further, Table: 5.58 provides the year of time and cost over-run of their project. The majority of the respondents (74.2 percent) did not provide the comment on the time and cost over-runs during the review period.

Table: 5.58

Year of Time and Cost Over-run

Year ending mid-July	Frequency	Percent
1998	1	0.8
1999	2	1.7
2000-2005	4	3.3
2000	6	5.0
2001 - 2004	5	4.2
2001	2	1.7
2002	5	4.2
2003	3	2.5
2004	2	1.7
2005	1	0.8
No Comment	89	74.2
Total	120	100.0

Source: Primary Survey, 2006

However, the response showed that there had been many time and cost over-runs in Fiscal Year 1999/2000 whereas very few in 2004/05.

Table: 5.59 depicts the reasons for the time and cost over-runs during the period under study. The major reason for the time and cost over-runs was related to the national and international factor. National factors basically, contained Strike and Bandha whereas international factors contained terrorism and natural calamities. Other reasons for the time and cost over-runs were general ranging from the legal and banking processing to cash shortages and security problems.

Table: 5.59

Reason for Time and Cost Over-Run

Reasons	Frequency	Percent
Cash shortage	3	2.5
Legal processing for the guarantee	3	2.5
National and International factors	11	9.2
Banking processing	6	5.0
Security situation	5	4.2
Slow Processing and Poor Response	3	2.5
No Comment	89	74.2
Total	120	100.0

Source: Primary Survey, 2006

5.10 BORROWING NEED AND PROSPECTS OF TOURISM FINANCING

As the size of the business grows own funds as well as the loans from friends and relatives would be insufficient. Borrowing appears to be an endurable source of financing whether to increase the production; promote the market or to exploit emerging opportunities. In some cases such as in seasonal production, expansion of the business or promotion of the products and services borrowing becomes desirable. However, in other cases such as in the liquidity crunch, debt servicing and cutthroat competition, it becomes unavoidable/inevitable.

In this section, an attempt is made to determine the prospects of tourism financing from the survey finding on business prospects and borrowing need of the tourism business enterprises. Therefore, this section largely employs the data generated from the field survey through the structured questionnaire.

A.   EXISTENCE OF OTHER BUSINESS RELATED TO TOURISM

During the survey, it was tried to find out the exposure of other business related to tourism because it indicates the business prospects of the companies. It also hints about the need for borrowing or financing. Table: 5.60 summarizes the result of the survey.

The majority of the surveyed tourism business enterprises were found to be largely engaged in their core business activities because 64.2 percent respondents did not have other business related to tourism. The survey also showed that about 35.8 percent of the tourism business enterprises have other business related to tourism.

Table: 5.60

Enterprises having other Business Related to Tourism

Response	Frequency	Percent
Yes	43	35.8
No	77	64.2
Total	120	100

Source: Primary Survey, 2006

Another question may arise naturally about the types of business they were engaged in or dealing over the years. Table: 5.61 summarizes the result about the type of business related to the tourism.

Table: 5.61

Types of Other Business Related to Tourism

Response	Frequency	Percent
No other Business	79	65.8
Booking Facility	6	5.0
Export Business	1	0.8
Other related facilities	14	11.7
Reservation Services	6	5.0
Sister Concern	14	11.7
Total	120	100.0

Source: Primary Survey, 2006

The companies both providing other related facilities for the tourist and having sister concerns stood to be major with 11.7 percent share in total response. They are followed by the companies having both the booking facilities and reservation services with 5.0 percent share in total distribution. However, there is only one company which has an export business related to the tourism business holding just minor 0.8 percent share.

B. BUSINESS AGREEMENTS (TSA OR FRANCHISE)

The business agreement of the enterprises with related business inside and outside the country provides a continuous support for the marketing and operation of the services. The business agreement can be of various types ranging from simple agreement to Technical and Service Agreement. The franchising is also taken as a kind of business agreement. Table: 5.62 is designed to provide the status of the business agreement of the tourism business enterprises during the review period whereas Table: 5.63 provides the details of the business agreements.

Table: 5.62

Business Agreements (TSA or Franchise)

Response	Frequency	Percent
Yes	36	30.0
No	84	70.0
Total	120	100.0

Source: Primary Survey, 2006

Out of the total respondents, the majority of the tourism business enterprises did not have the business agreements in this way or the other. In other words, only 30.0 percent of the respondents had engaged in business agreements.

Table: 5.63

Details of Business Agreement (Franchise or TSA)

Response	Frequency	Percent
No Agreement	84	70.0
Business Agreement	15	12.5
GSA	8	6.7
GSA, PSA	4	3.3
PSA	6	5.0
Stockist	3	2.5
Total	120	100.0

Source: Primary Survey, 2006

Out of the total tourism business enterprises (respondents), only 36 provided the details of the business agreements. Out of such response, the majority of the enterprises i.e. 15 in number had business Agreement (including technical and service agreement). There are 6.7 percent and 5.0 percent respondents with GSA status (General Sales Agent) and or PSA status (Passenger Sales Agent) respectively. There are 3.3 percent respondents having both the agreements of GSA and PSA. Only 2.5 percent of the respondents had enjoyed the status of stockist during the review period.

C. PROPOSED INVESTMENT OF TOURISM BUSINESS ENTERPRISES

During the survey, an attempt has been undertaken to find out demand of financing in terms of proposed investment in near future. The detail of the proposed investment essentially discloses the additional investment of the tourism business enterprises. The proposed investment is the financing in addition to the financing in normal course of the business operation.

The following section attempts to find out the purposes of the proposed investment, amount of proposed investment and financial planning to acquire the proposed amount. Table: 5.64 summarizes the aims of the proposed investment.

Table: 5.64

Purpose of Proposed Investment

	Frequency	Percent
No Propose Investment	89	74.2
Business Promotion	4	3.3
Purchase or Increase Stock	5	4.2
To aid in construction	3	2.5
To Expand the Business	5	4.2
To open sister concern	2	1.7
To Purchase Equipments	12	10.0
Total	120	100.0

Source: Primary Survey, 2006

From the analysis, it is seen that though majority of the tourism business enterprises did not have an immediate planning of further investment, they have shown great interest to resume the emerging changes with further investment given the improvement in law and order situation and economic activities.

Only 25.8 percent of the respondents have disclosed the details of the further investment. The majority of respondents i.e. 10.0 percent want to purchase the equipments in near future. Businesses looking forward to either purchase or increase the stock of the ticket and to expand the business registered 4.2 percent share. Other purposes hold minor position in the total distribution, as such 3.3 percent, 2.5 percent to promote the business and to aid the construction respectively. Remaining 1.9 percent of the respondents showed the interest to open a sister concern in near future.

Similarly, Table: 5.65 summarizes the amount of the proposed investment of tourism business enterprises in near future.

The majority of the tourism business enterprises (19.1 percent) have a plan to spend the amount in between Rs. 801 to 1000 thousand. Similarly, 17 percent respondents have a plan to spend Rs 2001 thousand and more. The respondents with an intention to invest in between Rs. 201 to 400 thousand, 601 to 800 thousand and 1801 to 2000 thousand hold same share (4.3 percent) whereas the respondents to invest in between Rs. 1400 to 1600 thousand hold just 2.1 percent share. However, there is no tourism business having the proposed investment in between Rs. 1001 to 1200 and 1201 to 1400 thousand. To be more specific, 27.7 percent respondents did not mention the amount of the proposed investment.

The proportion of proposed investment in total assets of the business indicates the relative size of investment. Thus, it is better to compute the proportion than just to mention the absolute figures. Here, out of 47 tourism businesses that disclosed the information related to the amount of proposed investment, only 34 respondents have supplied the amount of proposed investment. Further, amongst these, two respondents did not supply the balance sheet details hence the analysis is only for the 32 respondents. Out of this, 8 respondents have proposed investment plan more than their existing asset. This ranges from one time to 8 times of their total assets. Similarly, other 4 respondents have the investment more than 50 percent and remaining 20 have less than less than 50 percent of their existing assets.

Table: 5.65

Amount of Proposed Investment (In '000 Rs)

Class	Frequency	Percent
Rs. 200 and Below	5	10.6
201 - 400	2	4.3
401 - 600	5	10.6
601 - 800	2	4.3
801 - 1000	9	19.1
1001 - 1200	0	0.0
1201 - 1400	0	0.0
1401 - 1600	1	2.1
1801 - 2000	2	4.3
2001 and Above (up to Rs. 10000)	8	17.0
Amount Not Mentioned	13	27.7
Total Response	47	100.0
Percent in Grand Total		**36.2**
No Response	73	60.8
Total Business Enterprises	**120**	**100.0**

Source: Primary Survey, 2006

The discussion continues to find out the financial planning for the proposed investment of tourism business enterprises in near future. Table: 5.66 attempts to disclose such information. Only 35 have furnished the information about the financial planning for the proposed project(s).

The majority of the tourism business enterprises have planned to acquire the funding from the combination of various sources. Thus, 21.3 percent of the respondent would raise the financial resources from internal funds, equity by promoters and loans from the banks and financial institutions.

It is followed by the 17.0 percent of the businesses enterprises who look forward to mobilize equity financing and loan from banks and financial institutions. There is a small portion of the enterprises looking forward to generate the funds either from equity finance or from loan finance from banks and financial institutions.

Table: 5.66

Financial Planning for Proposed Project

Financial Sources	Frequency	Percent
Equity by promoter, Loan from Bank and FI	8	17.0
Equity by Promoters	1	2.1
Internal Fund	3	6.4
Internal fund and Loans from BFI	5	10.6
Internal fund, Equity by promoters and loans from Bank and Financial Institution	10	21.3
Internal fund, Loans from BFI, Equity Capital and Loan from Director	1	2.1
Loan from Bank and Financial Institutions	7	14.9
No Comment	12	25.5
Total	**47**	**100.0**

Source: Primary Survey, 2006

Further, the companies intending to raise the finance from internal fund and loan from BFI as well as from loans from banks and financial institutions accounted for 10.6 percent and 14.9 percent share respectively. However, 25.5 percent respondents did not provide the comment.

D. EMPLOYEES AND LABOUR RELATION

In fact, sound labour relation is desirable for the successful operation of the business enterprise and it definitely provides the prospects of financing. It is essential in tourism business because it is a service industry. Tourism is rightly named as hospitality industry simply describing the importance of the human resources in the business operation.

An attempt was undertaken in order to find out the labour relation in the surveyed tourism business enterprises. Thus, the following sections attempt first to find out the size of employees and second to find out the labour relation in the business.

There were 36 tourism business enterprises having less than 10 employees. They had 30.0 percent share in total distribution. The enterprises having employees in between 11 to 20 are in the second position with 27.5 percent share. It also showed that most of the tourism business enterprises are small size companies having less than 30 employees (71.7 percent).

However, there are 15 business enterprises having more than 71 employees. These enterprises are hotels, resorts and airlines. They have assumed 12.5 percent share in total. Other enterprises (19) having employees in between 31 and 70 altogether are in minor position with 15.8 percent share.

Further, in order to compare the types and ownership pattern of tourism business with the number of employees, Table: 5.68 is designed. The table also provides the information about the average sales and average asset per employee for surveyed enterprises. Accommodation, travel, adventure and other business, on an average have 74.1, 10.5, 15.9 and 30.5 employees whereas proprietorship and partnership firms, private and public limited companies have 14.7, 16.6, 33.1 and 380 employees respectively.

Table: 5.67

Number of Employees in the Tourism Business

Class	Frequency	Percent
Below 10	36	30
11 - 20	33	27.5
21 - 30	17	14.2
31 - 40	9	7.5
41 – 50	5	4.2
51 - 60	4	3.3
61 - 70	1	0.8
71 and Above (Up to 422)	15	12.5
Total	120	100

Source: Primary Survey, 2006

The average sales per employee stood to be highest of Rs. 532.3 thousand for travel agency and lowest of Rs. 112.2 thousand for adventure business whereas it stood Rs. 122.2 thousand and Rs. 525.0 thousand for accommodation and other business respectively. However, the accommodation business stood at the top in terms of average assets per employee with Rs. 734.7 thousand followed by travel agency and other business with Rs. 699.5 thousand and 377.9 thousand respectively. The ratio stood at the bottom with Rs. 144.8 thousand for adventure business.

Table: 5.68

Average Number of Employees and Ratio

(Rs. In '000)

Particulars	No. of Employee (Average)	Sales/Employee (Average) Rs.	Total Assets/ Employee (Average) Rs.
On the Basis of Type of Business			
Accommodation	74.1	122.2	734.7
Travel agency	10.5	532.3	699.5
Adventure	15.9	112.2	144.8
Others	30.5	525.0	377.9
On the Basis of Ownership of Business			
Proprietorship	14.7	91.0	144.6
Partnership	16.6	84.2	216.8
Private Limited	33.1	278.8	479.9
Public Limited	380.0	730.8	4570.2
Aggregate	**38.3**	**251.9**	**521.7**

Source: Primary Survey, 2006 and calculation

The average sales and average asset per employee based on ownership pattern showed an interesting picture. In fact, as the ownership pattern moves from proprietorship firm to partnership firm, private limited company and finally to public limited company, the ratio increases significantly in both the cases. Thus, these ratios stood at the highest with Rs. 730.8 and Rs. 4570.2 thousand for public limited companies whereas stood at the lowest with Rs. 91.0 thousand and Rs. 144.6 thousand for proprietorship firms respectively. Further, partnership firms and private limited companies recorded average sales of Rs. 84.2 thousand and Rs. 278.8 thousand compared to the average asset of 216.8 thousand and Rs. 479.9 thousand respectively.

The survey also attempted to find out the existence of the trade union in the tourism business enterprises. The existence of trade union unites the employees and empowers them. It does not necessarily ensure the sound labour relation in the companies. There can be various determinants of the sound labour relation, which is beyond the scope of the present discussion. However, the labour relation also indicates the prospects of the business.

Table: 5.69 simply summarizes existence of trade union and prevailing status of the labour relation in surveyed tourism business enterprises. The majority of the tourism business enterprises (82.5 percent) do not have registered (formal) trade union. However, there are only 17.5 percent companies having trade union.

Table: 5.69

Existence of Trade Union and Labour Relation

Existence of Trade Union	Labour Relation in a Company			Total
	Excellent	Average	Very Poor	
Yes (Frequency)	8	13		21
Percentage in Total	**6.7**	**10.8**		**17.5**
No (Frequency)	63	35	1	99
Percentage in Total	**52.5**	**29.2**	**0.8**	**82.5**
Total (Frequency)	71	48	1	120
Percentage in Total	**59.2**	**40.0**	**0.8**	**100.0**

Source: Primary Survey, 2006

The majority of tourism business enterprises (59.2 percent) have an excellent labour relation. The companies having average labour relation with 40.0 percent follow it. However, there was only one company (0.8 percent) having very poor labour relation among the surveyed enterprises.

In order to find out the association between the existence of trade union and labour relation Phi-Coefficient is undertaken. Here, it is assigned Yes (1) for an excellent labour relation and No (0) for both - an average and very poor. The 'Yes' for existence of trade union is compared with 'Yes' or 'No' for the labour relation. The calculated value of the Phi-Coefficient (4.66) is more than the tabulated value (3.84, df. = 1) at 5 percent level of significance. Therefore, it is clear that there is a significant relationship between the existence of trade union and sound labour relation (excellent).

188 Opportunities and Challenges of Tourism Financing

E. LACKS OR PROBLEMS FOR THE BUSINESS

During the survey, an attempt has been particularly made to find out the major problems that these tourism business enterprises are facing in their business operation. In fact, these factors are related to the infrastructure and products of the tourism industry and provide indication for the requirement of further financing.

Further, during the survey the respondents were also asked to rank the problems if they choose more than one problem. While analyzing such factors, the study will incorporate the intensity of the problem on one hand show the further need of financing (both equity and borrowing) on the other. Table: 5.70 provides the detail of the response and ranking provided by the surveyed tourism business enterprises. In fact, majority of the respondents though have provided the information they have not provided the ranking for all the factors.

Table: 5.70
Lacks or Problems

	Rank 1	Rank 2	Rank 3	Rank 4	Rank 5	Rank 6	Total*
Lack of Promotion Budget	45	18	7		2		72
Lack of New Product	7	16	1	3			27
Insufficient Infrastructure	16	31	17	2			66
Lack of Quality Product	1	5	11	12	3		32
Lack of Trained HRs	3	3	9	5	9	3	32
Strike and Bandha	7	3	12	6		6	34

Note: * Refers to the number of respondents.
Source: Primary Survey, 2006

In fact, it has been clear that these factors have been the major problems for the surveyed tourism business enterprises. Lack of promotion budget stood as a major problem because the highest number of respondents (45) provided the first ranking followed by 18 respondents with second ranking. Further, insufficient infrastructure received the second ranking because a large number of respondents, 31 (plus 16 others that provided the first ranking).

F. HINDERING FACTORS

During the survey, tourism business enterprises were asked to furnish the information related to the factors that hinder the growth or the development of the business. Table: 5.71 summarizes the response.

Table: 5.71
Comments on Hindering Factors

Response	Frequency	Percent
Hinder the development	75	62.5
Do not Hinder development	2	1.7
No Comment	29	24.2
Hinder to some extent	14	11.7
Total	120	100

Source: Primary Survey, 2006

Majority of the tourism business enterprises clearly provided the response to the hindering factors for the development and growth of the business. In fact, 62.5 percent enterprises felt that such factors hinder the growth of the business strongly whereas 11.7 percent felt that impact would be to some extent only. However, 24.2 percent respondents did not provide any comment on the question and only 1.7 felt that the factors do not hinder the growth of the business.

Further, the business enterprises were asked to furnish the information related to the factors that hinder the growth and impact in 5-point rating scale. The response thus collected is summarized in Table: 5.72 as follows.

The cost of land and rent seemed to be a major hindering factor for the growth of the business with a response of about 41.0 percent. In fact, it has been affecting over the period as it was confirmed by 72 out of 83 respondents.

The credit facility seemed to be less strong to hinder the growth of the business with 29.4 percent respondents viewing a large effect in contrast to the 22.4 percent respondents viewing no effect at all.

Table: 5.72
Hindering Factors for the Development of Business

	Significantly	Largely	Fairly	Poorly	Not at all	Total
Cost of Land and Rent						
No. of Agencies	34	29	8	1	11	83
Percentage	41.0	34.9	9.6	1.2	13.3	100.0
Credit Facility						
No. of Agencies	19	25	15	7	19	85
Percentage	22.4	29.4	17.6	8.2	22.4	100.0
Community Attitude						
No. of Agencies	7	10	12	7	44	80
Percentage	8.8	12.5	15.0	8.8	55.0	100.0
Related Service Facilities						
No. of Agencies	13	25	32	5	13	88
Percentage	14.8	28.4	36.4	5.7	14.8	100.0

Source: Primary Survey, 2006

The community attitude did not appear to be a strong hindering factor. The majority of the enterprises (55.0 percent) did not view the community attitude as a hindering factor for the growth and development of the business.

However, the availability of the related service facilities appeared to be strong hindering factor. In fact, the majority (85.2 percent) of the tourism business enterprises viewed the effect at various levels while leaving just 14.8 percent respondents aside.

In order to map out the intensity of hindering factors, Chi-square (χ^2) Test is undertaken. In other words, the test is applied to find whether the hindrance is equally appealing to the respondents or not. The analysis is undertaken separately for four factors viz. credit facility, related service facility, cost of land/rent and community attitude. Thus, it is hypothesized (usually referred as null hypothesis) that the level of hindrance is equally distributed in each factor i.e. A:B:C:D:E = 1:1:1:1:1. Table: 5.71 summarizes the result of calculations for the test statistics.

Table: 5.73

Results of Test Statistics on Hindering Factors

Test Statistics	Credit Facility	Related Service Facilities	Land and Rent	Community Attitude
Chi-Square	10.35*	26.32*	48.51*	62.38*
Mean	2.79	2.77	2.11	3.89
Standard Deviation	1.46	1.22	1.33	1.41
Tabulated Value (d.f.= 4) at 5 percent level of Significance				9.49

Note: The symbol '*' denotes the result is significant at 5 percent level of Significance

Since, the computed value χ^2 in all the cases is greater than the critical value (9.49) at 5 percent level of significance, the assumption is rejected and concluded that the level of hindrance is not equally distributed (A:B:C:D:E ≠ 1:1:1:1:1). Thus, on the basis of the data, it can be concluded that the intensity of the hindrance within a particular factor differs significantly with the distribution. Further, it also means that the intensity is not uniformly distributed in the population.

G. FACTORS FOR THE DEVELOPMENT OF BUSINESS

Similarly, the business enterprises were asked to provide the rating for the factors that have direct linkage in the growth and development of the business. The rating was designed in 5-point rating scale. The response thus collected is summarized in Table: 5.74 as follows.

The majority of the tourism business enterprises confirmed that there exists a strong business prospect. In fact, 34.3 percent viewed the effect largely followed by 27.6 percent fairly and 18.1 percent strongly. However, only 13.3 percent viewed the effect poorly and 6.7 percent viewed no effect at all.

The availability of the funds also became the hindering factor but in lesser degree with 48.4 percent respondents viewing the effect fairly. There were very few enterprises to confirm that the factor did not hinder the growth.

There has been a sharp competition among tourism business in recent years. The response did support the assumption. The majority of the tourism business enterprises confirmed that there exists a strong competition. In fact, 54.7 percent viewed the significant effect followed by 34.0 percent with large effect and 8.5 percent that of fair. However, only 1.9 percent viewed the effect poorly and 0.9 percent viewed no effect at all.

Table: 5.74

Rating of the Factors for the Development of Business

	Significantly	Largely	Fairly	Poorly	Not at all	Total
Business Prospects						
No. of Agencies	19	36	29	14	7	105
Percentage	18.1	34.3	27.6	13.3	6.7	100.0
Availability of funds						
No. of Agencies	6	26	46	13	4	95
Percentage	6.3	27.4	48.4	13.7	4.2	100.0
Level of Competition						
No. of Agencies	58	36	9	2	1	106
Percentage	54.7	34.0	8.5	1.9	0.9	100.0
Market Potential						
No. of Agencies	17	66	20	3	1	107
Percentage	15.9	61.7	18.7	2.8	0.9	100.0

Source: Primary Survey, 2006

In addition, the tourism business enterprises were asked to state the view for the market potential of the business. The majority (61.7 percent) viewed there is a large market potential followed by 15.9 percent and 18.7 percent viewing the significant and fair potential respectively.

In order to map out the intensity of factor in the development of the business, Chi-square (χ^2) Test is undertaken. In other words, in order to determine whether the intensity of the particular factor differs significantly with the distribution or not, the Test (χ^2) is undertaken. The analysis is undertaken for only one factor – Business Prospects related to the development of the business. Here, it is hypothesized that the level of rating (certainly of the sample) is equally distributed in the population i.e. A:B:C:D:E = 1:1:1:1:1.

Since, the computed value χ^2 (25.62) is greater than the critical value (9.49) at 5 percent level of significance, the assumption is rejected and concluded that the level of rating is not equally distributed (A:B:C:D:E ≠ 1:1:1:1:1). Therefore, the result indicates the difference in the intensity of the factor in the development of the business.

5.11 CONCLUSION

It has been crystal-clear that every enterprises need capital (financial resources) to operate the business and achieve the stipulated objectives. Tourism business enterprises cannot be the exceptions, they certainly need finance to establish and operate the business. They have to purchase the fixed assets, install them properly; purchase and manage raw materials for the production and hire the human resources to carry out activities ensuring the successful running of the organization.

The business enterprise needs to frame a sound financial policy ensuring the wise use of funds, on one hand incorporating a rational matching of short-term and long-term funds, on the other. In addition, it needs to determine the proportion of equity and debt. A business enterprise can mobilize various types of finance such as internal-external, formal-informal, domestic-foreign and commercial-non commercial. The basic source comprise equity share, debentures, borrowing (loans), advances, bill of exchange and venture capital though the proportion of various sources and selection highly depends upon the purpose and size of financing, cost of funds and time duration.

The financing pattern of surveyed tourism business enterprises (in aggregate) showed the gradual growth in all constituents of sources and uses of funds except in reserve and surplus. Accommodation business and private limited companies based on types of business and ownership pattern, had an overwhelmingly majority share in aggregate sources and uses of funds respectively.

The analysis (ANOVA) on the structure of financing based on the average amount considering the actual number of respondents for each and every item showed a significant variation among various types and ownerships of businesses during the analysis. However, the variations among the various types of business and ownership pattern stood significant in most of the cases just indicating the significant variations in the distribution among the business enterprises. Similarly, the t-Test as undertaken to find out the variations between two items of sources or uses of funds incorporating the data for the entire review period clearly showed a significant variations. It also showed significant variations in both the analysis (comprising common size statements and average amount by the actual respondents) and in both the cases based on the types and ownership pattern of the tourism business enterprises. Moreover, the result supported a priori notion of the difference between the distribution and among the business.

The analysis on the composition of financing showed almost a half portion for debt financing whereas remaining portion for equity and current asset financing. Further, debt financing registered a remarkable growth of 28 percent during the review period. Similarly, the analysis on structure of balance sheet showed majority share of fixed assets (79.8 percent on an average) on assets side and that of borrowing (51.3 percent, on an average) on liability side. There has been more than 1.6 fold increase in total assets and 1.7 fold in fixed assets over the period.

The operating performance of tourism business enterprises in terms of sales revenue showed 6.1 percent growth over the period. The growth remained variable for different business groups. 'Other business' registered remarkable growth followed by travel and adventure business against accommodation business registering a considerable decline. The ratio analysis indicated satisfactory position regarding debt equity ratio, turnover ratio and proprietorship ratio compared to current ratio, net profit to sales (profitability) and other ratio that require further analysis and concerns. However, tourism financing analysis based on the field survey provided a clear picture for different variables as discussed in the chapter; it certainly needs certain cautions to draw interpretations otherwise.

Further, the chapter also provided with some fundamental findings for the questions regarding adequacy of financing and the need of financing. In addition, it also incorporated the indicators of financing and assessed the effectiveness.

The analysis on average sales and average asset per employee based on ownership pattern showed an interesting picture. In fact, as the ownership pattern moves from proprietorship firm to partnership firm, private limited company and finally to public limited company, both the ratios increase significantly. However, the ratios based on the types of business showed a different picture with considerable variations between the variables and among the businesses. The Phi-Coefficient as undertaken to find out the association between the existence of trade union and labour relation clearly showed a significant relationship between the variables.

The result of the Chi-square (χ^2) Test simply proved the significant variations in the distribution and thus on the intensity of the hindering factor for the development of the business. It also proved that the factors were not equally appealing to the respondents and permitted to conclude that each type of the rating is not uniformly distributed in the population. In other words, the test showed a significant variation in the intensity of the hindrance within the particular factor and permitted to conclude that the level of hindrance is not uniformly distributed in the population.

Similarly, another analysis attempted to map out the level of intensity for a particular factor for the development of the business. The test is undertaken for Business Prospects in order to determine whether the intensity differs significantly with the distribution or not. The analysis showed a significant variation in the ratings and permitted to conclude that the level of hindrance is not equally distributed in the population. Further, it also indicates the significance of the factor in the development of the business.

The analysis examined the views of the respondents about the borrowing need prospects of further financing. It observed that there is ever growing borrowing need however it depends heavily upon the law and order situation and the growth of tourism business. It is felt that the tourism business enterprises are ready to lean more for further financing whenever they feel possible growth in tourism business.

REFERENCES

Bernstein, L.A. (1993). **Financial Statements Analysis**. USA: IRWIN

Chandra, Prasanna (1998). Fundamentals of Financial Management. New Delhi: Tata McGraw-Hill Publishing Company.

Gitman, Lawrence J. (2004). **Principles of Managerial Finance**. 10th Edition. Pearson Education, Inc.

Gupta, S. P. (2002). Statistical Methods. New Delhi: Sultan Chand and Company.

Hildebrand, David H. and R. Lyman Ott (1998). **Statistical Thinking for Managers**. Duxbury Press An International Thompson Publishing Company.

Kantawala, Amita S. (1996). **Management Accounting Techniques for Lending Decisions by Banks**. Baroda: M. S. University of Baroda.

Kishore, Ravi M. (2004). Financial Management. New Delhi: Taxmann Allied Services Pvt. Ltd.

Manjit Singh (2001). **Financial Organization and Working of State Tourism Development Corporations**: A Study of Punjab, Haryana and Himanchal Pradesh. A Ph. D. thesis submitted to the Faculty of Commerce and Business Management of Kuruchhetra University

MOCTCA (2005). **Nepal Tourism Statistics**. Kathmandu: Ministry of Culture, Tourism and Civil Aviation, Government of Nepal.

Pandey, I. M. (1999). **Financial Management.** New Delhi: Vikas Publishing House Private Limited.

Pandey, I. M. (2004). **Financial Management** 9th edition. New Delhi: Vikas Publishing House Private Limited.

Sharma, Anil (2006). **Tourism for Economic Development.** New Delhi: Maxford Books.

Siddiqui, S. A. and A. S. Siddiqui (2005). **Managerial Economics and Financial Analysis**. New Delhi: New Age International (P) Limited, Publishers.

Soloman, Ezra (1969). **The Theory of Financial Management**. Columbia University Press.

UNCTAD and ICC (2003) **An Investment Guide to Nepal: Opportunities and Conditions.** New York: United Nations.

Van Horne, James C (1995). Financial Management and Policy. New Delhi: Prentice Hall of India Private Limited

Whitehouse, Jan and Colin Tilley (1993). **Finance and Leisure: Leisure Management Series**. London: Financial Times, Pitman Publishing.

Witt, S. F.Y.; M. Z. Brooke; and P. Busklay (1997). **Finance and Control: The Management of International Tourism**. New York: Rutledge.

CHAPTER

TOURISM FINANCING: AN ANALYSIS OF RESPONDENTS FROM BANKS AND FINANCIAL INSTITUTIONS

6.1 INTRODUCTION

6.2 PROFILE OF THE RESPONDENTS (BFIs)
- Distribution of the Respondents
- Duration of Tourism Financing

6.3 FINANCING PRACTICES OF BANKS AND FINANCIAL INSTITUTIONS
- Loan Processing
- Negotiations with the Clients
- Intimation to the Customers
- Credit Disbursement Practice
- Difference in Loan Processing for Tourism Sector

6.4 PROPOSAL ASSESSMENT AND CREDIT APPRAISAL
- Analysis of the Credit Proposal
- Credit Appraisal (Financial Aspects)
- Relationship between Proposal Analysis and Credit Appraisal

6.5 RESPONSE ON EFFECTIVENESS OF TOURISM FINANCING
- Supply of Financial Information
- Credit Documentation
- Rescheduling/Restructuring
- Quality of Tourism Sector Loan

6.6 CONCLUSION

CHAPTER

VI

TOURISM FINANCING: AN ANALYSIS OF RESPONDENTS FROM BANKS AND FINANCIAL INSTITUTIONS

6.1 INTRODUCTION

The primary purpose of this chapter is to examine the system of tourism financing and practices of banks and financial institutions related to the financing in tourism industry. Other purposes are to inquire about their practices of loan processing, proposal analysis and credit appraisal as well as about their ratings on the effectiveness of tourism financing.

The chapter basically, employs the data collected from the field survey using the structured questionnaire. Therefore, it is based on the analysis of the data and perception of the surveyed banks and financial institutions (BFIs). In addition, it employs some relevant secondary data for the analysis and various mathematical and statistical tools to get at the conclusion.

It has been already mentioned that proper finance is necessary for the establishment, nursing and growth of the tourism business/industry. It is required to commence and to operate the business. The financing requirement of the tourism business enterprises and its composition heavily depends upon the business prospects and borrowing need. Borrowing need depends upon the performance or the potential business opportunities. Business opportunities of tourism business enterprises depend on the growth and development of the tourism industry and economy. Therefore, there is a revolving relationship between all these activities and economic variables.

The fourth Chapter examined the existing status of tourism financing from various sources i.e. the existing supply whereas the fifth Chapter enumerated the details of tourism investment and also inquired about the borrowing need of tourism business and prospects of tourism financing. Here, one question is still intact i.e. how these tourism businesses mobilize the borrowings from the banks and FIs. Not only this, it is desirable to inquire about the perception and practices of banks and financial institutions regarding the loan processing ranging from proposal analysis, credit appraisal to the disbursement practice. In addition, it is desirable to inquire about the effectiveness of financing based on the response of these surveyed banks and financial institutions.

Financing incorporates several activities related to acquisition, utilization and management of funds (Siddiqui and Siddiqui, 2005: 273). The acquisition of funds depends upon various factors such as the availability of funds, cost of funds, repayment capacity of the borrower etc. Precisely, it depends on the

198 *Opportunities and Challenges of Tourism Financing*

project itself, its viability and formalities. Therefore, present chapter examines the financing practices of banks and financial institutions considering these factors and provide the hints for further tourism financing in an effective manner.

6.2 PROFILE OF THE RESPONDENTS (BANKS AND FIS)

Considering the importance of the bank finance, the primary survey has attempted to include various banks and financial institutions. The study basically requires figures and information related to the investment finance. Therefore, it has selected all commercial banks (17) and 17 financial institutions consisting 4 development banks and 13 finance companies (refer Appendix: F.1). Basic thrust of such selection was to cover majority of the tourism financing, on one hand and the availability of detailed financial information, on the other.

A. DISTRIBUTION OF RESPONDENTS

One of the important purposes of the survey was to incorporate the financing practices of selected banks and financial institutions.

Table: 6.1

Distribution of Respondents (Banks and Financial Institutions)

Institutions	Sample		Response		Response Rate
	Number	Percent of Total Sample	Number	Percent of Total Respondents	Percent of Sample
Commercial Banks	17	50	15	54	88
Development Banks	4	12	4	14	100
Finance Companies	13	38	9	32	69
Total	34	100	28	100	82

Source: Primary Survey, 2006

Table: 6.1 summarizes the distribution of the sample and respondents whereas the Figure: 6.1 and Figure: 6.2 present such information in terms of percentage.

Figure: 6.1
Sample of the BFI

Figure: 6.2
Response of the BFI

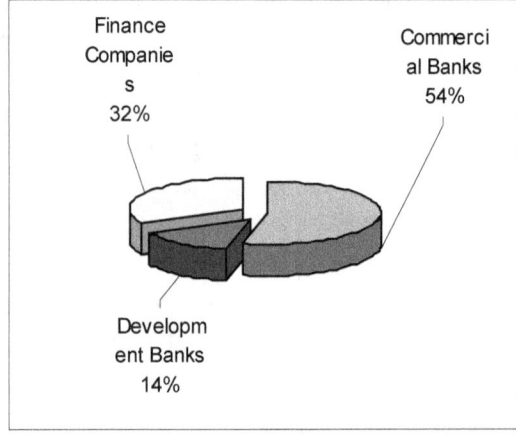

Thus, the response of the survey comprised commercial banks with 54.0 percent share followed by finance companies with 32.0 percent share. Likewise, the development banks have 14.0 percent share in total distribution. However, the distribution indicates the majority share of commercial banks. It is in line with the importance of such transaction and level of credit exposure, too.

B. DURATION OF TOURISM FINANCING

To examine the experience of Banks and Financial Institutions for lending to tourism industry the questionnaire inquired about the number of years of financing in tourism. Banks and financial institutions have been financing the tourism sector for quite a long time. During the survey, it was tried to incorporate the duration of tourism financing. Figure 6.3 summarizes the result about the duration of financing in tourism business enterprises by BFIs.

The figure depicts that majority of the commercial banks and financial institutions (35.7 percent) have been found to be financing the tourism business enterprises for the period of 6 to 10 years. It is followed by another group of banks and FIs (32.1 percent) that is financing the ventures for the period of 5 years and less. Similarly, another group (10.7 percent) has been financing for the period of 16 to 20 years. Remaining groups with 7.1 percent shares in total have been found to be financing for both the period 11 to 15 years and 21 years and more. However, another group having 7.1 percent share has never financed the tourism business enterprises.

Figure 6.3

Duration of Tourism Financing by Banks and Financial Institutions

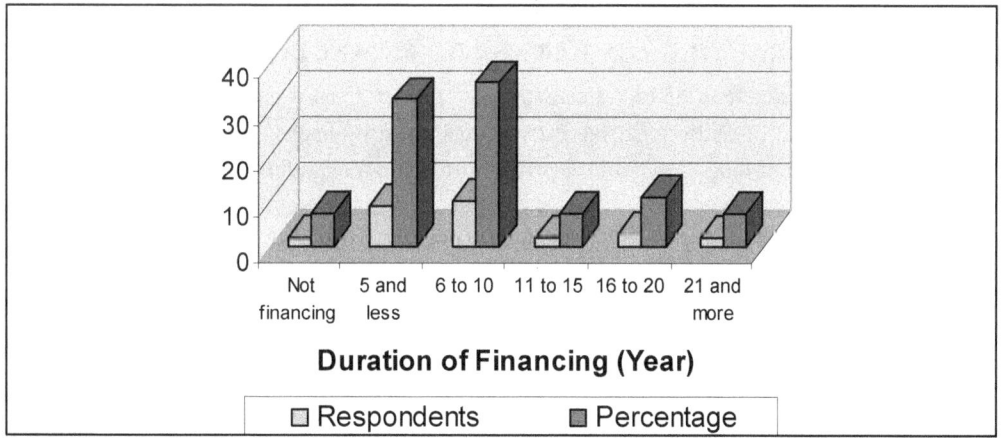

In order to find out the relationship between the establishment of the banks and financial institutions and duration of the tourism financing Table: 6.2 is designed. The table depicts the fact that BFIs start financing the tourism business after their establishment. However, there was one development bank that started tourism financing after 20 years of operation.

Table: 6.2

Establishment vs. Duration of Tourism Financing

Bank and Financial Institutions		Year of Tourism Financing						
Year of Establishment	Not financing	1960–1965	1966–1970	1986–1990	1991–1995	1996–2000	2001–2005	Total
1960 – 1965		1						1
1966 – 1970			1				1	2
1981 – 1985				1				1
1986 – 1990				2				2
1991 – 1995	2				2	7	1	12
1996 – 2000						5	2	7
2001 – 2005							3	3
Total	2	1	1	3	2	12	7	28

Source: Primary Survey, 2006

6.3 FINANCING PRACTICES OF BANKS AND FINANCIAL INSTITUTIONS

It is already mentioned that the broad categories of finance consist equity finance and loan finance from banks and financial institutions. In fact, term loans given by banks and financial institutions have been the primary source of long-term debt for private firms and most public firms (Chandra, 2002: 538). Hence, it is desirable to assess the loan processing and credit appraisal practices of the banks and financial institutions. This section of the chapter, thus presents the profile of the banks and financial institutions along-with their response on the structured questionnaire administered during the primary survey (Please refer to the Appendix: A.2 for the questionnaire).

Some banks and financial institutions did not supply the complete information despite of vigorous efforts (please refer Appendix: F.1 for the details). Whatever the information was received during the survey is presented at appropriate sections.

A. LOAN PROCESSING

During the survey, one section of the questionnaire was specially designed to find out the practices of the banks and financial institutions related to the loan application, its requirement with reference to the amount and type of loan as well as with feasibility report.

Specific Formats for Loan Application

Table: 6.3 summarizes the result along-with some other details. The majority of the banks and financial institutions (85.7 percent) use the specific format for the loan application in contrast to 14.3

percent respondents that do not use such format. Among the BFIs using the specific format, about 36 percent use it as per the amount whereas 67.9 percent use it as per loan type. However, the majority i.e. 53.6 percent use the specific application as per both amount and type of the loan. Notwithstanding the above, 53.6 percent and 28.6 percent of respondents did not provide the comment on the usage of specific format as per loan amount and loan type respectively. Further, 35.7 percent respondents also did not provide the comment for the use of format as per both the amount and type of loan.

Table: 6.3

Specific Formats for Loan Application

Format for Loan Application	Yes	No	No Comment	Total
Using Specific Format for Loan	24	4	0	28
Percentage	*85.7*	*14.3*	*0.0*	*100.0*
As per Loan Amount	10	3	15	28
Percentage	*35.7*	*10.7*	*53.6*	*100.0*
As per Loan Type	19	1	8	28
Percentage	*67.9*	*3.6*	*28.6*	*100.0*
As per both Loan Amount and Type	15	3	10	28
Percentage	*53.6*	*10.7*	*35.7*	*100.0*

Source: Primary Survey, 2006

Requirement of Feasibility Report

The survey attempted to find out the requirement of feasibility report along with the loan application. The overwhelming majority of the BFIs (above 90 percent) responded that they require it during the loan processing. When they were asked about the type of loan that requires the feasibility report, only 39.3 percent told that it is required in all loans. More specifically, 32.1 percent and 28.6 percent respondents mentioned that it was required in project loan and term loan respectively.

In the other fold, the respondents were also asked to mention the type of loan that does not require the feasibility report to be attached. The majority (71.4 percent) mentioned that it is required to be attached with the loan application whereas 28.5 percent mentioned that consumer loan, hire purchase loan and other small loan do not require the feasibility report along-with the loan application.

Table: 6.4
Response on Feasibility Report or Project Proposal

S. N.	Particulars	Frequency	Percent
1.	**Required**		
	Yes	26	92.9
	No	2	7.1
	Total	28	100
2.	**Type of Loan Requiring the Feasibility**		
	Term Loan	8	28.6
	Project Loan	9	32.1
	all loan	11	39.3
	Total	28	100
3.	**Type of Loan Not Requiring the Feasibility**		
	Consumer Loan	2	25
	Hire Purchase	2	25
	Small loan	4	50
	Total	8	100

Source: Primary Survey, 2006

Average Time for Loan Processing

During the survey, commercial banks and financial institutions were asked to furnish the information regarding the average time required for the loan processing.

Table: 6.5 summarizes the response and depicts that working capital takes less than one week whereas term loan and project loan take two week or more for the loan processing. It was the term loan that received the response from most of the banks and financial institutions followed by working capital loan.

The majority of the respondents did not provide the comments for the retail loan, corporate loan and consortium loan.

Table: 6.5
Average Time for Loan Processing (in Week)

Loan Type	Up to 1	2	3	4	More than 5	No Comment	Total
Working Capital Loan	9	4	1	0	1	13	28
Percentage	*32.1*	*14.3*	*3.6*	*0.0*	*3.6*	*46.4*	*100.0*
Project Loan	1	5	2	3	0	17	28
Percentage	*3.6*	*17.9*	*7.1*	*10.7*	*0.0*	*60.7*	*100.0*
Term Loan	9	10	1	3	1	4	28
Percentage	*32.1*	*35.7*	*3.6*	*10.7*	*3.6*	*14.3*	*100.0*
Retail Loan	2	7	1	0	0	18	28
Percentage	*7.1*	*25.0*	*3.6*	*0.0*	*0.0*	*64.3*	*100.0*
Corporate Loan	2	7	1	0	0	18	28
Percentage	*7.1*	*25.0*	*3.6*	*0.0*	*0.0*	*64.3*	*100.0*
Consortium Loan	4	3	0	2	0	19	28
Percentage	*14.3*	*10.7*	*0.0*	*7.1*	*0.0*	*67.9*	*100.0*

Source: Primary Survey, 2006

B. NEGOTIATIONS WITH THE CLIENTS

Negotiation is one of the important aspects of loan processing. During the survey, the commercial banks and financial institutions were asked to furnish the information regarding the negotiation with the client about the terms and conditions of the loan.

Table: 6.6 summarizes the response. All the respondents described that they always negotiate with the customers. Further, when they were asked to mention the details of terms and conditions, interest rate and amount of loan stood at the top of the hierarchy whereas repayment schedule remained just behind that. However, the respondents also negotiate with their customers for other factors such as collateral/security, processing charges, service charges and other conditions depending upon the situation and requirement of the clients.

Table: 6.6
Negotiations with the Clients

	Yes	No	No Comment	Total
Negotiation	28	0	0	28
Percentage	*100.0*	*0.0*	*0.0*	*100.0*
For Interest Rate	22	6	0	28
Percentage	*78.6*	*21.4*	*0.0*	*100.0*
Amount of the Loan	22	2	4	28
Percentage	*78.6*	*7.1*	*14.3*	*100.0*
For Repayment Schedule	20	4	4	28
Percentage	*71.4*	*14.3*	*14.3*	*100.0*
For Other Factors	28	0	0	28
Percentage	*100.0*	*0.0*	*0.0*	*100.0*

Source: Primary Survey, 2006

C. INTIMATION TO THE CUSTOMERS

The intimation to proposed borrower about loan processing plays a crucial role in convincing the borrowers about loan sanction, interest rates, time taken for processing etc. The majority of the respondents mentioned that they intimate their clients about the loan processing.

Table: 6.7

Intimation to Customers about Loan Processing

Particulars	Frequency	Percent
Yes	25	89.3
No	1	3.6
To some Extent	1	3.6
No Comment	1	3.6
Total	28	100

Source: Primary Survey, 2006

D. CREDIT DISBURSEMENT PRACTICE

The credit disbursement practice plays important role in the liquidity position in of banks and the interest burden of clients. Generally, the disbursement depends on the requirements of the clients and it also depends on the kind of the projects. On inquiring about the same it is observed that 50 percent respondents disburse the loan phase wise. Further, 21.4 percent respondents mentioned that they disburse the total amount in one go whereas 28.6 percent disburse it on the combination of the both. Table: 6.8 and Figure: 6.4 present the response about such disbursement practice.

Table: 6.8

General Practice of Credit Disbursement by banks and FIs

Response	Frequency	Percent
Full Amount Disbursement	6	21.4
Phase-wise Disbursement	14	50
Both	8	28.6
Total	28	100

Figure 6.4

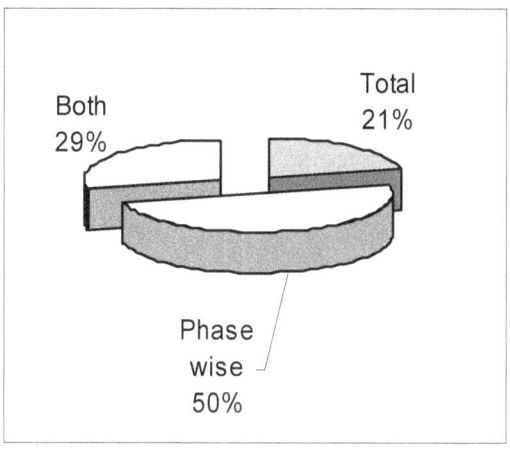

Source: Primary Survey, 2006

E. DIFFERENCE IN LOAN PROCESSING FOR TOURISM SECTOR

This being specific study with reference to tourism, a further inquiry was made about the difference in the processing of tourism loan proposal.

Table: 6.9

Difference in Loan Processing between Tourism and Other Loans

Difference	Frequency	Percent
Yes	4	14.3
No	24	85.7
Total	28	100

Source: Primary Survey, 2006

Figure 6.5

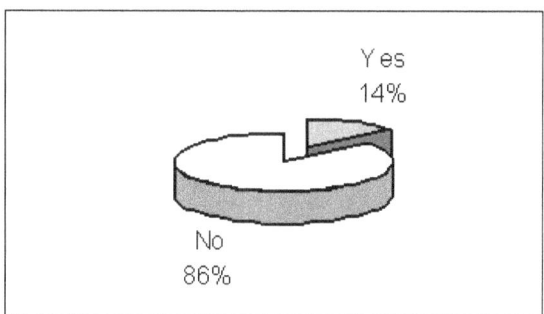

Only 4 respondents (14.3 percent) stated that they process the loan differently because of the down turn in tourism industry in recent years. Here, three commercial banks and one finance company also provided the points of difference in loan processing for the tourism. They mentioned that they consider the category of tourism business, market survey, peculiarity of the hotel business and the factors related to the security situation.

6.4 PROPOSAL ANALYSIS AND CREDIT APPRAISAL

The appraisal process of the loan has far reaching implication on the earning of the bank as well as the soundness of the bank. The credit appraisal has to take into consideration, certain general aspects of the business as well as the financial strength of the proposed borrower. Various factors have been identified with reference to business in general viz. business prospects, market position, management of the company, relation with affiliated company and labour relation. With reference to financial aspects, factors identified are profitability, capital structure, liquidity position, working capital and cash flow and ability to pay.

For both, the extent of importance assigned is also examined. Here, the five points scale is given, which ranges from extremely importance to the least importance.

A. ANALYSIS OF THE CREDIT PROPOSAL

Table: 6.10 depicts the result along-with the level of importance accorded by the banks and financial institutions during the analysis of the proposal for business aspects in general.

Business prospects and management of the company stood as most important factors during the analysis of the credit proposals whereas market position and relation with affiliated company stood at largely important position. Similarly, labour relation received more than average importance whereas collateral did not receive much importance as the majority of BFIs did not provide the comment.

Table: 6.10
Proposal Analysis

Particulars	Extremely Important	Largely Important	Average	Fairly Important	Least Important	Total
Business Prospects						
No. of Agencies	19	6	1	2	0	28
Percentage	*67.9*	*21.4*	*3.6*	*7.1*	*0.0*	*100*
Market Position						
No. of Agencies	11	13	2	2	0	28
Percentage	*39.3*	*46.4*	*7.1*	*7.1*	*0.0*	*100*
Management of the Company						
No. of Agencies	22	4	2	0	0	28
Percentage	*78.6*	*14.3*	*7.1*	*0.0*	*0.0*	*100*
Relation with Affiliated Company						
No. of Agencies	3	13	9	3	0	28
Percentage	*10.7*	*46.4*	*32.1*	*10.7*	*0.0*	*100*
Labour Relation						
No. of Agencies	2	12	10	3	1	28
Percentage	*7.1*	*42.9*	*35.7*	*10.7*	*3.6*	*100*
Collateral/security						
No. of Agencies	3	4	2	2	17*	28
Percentage	*10.7*	*14.3*	*7.1*	*7.1*	*60.7*	*100*

* No comment.

Source: Primary Survey, 2006

B. RELATIONSHIP BETWEEN THE BUSINESS ASPECTS

To examine the degree of association, in the importance assigned to various business aspects, the tool of Phi-Coefficient (r_ϕ) is applied (Edwards, 1958: 162-163). The point of examination is when 'business prospects' is considered extremely important for proposal analysis whether 'market position' is considered extremely important or not.

The first analysis is undertaken considering the response for the factor as 'extremely important.' Here, the 'yes' means it is extremely important and 'no' means it is not extremely important (rather may it be largely important, average or otherwise). Further, the 'yes' for one factor is compared with 'yes' or 'no' for another factor and the 'no' for one factor with the 'no' or the 'yes' for another factor. Thus, the combination of the responses will be (i) Yes, Yes (ii) Yes, No (iii) No, Yes (iv) No, No. Thereafter, the calculation is undertaken employing the following formula (also refer Chapter – I).

$$r_\phi = \frac{bc - ad}{\sqrt{(a+c)(b+d)(a+b)(c+d)}}$$

where, r_ϕ = Phi-Coefficient, a, b, c and d are represented in following manner:

	X_0	X_1	
Y_0	a	b	(a+b)
Y_0	c	d	(c+d)
	(a+c)	(b+d)	n

Hence, Table: 6.11 presents the calculated value of Phi-Coefficient. Since, the calculated value is greater than the tabulated χ^2 value (3.84) there is significant relationship between business prospects and market position as well as between business prospects and management of the company. However, the relationship is not significant between market position and management of the company.

Table: 6.11
Relationship between the Factors Related to Proposal Analysis
(Result of the Phi-Coefficient for Extremely Important)

Techniques	Business Prospects	Market Position	Management of the Company
Business Prospects	1		
Market Position	0.397* (3.895)	1	
Management of the Company	0.386* (4.173)	0.242 (1.638)	1

Note: Figures in the brackets represent the estimated value of χ^2 and '*' indicates the significant relationship at 5 percent level of significance.

The second calculation was undertaken considering the response as largely important and more (taking both the response for extremely and largely important) for all the factors related to the Proposal Analysis by the banks and financial institutions. Table: 6.12 summarizes the results.

Table: 6.12
Relation between the Aspects Related to Proposal Analysis
(Result of the Phi-Coefficient for Largely Important and More)

Factors	Business Prospects	Market Position	Management of the Company	Relation with Affiliated Com.	Labour Relation
Business Prospects	1				
Market Position	0.519* (7.529)	1			
Management of the Company	0.801* (17.949)	0.679* (12.923)	1		
Relation with Affiliated Company	0.167 (0.778)	0.265 (1.969)	0.320 (2.872)	1	
Labour Relation	0.115 (0.373)	0.204 (1.167)	0.277 (2.154)	0.722* (14.583)	1

Note: Figures in the brackets represent the estimated value of χ^2 and '*' indicates the significant relationship at 5 percent level of significance.

From the table, it is clear that there exists a significant relationship between (a) business prospects and market position and (b) business prospects and management of the company. Similarly, there also exists significant relationship between (c) market position and management of the company as well as (d) labour relation and relation with affiliated company. However, the relationship of business prospects with relation with affiliated company and labour relation is found insignificant. Further, a weak relationship is found for both of market position with relation with affiliated company and labour relation followed by that of labour relation with market position and management of the company.

C. CREDIT APPRAISAL (FINANCIAL ASPECTS)

As mentioned in preceding paragraphs another question was designed to enquire about the views of financing institutions for the financial aspects of the borrowing company during the credit appraisal. Table: 6.13 depicts the result along-with the level of importance accorded by the banks and financial institutions during the year.

Cash flow and ability to pay received overwhelming importance (82.1 percent) and stood at the apex position whereas profitability and liquidity position received remarkable importance (57.1 percent and 50.0 percent respectively) to stay also at the extremely important position. However, capital structure and working capital stood at largely important position though capital structure also maintained almost similar ranking in the distribution i.e. extremely important position.

Table: 6.13

Credit Appraisal

Particulars	Extremely Important	Largely Important	Average	Fairly Important	Least Important	Total
Profitability						
No. of Agencies	16	9	1	2	0	28
Percentage	57.1	32.1	3.6	7.1	0.0	100
Capital Structure						
No. of Agencies	12	12	3	1	0	28
Percentage	42.9	42.9	10.7	3.6	0.0	100
Liquidity Position						
No. of Agencies	14	6	7	1	0	28
Percentage	50.0	21.4	25.0	3.6	0.0	100
Working Capital						
No. of Agencies	10	15	1	2	0	28
Percentage	35.7	53.6	3.6	7.1	0.0	100
Cash Flow and Ability to Pay						
No. of Agencies	23	3		2	0	28
Percentage	82.1	10.7	0.0	7.1	0.0	100

Source: Primary Survey, 2006

D. RELATIONSHIP BETWEEN THE APPLICATIONS OF TOOLS

In order to examine the degree of relationship between the application of various tools to examine the financial position of the borrowing company by banks and financial institutions, Phi-Coefficient is undertaken. It analyzes the association between the financial aspects.

The Table: 6.14 depicts that there exists a significant relationship in importance assigned to the application of various tools to examine financial position in eight situations out of 10. This implies that when the profitability is considered extremely important as a credit appraisal techniques; liquidity position, working capital and ability to pay are also considered extremely important for credit appraisal. Similarly, when capital structure is considered extremely important for credit appraisal; liquidity position, working capital and ability to pay are also considered extremely important for credit appraisal. Further, when liquidity position is considered extremely important; working capital and ability to pay are also considered to be extremely important.

Table: 6.14
Relationship between the Aspects Related to Credit Appraisal

(Result of the Phi-Coefficient for Extremely Important)

Aspects	Profitability	Capital Structure	Liquidity Position	Working Capital	Cash Flow/ Ability to Pay
Profitability	1				
Capital Structure	0.167 (0.778)	1			
Liquidity Position	0.433* (5.250)	0.433* (5.250)	1		
Working Capital	0.495* (6.857)	0.409* (4.680)	0.596* (9.956)	1	
Cash Flow/Ability to Pay	0.538* (8.116)	0.404* (4.565)	0.466* (6.087)	0.348 (3.382)	1

Note: Figures in the brackets represent the estimated value of χ^2 and '*' indicates the significant relationship at 5 percent level of significance.

Further calculation is also undertaken considering the response as largely important and more (taking both the response for extremely and largely important from Table: 6.13) for all the aspects related to the credit appraisal. Table: 6.15 summarizes the result. From the table, it is clear that there exists a significant relationship between the techniques of financial analysis in four situations out of ten. This implies that when the profitability is considered largely important as a credit appraisal technique; liquidity position and ability to pay are also considered largely important for credit appraisal. Similarly, when the liquidity position is considered largely important; working capital and ability to pay are also considered to be largely important.

Table: 6.15
Relationship between the Aspects Related to Credit Appraisal

(Result of the Phi-Coefficient for Largely Important and More)

Aspects	Profitability	Capital Structure	Liquidity Position	Working Capital	Cash Flow/ Ability to Pay
Profitability	1				
Capital Structure	(-)0.141 (0.560)	1			
Liquidity Position	0.548* (8.400)	(-)0.242 (1.638)	1		
Working Capital	0.253 (1.797)	(-) 0.141 (0.560)	0.548* (8.400)	1	
Cash Flow/Ability to Pay	0.801* (17.949)	(-) 0.113 (0.359)	0439* (5.385)	(-) 0.096 (0.258)	1

Note: Figures in the brackets represent the estimated value of χ^2 and '*' indicates the significant relationship at 5 percent level of significance.

However, the relationship is not significant between the techniques of credit appraisal in majority of the situations (six out of ten). Not only this, a negative relationship is also found between some techniques of financial analysis. This implies that when a technique is considered largely important or more, another technique is not considered largely important in all cases.

E. RELATIONSHIP BETWEEN PROPOSAL ANALYSIS AND CREDIT APPRAISAL

For the purpose of credit appraisal, both business aspects and financial aspects are important. It is also found that most of the business aspects are considered 'extremely important' with other. This is also observed for the financial aspects. In the next stage, cross verification is carried out to examine, with which business aspects, which of the financial aspects is considered 'extremely important.' Here, again the tool of Phi-Coefficient (r_ϕ) is applied. The results are presented in Table: 6.16.

From the table it is clear that there exists a significant relationship between business prospects and all financial aspects (profitability, capital structure, liquidity and cash flow) except working capital. This implies that when the 'business prospects' is considered 'extremely important' for credit analysis; the financial aspect such as profitability, capital structure, liquidity position and ability to pay is also considered 'extremely important' for credit appraisal.

The relationship is insignificant for both 'market position' and 'management of the company' with the financial aspects (except that with cash flow). Similarly, the relationship was poor between labour relations with all financial aspects except with working capital. However, there is significant relationship between market position and cash flow/ability to pay because banks/FIs particularly look for this situation (cash-cow)[1]. Thus, it is important to note that the importance assigned to some of the business aspects and the financial aspects behave independently.

Table: 6.16

Relationship between Proposal Analysis and Financial Aspects

(Result of the Phi-Coefficient for Extremely Important case)

Aspects	Profitability	Capital Structure	Liquidity Position	Working Capital	Cash Flow and Ability to Pay
Business Prospects	0.486* (6.604)	0.442* (5.458)	0.535* (8.023)	0.353 (3.497)	0.677* (12.850)
Market Position	0.106 (0.312)	0.190 (1.011)	0.219 (1.348)	0.011 (0.003)	0.375* (3.939)
Management of the Company	0.251 (1.768)	0.276 (2.139)	0.174 (0.848)	0.208 (1.207)	0.438* (5.379)
Relation with Affiliated Company	0.067 (0.124)	(-) 0.067 (0.124)	(-) 0.115 (0.373)	0.224 (1.402)	0.162 (0.730)
Labour Relation	0.240 (1.615)	0.320 (2.872)	0.277 (2.154)	0.372* (3.877)	0.129 (0.468)

Note: Figures in the brackets represent the estimated value of χ^2 and '*' indicates the significant relationship at 5 percent level of significance.

---

[1] It is called cash-cow in BCG Matrix when market share is high and cash flow is low (Robins and Coulter, 2002:)

6.5 RESPONSE ON THE EFFECTIVENESS OF TOURISM FINANCING

The effectiveness of the financing can be gauzed by and through various methods. Financing itself is a broad term thus requires proper analysis to conclude the discussion. However, an attempt was made to discuss the response related to some issues pertaining to the effectiveness of financing in one way or the other. This analysis is based on the response of the banks and financial institutions during the primary survey.

A. REPAYMENT HABIT OF THE BORROWER

Bank and Financial Institutions were asked to furnish the information related to the repayment habit of the borrower because it clearly shows the effectiveness of the tourism financing. Out of 28 respondents the majority (71.4 percent) perceived the habit as average compared to 25 percent respondents viewing it poor. However, there is only one respondent that perceived the habit as an excellent.

Table: 6.17

Repayment Habit of the Borrower

Response	Frequency	Percent
Excellent	1	3.6
Average	20	71.4
Poor	7	25.0
Total	28	100.0

Source: Primary Survey, 2006

B. CREDIT DOCUMENTATION

As the status of credit documentation expected to indicate the effectiveness, the result showed that overwhelming majority of bank and financial institutions perceived that quality as average and more than average.

Table: 6.18

Quality of Credit Documentation

Response	Frequency	Percent
Complete	13	46.4
Average	14	50.0
No Comment	1	3.6
Total	28	100.0

Source: Primary Survey, 2006

C. RESCHEDULING/RESTRUCTURING OF THE LOANS

The information related to the rescheduling and restructuring generally provide the effectiveness of the financing. During the review period, very few companies had applied for the rescheduling of restructuring of the loans. Table: 6.19 is designed to provide the summary of the response about the abovementioned subject. In fact very few tourism business enterprises (14.3 percent) have applied in banks and financial institutions for the restructuring of the loans during the review period.

Table: 6.19

Existence of Restructuring of Loan

Existence	Frequency	Percent
Yes	4	14.3
No	21	75.0
No Comment	3	10.7
Total	28	100

Source: Primary Survey, 2006

D. QUALITY OF TOURISM SECTOR LOAN

Difference in Loan Quality

During the survey the banks and financial institutions were asked to furnish the information related to the loan classification related to the tourism sector only. The attempt was especially undertaken to find out whether there exist any significant difference between the overall non-performing loan and tourism sector loan, in particular. The majority of BFIs (46.4 percent) did not feel the difference compared to 39.3 percent feeling the difference in the loan quality. However, 14.3 percent respondents did not provide the response in this connection.

Table: 6.20

Difference in Loan Quality

Existence	Frequency	Percent
Yes	11	39.3
No	13	46.4
No Comment	4	14.3
Total	28	100

Source: Primary Survey, 2006

Loan Classification Related to Tourism

The response of commercial banks and financial institutions regarding the tourism sector loan classification is summarized in Table: 6.21.

In the fiscal year ending mid-July 2000, the pass loan has 86.6 percent share whereas the bad loan had 10.9 percent share in total loan outstanding of tourism sector. The size of the bad loan gradually rose during review period and went up to 40.4 percent at the end of fiscal year 2004/05 from 10.9 percent of F. Y. 1999/00. One of the reasons for such gradual increase can be the increasing respondents for the later year (2000/05 - 16) form earlier year (2000/01- 10)

214 *Opportunities and Challenges of Tourism Financing*

To sum up the average percentage of pass loan, substandard, doubtful and bad (loss) loan stood at 67.9 percent, 3.0 percent, 5.2 percent and 24.0 percent respectively during the review period.

Table: 6.21

Loan Classification Related to Tourism

Year ending mid-July	Percentage in total loan (tourism)				Total Amount (Rs. Million)	Growth %
	Good/Pass	Substandard	Doubtful	Bad		
2000	86.6	0.9	1.7	10.9	2,977,329	
2001	81.1	1.3	1.6	16.0	2,624,308	88.1
2002	78.2	2.7	2.6	16.5	3,686,124	140.5
2003	63.1	5.9	9.4	21.9	2,846,827	77.2
2004	56.6	3.4	9.1	30.9	4,135,170	145.3
2005	50.6	3.4	5.6	40.4	3,965,450	95.9
Average	**67.9**	**3.0**	**5.2**	**24.0**	20,235,208	

Source: Primary Survey, 2006

Further calculation is undertaken to find out the ratio of NPA in total credit outstanding in tourism sector based on the response of the surveyed commercial banks. Figure 6.6 presents the details about such analysis and calculation.

Figure: 6.6

Total Loan, Non-Performing Assets and NPA Ratio (Tourism Sector)

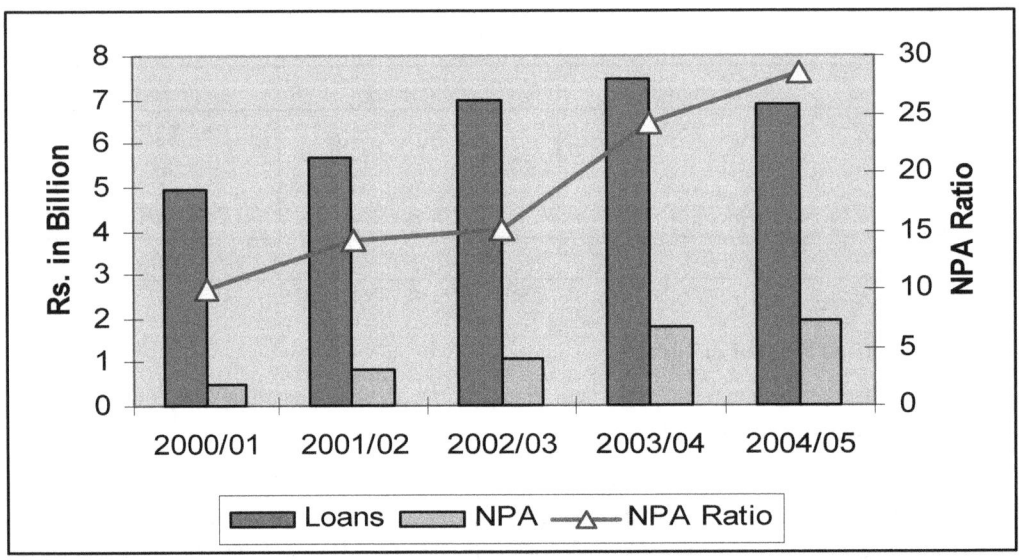

During the review period (from F.Y. 2000/01 F.Y. 2004/05) Tourism Sector NPA ratio stood more than 10 percent. It remained at 10.1 percent in F.Y. 2000/01 (the lowest) and at 28.5 percent (the highest)

in F.Y. 2004/05. The ratio is derived dividing the tourism sector NPA (based on survey, Table: 6.21) by the Tourism Sector Loan Outstanding (Chapter – IV, Table: 4.4)

E. IMPACT OF LENDING

The majority of commercial banks and financial institutions (57.1 percent) perceived the overall impact of tourism sector lending as an average during the review period. It was perceived as poor by 28.6 percent respondents whereas 14.3 percent did not provide the comment in this matter.

Table: 6.22

Impact of the Lending

	Frequency	Percent
Average	16	57.1
Poor	8	28.6
No Comment	4	14.3
Total	28	100

Source: Primary Survey, 2006

6.6 CONCLUSION

The practices of banks and financial institutions regarding the loan processing and credit appraisal provide with relevant information of financing. Field research, thus, surveyed the practices and perception of banks and financial institutions and assessed them. The profile of respondents showed that most of them have furnished the information for the study and were engaged in financing of tourism business. The majority of the respondents use specific formats for the loan application though it largely depends upon the amount and type of the loan or both. They usually require feasibility report or project proposal and take 1-2 weeks for loan processing, on an average. They usually negotiate for the interest rate, amount and repayment schedule and intimate the customers about the loan processing and decision. They generally disburse the loan 'phase-wise' and treat the tourism sector loan similarly as others. They carry the credit appraisal considering the factors related to the business affairs and financial aspects of the borrowing company.

The result of Phi-Coefficient (r_ϕ) clearly showed that there exists strong relationship between various aspects examined during the proposal analysis and credit appraisal. It also showed that there exists a significant relationship between business prospects with most of the financial aspects. Similarly, market position, management of the company and labour relation has positive relationship with the financial factors (though not significant except for one in each combination). However, the negative relationship from the calculation proved that there does not exist a relationship between affiliated company and capital structure as well as that with liquidity position.

In addition, the study examined various aspects of tourism financing and incorporated the views of the banks and financial institutions (supply side) about indicators of tourism financing and assessed the effectiveness.

A considerable difference is observed when the tourism sector NPA ratio (based on the survey) is compared with the overall NPA ratio of the commercial banks. In early years of review period i.e. during F.Y. 2000/01 to F.Y. 2002/03 the ratio stood less than the overall NPA ratio in contrast to the later years of review period i.e. during F.Y. 2003/04 to 2004/05 in which the ratio stood more than the overall ratio.

REFERENCE

Chandra, Prasanna (2002). Projects: Planning, Analysis, Financing, Implementation and Review. New Delhi: Tata McGraw Hill Publishing Company Limited.

Edwards, Allen E. (1958). **Statistical Analysis**. New York: Reinhart and Company, Inc.

Gujarati, Damodar (1996). **Basic Econometrics** Third Edition. New York: McGraw-Hill Inc.

Gupta, S. P. (1987). **Statistical Methods**. New Delhi: S. Chand and Company.

Hildebrand, David H. and R. Lyman Ott (1998). Statistical Thinking for Managers. Duxbury Press An International Thompson Publishing Company.

NRB (2006). Nepal Rastra Bank Banking Supervision Annual Report, 2005. Kathmandu: Nepal Rastra Bank Banking Supervision Department.

Sharma, Om Prakash (2001). **Tourism Development and Planning in Nepal**. A Ph. D. Thesis presented to Faculty of Social Sciences, Banaras Hindu University India.

Shrestha, Sunity (1995). **Portfolio Behaviour of Commercial Banks in Nepal**. Kathamandu: Mandala Book Point.

Siddiqui, S. A. and A. S. Siddiqui (2005). **Managerial Economics and Financial Analysis**. New Delhi: New Age International (P) Limited, Publishers.

VII
CHAPTER

SUMMARY OF FINDINGS AND SUGGESTIONS

7.1 SUMMARY OF THE STUDY IN GENERAL

7.2 FINDINGS AND CONCLUSION

7.3 LIMITATION OF THE STUDY

7.4 POLICY IMPLICATION AND SUGGESTIONS

CHAPTER VII
SUMMARY OF FINDINGS AND SUGGESTIONS

7.1 SUMMARY OF STUDY IN GENERAL

Tourism has emerged as an important sector in the economy of every country. It has become a subject of considerable interest for academicians as well as for the policy makers on account of the contribution that it makes to the economic growth of the nation.

Consequently, various aspects of tourism viz. the contribution, impacts, problems and prospects become the area of concern. Several evaluations have been performed to find out the forward and backward linkages of tourism. Financing being the lifeblood of industry holds the place of prime importance for tourism industry also.

Tourism industry, being capital-intensive, requires substantial amount of investment for the erection of infrastructure and superstructure. In addition, more investment and financing is also necessary for the successful operation of tourism business enterprises and for the promotion of other related industries/businesses. Nepal being a developing country with limited infrastructure and lack of accumulated capital could not provide sufficient financing in the long run. During the review period it is found to be allocating less than one percent of total development budget for the tourism sector. Rather it can create an environment, act as a catalyst and promote the private and foreign investment.

The government and financial system have a vital role in providing the financial assistance and support for tourism. As such, the role is distinct in terms of funding sources comprising budget allocation of the government, credit disbursement of bank and financial institutions and magnitude of foreign investment.

Present study attempted to inquire about the direct investment in the tourism sector, to analyze it in terms of requirement, to account the lending in tourism sector from various commercial banks and other financial institutions and to perform the corresponding analysis.

After a preliminary discussion of tourism in general, and tourism financing in particular, the study goes on to take the stock of the research work carried out on tourism financing at a global level, spread over various countries. Nepal, being a typical tourism centre, and finding a gap for a study focused on tourism financing, the present study focused on various aspects of tourism financing.

The study starts with the secondary data on tourism, tourism financing and indicators of economic growth. It attempts to examine the impact of tourism and tourism financing on economic growth. To reach to the root, the primary data collection is also carried out, of those demanding tourism finance viz. various tourism business enterprises and of those supplying finance viz. banks and financial institutions.

Having discussed the profile of the respondents, the study goes on to examine the finer aspects of tourism financing, with reference to respondents.

Thus, the study turns out to be the analysis in a triangular form. The first is the impact of tourism and tourism financing on the development of tourism and economic growth. The second is views of the TBE (demand side) about the effectiveness of financing and the third is the views of the banks and financial institutions (supply side). The study also incorporated the magnitude of tourism financing, structure, pattern and the indicators of financing as well as the effectiveness of tourism financing.

7.2 SUMMARY OF FINDINGS AND CONCLUSION

The review on tourism, tourism financing and economic impact of tourism provided a strong basis for the study in two ways. The first one is related with the concept and where-about of the tourism and has provided a clear path for the study whereas the second one is related with the availability of existing works to indicate the requirement for the fresh discussions and analysis. The study carried out is summarized in the following lines:

A. To begin with, the study attempted to examine the profile of tourism industry in Nepal (Chapter – III). It basically employed the secondary data to analyze he trend of tourist arrival, tourism products and infrastructure as well as planning practices and the organizational setting related to the tourism. The findings are summarized as follows:

The tourist arrival in recent years particularly after 2000 showed a sharp decline. The major reason behind this was the ever-spreading terrorism around the world and Maoist insurgency inside the country.

The largest number of tourists was found to be visiting Nepal only for recreational purposes. However, the trend is changing over the years. Earlier, majority of the tourists were visiting the country particularly for holiday as well as for convention and official purposes.

The tourists visiting for adventure are important in terms of the both, duration of stay and foreign exchange income. They visit far distant (remote) places, generate the employment even for the local people and use local goods and services during the visit. This has a multiple economic impact in the economy.

The length of stay has remained stagnant over the years. It is the main reason why accommodation businesses are suffering with growing loss and could not generate sufficient revenue.

B. The study attempted to assess the tourism financing from the supply side employing the secondary data related to the financing of tourism industry, trend, magnitude and ratio of tourism financing in total financing from various sources. It has incorporated the investment from government budget and foreign aid and loan assistance, lending (loan disbursement) of commercial banks and financial institutions as well as foreign direct investment in tourism. In addition, it has undertaken empirical analysis for the impact of tourism and tourism financing on economic growth of the country. Major findings can be summarized as follows:

The budget allocation of the government to tourism sector had hardly been 0.54 percent, on an average in total development budget during the review period. The role of the government appeared to be very limited leaving tourism industry operation in the private sector, particularly during the review period. Despite of this, the government has been providing investment promotion incentives, formulating investment legislation, and publishing trade and business directories.

The investment in civil aviation also has been in similar fashion but relatively at a higher level of 2.24 percent on an average during the review period.

The foreign aid and loan disbursement in other sector (including tourism) has been variable during the review period and stood at 10.1 percent on an average in total foreign aid and loan disbursement.

The extent of foreign direct investment in tourism was only 3.9 percent on an average during the review period. This can be attributed to the difficulties related to investment policy environment and inadequate infrastructure.

On examining the impact of tourism earning (foreign exchange from tourism - FXET) on the various development indices such as government internal revenue (GIR), tax revenue (TAXR), trade volume (TRAV), contribution of hotel, trade and restaurant on GDP (GDPT), gross domestic product (GDPN) and Ratio of GDPT on GDPN, it was found to have a significant positive impact. Therefore, the foreign exchange earning from tourism plays a significant role in the economy. Moreover, it was also observed that the tourism sector in Nepal has a significant impact on the economic growth.

It was found that the tourism development has a significant impact on the economic growth of the country. It is found to be explained by the indicators of tourism development such as foreign exchange from tourism (FXET), total no. of tourists' arrival (TTAR), total no. of tourism business (TNTB), total no. of trained human resources (TNHR) and total no. of hotel beds (TNHB).

Focusing on the impact of tourism financing on certain growth variables viz. Contribution of hotel trade and restaurant on GDP (GDPT), Gross domestic product at nominal price (GDPN) and Ratio of GDPT to GDPN (RGDPT) it is found to have a significant impact. Moreover, it is found that the indices of development are sensitive to the tourism financing.

On taking the tourism financing from various sources like, Tourism sector loan disbursement of NIDC (LDTNIDC), Service sector loan disbursement of commercial banks (LDSCB), Development expenditure of the government in tourism sector (TEXP), Government investment in civil aviation (GICA) and Foreign aid and loan disbursement in other sector including tourism (FADOT) as independent variables it is found to have significant impact on contribution of hotel, trade and restaurant on GDP (GDPT).

On further dividing tourism financing from banks and FIs by way of loan in one group and government annul budget allocation in second group, also the impact of tourism financing is found to be significant and positive on GDPT. Moreover, when the impact of foreign aid and loan disbursement through government to other sector including tourism (FADOT) is examined, it is found to have positively significant impact on GDPT.

C. Further the study attempted to identify the various aspects of financing and financing practices of tourism business enterprises (TBE) digging through the field survey (Chapter – V). It has incorporated the pattern, composition and structure of financing during the review period. The results are summarized as under:

The analysis for the magnitude of equity financing of tourism business enterprises showed a gradual increase (23.62 percent, on an average) during the review period.

On examining the composition of equity financing, it is found that the majority of the finance (82 percent, on an average) has been from the domestic promoters. The proportions of the equity share from foreign capital and from the public issue found to be 12 percent and 6 percent, on an average respectively.

The analysis for the magnitude of debt financing of tourism business enterprises showed an increase of 25.32 percent, on an average during the review period.

The composition of the debt financing showed that a major portion of the borrowing (96 percent, on an average) was from the banks and financial institutions whereas a minor portion (4 percent, on an average) was from other sources (informal).

Current assets financing of the tourism businesses registered quite a high growth rate i.e. more than three folds (318 percent) over the review period.

The total financing of the tourism business enterprises during the review period registered an average growth rate of 28.6 percent while the average share of equity financing, debt financing and current assets financing stood at 30.1 percent, 46.8 percent and 23.1 percent respectively.

The structure of balance sheet based on the common size statements showed borrowing and fixed assets as the main constituents with the average share of 53.9 percent and 81.5 percent in the liabilities and assets side respectively.

Fixed assets remained as a major component in total assets of the tourism business enterprises during the period 2000-2005. Moreover, there has been a variation of fixed assets based on the type of tourism business. It is observed that the accommodation business has a large proportion of fixed assets.

Total assets of the surveyed tourism business enterprises are found to be increasing continuously during the review period (1.62 folds over the period).

Working capital of the tourism business enterprises extensively remained at negative balance during the review period (except in F.Y. 2000/01) and remarkably expanded (decreased either).

The aggregate sources or uses of funds of the surveyed tourism business enterprises have recorded a significant growth ranging from 3.6 percent to 112.7 percent during the review period except a decline of 1.7 percent in fiscal year 2004/05. The increase in sources and uses of funds is mainly attributed for the surge in tourism activities and establishment of new companies as well as the policy reforms to enhance the competition.

Among the constituents of sources and uses of funds, share capital, borrowing, current assets and fixed assets recorded a significant growth whereas others showed great variation. Negative balance of reserve and surplus for the accommodation business has been offsetting the growth in other variables.

Accommodation business among others, has an overwhelmingly majority share (85.7 percent) in aggregate sources and uses of funds. Similarly, private limited companies held majority share in terms of ownership pattern. However, some figures such as equity capital of public limited companies appeared to be more than that of private limited companies.

A significant variation is found in the structure of financing among various types of businesses (accommodation, travel, adventure and other business) based on the common size statements. The analysis based on the application of the ANOVA showed a significant variation in all the reviewed variables viz. share capital, reserve/surplus, borrowing, creditors, current assets and fixed assets.

Another analysis based on the application of t-Test also found a considerable variation in the reviewed variables between two types of business such as accommodation vs. travel business, adventure vs. other business and so on.

A significant variation is found in the structure of financing among various ownership forms of businesses based on the common size statements. The analysis undertaken with the application of the ANOVA showed a significant variation in the variables such as share capital, borrowing, current assets and fixed assets.

The examination undertaken using the ANOVA for the structure of financing among various types and ownerships of businesses based on the average amount considering the actual number of respondents for each and every item found a significant variation.

Another analysis undertaken with the application of the t-Test also found a significant variation in the reviewed variables in most of the cases based on the average amount of the sources and uses of funds for various types and ownership forms of the business.

The analysis with respect to the structure of financing supported a priori notion of the difference between and among the various types and ownership forms of the businesses.

The analysis on essential aspects of financing showed a mixed trend during the period whereas the operating performance remained quite unsatisfactory. In terms of sales revenue, accommodation business suffered while travel, adventure and other business gained significantly over the years.

Interest coverage, debt equity, debt to total assets and proprietorship ratio appeared to be satisfactory whereas profit margin and current ratio appeared to be weak. The ratio also indicated that adventure and travel agency business are strong whereas accommodation and others are very weak. The profitability position has clearly indicated an alarming situation in the financial health and soundness of the enterprises.

The study found a positive link and relationship between the duration of business operation and capital structure of the surveyed tourism enterprises using Karl Pearson's Correlation Coefficient.

Among the turnover ratios, current assets turnover showed quite satisfactory position while fixed assets and working capital turnover could not provide the impetus for the growth.

Regarding the financing indicators based on the perception of the surveyed business it has been difficult for them to raise the capital and get the loan.

The respondents perceive that they are unable to receive the loan proposed. However, they perceive that the amount of loan disbursed is utilized by them.

On the whole, the respondents perceived that the impact of loan financing is average.

The analysis on borrowing need provided the enough scope for the further tourism financing based on the proposed planning, labour relation and existence of hindering factors for the development of the business. Tourism business enterprises asked for the deliberate efforts to open up new vistas for further tourism financing.

The analysis for the average no. of employees among the tourism business showed dominant position of the accommodation business based on the types and of public limited companies based on the ownership pattern.

Further analysis for the average sales per employees found travel agencies at the top position among the types of business and public limited companies among the ownership forms of tourism business.

The analysis for the average assets per employee found accommodation business at the top position among the types and public limited companies among the ownership forms of tourism business.

The average sales and average assets per employees based on the ownership pattern showed an interesting picture. As the ownership pattern moves from the proprietorship firm to partnership, private ltd. and finally to public ltd., the ratio is also found to be increasing significantly.

The analysis based on the Phi-Coefficient found a significant relationship between the existence of the trade union and labour relation. However, there are large numbers of respondents, in which the trade unions are non-existing.

On inquiring about factors hindering the growth of tourism cost of land and rent was found to be the major factor. The study also found a significant variation in the intensity of the hindering factors viz. cost of land, credit facility, community attitude and related service facilities for the development of the business through the application of Chi-square (χ^2) test. It also proved that the factors are not equally appealing to the respondents.

The analysis examined the views of the respondents about the borrowing need and prospects for further financing. It is observed that there is a growing borrowing need however it depends heavily upon the law and order situation and the number of tourists' arrival in the country. It is felt that the tourism business enterprises are ready to lean more for further financing whenever they feel possibility of growth in tourism business and other economic activities.

D. The study attempted to analyze financing practices of banks and financial institutions based on the response of the field survey. It inquired about the loan processing, proposal analysis, credit appraisal and the effectiveness of tourism financing (Chapter – VI). The summary of the analysis of supply side of finance is presented here below:

The survey showed that the majority of the respondents use specific formats for the loan application though it largely depends upon the amount and type of the loan or both. They usually require feasibility report or project proposal and take 1-2 weeks for loan processing, on an average.

Bank and Financial institutions usually negotiate for the interest rate, amount and repayment schedule and intimate the customers about the loan processing and decision. They generally disburse the loan 'phase-wise' and treat the tourism sector loan similar as others.

During the proposal analysis and credit appraisal, they analyze various factors related to the business affairs of the borrowing enterprise and examine the financial aspects. They use these techniques to determine the repayment capacity of the borrower and risk associated with the disbursement of the credit.

Business prospects and management of the company stood as most important factors during the analysis of the credit proposals whereas market position and relation with affiliated company stood at largely important position. Similarly, labour relation received more than average importance whereas collateral did not receive much importance as the majority of BFIs did not provide the comment.

It is found that most of the business aspects are considered 'extremely important' with each other based on the analysis using Phi-Coefficient. Thus, there exists a significant relationship between business prospects and market position as well as between business prospects and management of the company. However, the relationship is not significant between market position and management of the company.

Another analysis based on the Phi-Coefficient also found that most of the business aspects are considered 'largely important or more' with each other (taking both the response for extremely and largely important) for all the factors related to the proposal analysis by the banks and financial institutions. Thus, there exists a significant relationship between (a) business prospects and market position and (b) business prospects and management of the company. Similarly, there also exists significant relationship between (c) market position and management of the company as well as (d) labour relation and relation with affiliated company.

It is found that most of the financial aspects are considered 'extremely important.' Cash flow and ability to pay received overwhelming importance (82.1 percent) and stood at the apex position whereas profitability and liquidity position received remarkable importance (57.1 percent and 50.0 percent respectively) to stay also at the extremely important position. However, capital structure and working capital stood at largely important position though capital structure also maintained almost similar ranking in the distribution i.e. extremely important position.

It is found that most of the financial aspects are considered 'extremely important' with each other based on the application of the Phi-Coefficient. There exists a significant relationship in importance assigned to the application of various tools to examine financial position.

It is also found that most of the financial aspects are considered 'largely important or more' with each other (taking both the response for extremely and largely important) for all the factors related to the Credit Appraisal by the banks and financial institutions. However, the relationship is not significant between the techniques of credit appraisal in majority of the situations (six out of ten) based on the result of the Phi-Coefficient. Not only this, a negative relationship is also found between some techniques of financial analysis. This implies that when a technique is considered largely important or more, another technique is not considered largely important in all cases.

For the purpose of credit appraisal, both business aspects and financial aspects are important. It is also found that most of the business aspects are considered 'extremely important' with other. This is also observed for the financial aspects. The result is based on the cross verification carried out to examine, with which business aspects, which of the financial aspects is considered 'extremely important.'

The analysis based on the Phi-Coefficient found that there exists a significant relationship between business prospects and all financial aspects (profitability, capital structure, liquidity and cash flow) except working capital.

The relationship is insignificant for both 'market position' and 'management of the company' with the financial aspects (except that with cash flow). Similarly, the relationship was poor between labour relations with all financial aspects except with working capital. However, there is significant relationship between market position and cash flow/ability to pay. Thus, it is important to note that the importance assigned to some of the business aspects and the financial aspects behave independently.

Based on the perception of the surveyed banks and financial institutions, the indicators of financing effectiveness showed the mixed result.

BFIs provided an average rating for repayment habit of the borrower, quality of credit documentation and impact of the lending in tourism.

They recorded very few cases of loan restructuring during the review period and did not find the difference in loan quality.

The size of the non-performing loan in tourism sector is found increasing during the review period from 10.1 percent in F.Y. 2000/01 to 28.5 percent in 2004/05.

1. The banks and financial institutions asked for the deliberate efforts to open up new vistas for further tourism financing.

7.3 LIMITATION OF THE STUDY

Tourism is a multi-faceted and complex industry. It embraces various sub sectors within it. Similarly, tourism financing is a wider term concerned with planning, acquisition, utilization and management of funds. It is also a complex activity comprising various activities from acquisition to the utilization of funds as well as from the determination of the purpose and composition of the financing to the methods and time duration of the financing. Considering the broad scope of tourism and tourism financing the major limitations of the study are listed as follows.

The study was largely confined within the scope of Tourism Financing in Nepal. It did not cover the entire financing policy and system to incorporate capital structure of the tourism business enterprises. Similarly, it did not cover all the activities pertaining to planning, acquisition, management and evaluation of the financing activity (practice) in the organization.

The study was mainly based on the available published secondary data and the primary data collected from the field survey. Thus, the study is confined to data available from these sources. Hence, the limitation of published secondary data and that of primary data is applicable.

7.4 POLICY IMPLICATION AND SUGGESTIONS

Rapid development in information and communication has brought about a revolution in every sector of the economy. After the liberalization, there has been a mushrooming in the opening of the financial institutions and tourism business. Hence, it is expected to increase the credit outreach for the tourism business. In addition, tourism business enterprises are expected to grow, adopt standard accounting/auditing practices as well as achieve the greater heights in their operation. Not only this, the recent peace agreement between the government of Nepal and Maoist is expected to improve the law and order situation inside the country on one hand and facilitate the development of every economic sector including tourism on the other.

Based on the findings of present study, both long term and short term measures are suggested in order to reap the tourism potentials and ensure efficiency. Long-term reform measures are necessary for the development of sound financing mechanism whereas short-term measures are for stability, efficiency and profitability of each individual business as well as of the tourism industry. Therefore, the tourism development must go simultaneously with that of other sectors in order to reap the growth potential and to reduce the poverty.

Tourism financing is broad and stands as an interesting area for further research. One can explore this in other countries as well. An effectiveness of tourism financing for developing countries is another area of further research. In addition, it could be highly demanding to explore prospects of tourism financing incorporating demand for and supply of tourism, impacts, inter-linkages and carrying capacity of tourism. The role of informal finance for the development of tourism can equally be another area of the research requiring considerable empirical analysis.

●

www.ingramcontent.com/pod-product-compliance
Lightning Source LLC
Chambersburg PA
CBHW082035300426
44117CB00015B/2490